Contemporary China
Society and Social Change

China's rapid economic growth, modernization and globalization have led to astounding social changes. *Contemporary China* provides a fascinating portrayal of society and social change in the contemporary People's Republic of China.

This book introduces readers to key sociological and anthropological perspectives, themes and debates about Chinese society. It explores topics such as family life, citizenship, gender and sexuality, ethnicity, labor, religion, education, class and rural–urban inequalities, youth identities and collective action for social change. It considers China's imperial past, the social and institutional legacies of the Maoist era, and the momentous forces shaping it in the present.

Contemporary China emphasises diversity and multiplicity, and encourages readers to consider new perspectives and rethink western stereotypes about China and its people. The authors draw on fieldwork to present contemporary, real-life case studies that illustrate the key features of social relations and change in China. Definitions of key terms, discussion questions and lists of further reading help students consolidate learning.

Written by experts in the field, and including full-colour maps and photographs, this book offers remarkable insight into Chinese society and social change. It is an excellent resource for university students of Chinese society.

Tamara Jacka is Senior Fellow in the Department of Political and Social Change, College of Asia and the Pacific at the Australian National University.

Andrew B. Kipnis is Professor of Anthropology in the College of Asia and the Pacific at the Australian National University.

Sally Sargeson is Fellow in the Department of Political and Social Change, College of Asia and the Pacific at the Australian National University.

Contemporary China

Society and Social Change

Tamara Jacka, Andrew B. Kipnis and Sally Sargeson

CAMBRIDGE
UNIVERSITY PRESS

CAMBRIDGE
UNIVERSITY PRESS

University Printing House, Cambridge CB2 8BS, United Kingdom

One Liberty Plaza, 20th Floor, New York, NY 10006, USA

477 Williamstown Road, Port Melbourne, VIC 3207, Australia

4843/24, 2nd Floor, Ansari Road, Daryaganj, Delhi - 110002, India

79 Anson Road, #06-04/06, Singapore 079906

Cambridge University Press is part of the University of Cambridge.

It furthers the University's mission by disseminating knowledge in the pursuit of education, learning and research at the highest international levels of excellence.

www.cambridge.org
Information on this title: www.cambridge.org/9781107600799

© Cambridge University Press 2013

First published 2013

Cover design by Anne-Marie Reeves
Typeset by Aptara Corp.

A catalogue record for this publication is available from the British Library

A Cataloguing-in-Publication entry is available from the catalogue of the National Library of Australia at www.nla.gov.au

ISBN 978-1-107-01184-7 Hardback
ISBN 978-1-107-60079-9 Paperback

Contents

Part 3: Inequalities, Injustices and Social Responses

Images

Maps

Figures

Tables

Acknowledgments

It takes a community to raise a child, and likewise to produce a book. We are fortunate in the College of Asia and the Pacific at the Australian National University (ANU) in having a wonderful community and a supportive environment for research and writing. We would particularly like to thank the following ANU colleagues for their contribution to this volume: Tom Cliff for advice on images; Kay Dancey and Jennifer Sheehan for the maps; Darrell Dorrington for help hunting down statistics; and Mary Walta for copy editing. And we'd like to thank our students for sharing their perspectives and serving as "guinea pigs" for early versions of many chapters.

We are extremely grateful to the following colleagues, friends and family members for taking the time to read and comment on the manuscript: Jonathan Unger, Luigi Tomba, Vanessa Fong, Shanfeng Li, Thomas Gold, Cao Nanlai, Tom Cliff, Sin Wen Lau, Sarah Gosper, Max Sargeson, Jamie Coates, Geng Li, Dorothy Solinger, Gerald Groot, Eleanor Jacka and Jonathan Kipnis. We would also like to thank the five anonymous reviewers of the manuscript for their suggestions. Thank you to Cao Nanlai, Tom Cliff, Haibird, and Gao Yanqiu for donating photographs, and to Max Sargeson and Misha Petkovic for help with the tables and figures. We greatly appreciate the support of Cambridge University Press for the project, and we would particularly like to thank Kim Armitage and Philippa Whishaw for their unfailing enthusiasm, patience, persistence and helpfulness.

We wish to acknowledge funding support from the Australian Research Council (grant nos DP0984510, DP0985775, DP0663389 and DP120104198) and the Ford Foundation (grant no. 1075–0591) for fieldwork research on which this book draws.

Permission to reprint has been gratefully received from the following: The Stephan Landsberger Collection, International Institute of Social History (Amsterdam) for Images 0.1 and 7.2; Princeton University Press for Map 0.4 (adapted from Ramsey 1987, Fig. 5 and Fig. 6, pp. 16–17); and Stanford University Press for Figure 12.1 (copied from Cohen & Wang 2009, Fig. 3.2, p. 43).

Abbreviations

ACFTU	All China Federation of Trade Unions
ADVN	Anti-Domestic Violence Network
BL	Boy Love (fan fiction)
CCP	Chinese Communist Party
CCTV	China Central Television
CNNI	China Net Network Information Center
CoPSI	Collective public security incidents
GDP	Gross domestic product
GL	Girl Love (fan fiction)
HDI	Human Development Index
LGBT	Lesbian, gay, bisexual, transgender
MPS	Ministry of Public Security
NBS	National Bureau of Statistics
NGO	Non-governmental organization
NPC	National People's Congress
PLA	People's Liberation Army
PRC	People's Republic of China
RAB	Religious Affairs Bureau
SARA	State Administration of Religious Affairs
SEPA	State Environmental Protection Agency
SEZ	Special Economic Zone
TVE	Township and village enterprise
UEE	university entrance exam
UNDP	United Nations Development Program

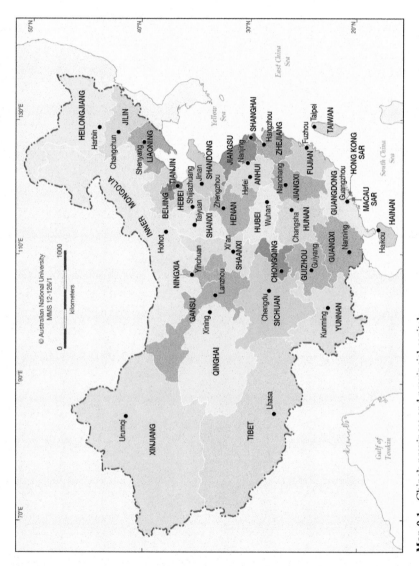

Map 0.1 China's provinces and provincial capitals.
Source: Australian National University Cartography 2012.

Introduction

Chinese society is changing at a breathtaking rate. At the same time as it undergoes what sociologists consider to be classic modernization, including industrialization and urbanization, it is globalizing and embracing new communication technologies. Few western theorists have dared to wrestle with the implications of these complex processes for Chinese society as a whole. Such analysis requires an engagement with the social and institutional legacies of China's revolutionary and pre-revolutionary, imperial past, as well as the momentous forces shaping the present. In this book, three social scientists come together to provide an analysis of Chinese society and social change, informed by anthropological and sociological theory.

The book has three parts. Part 1 examines the most fundamental institutions and forms of organization that shape the everyday lives and social relations of Chinese citizens. Part 2 focuses on the array of cultures and cultural life that may be found across China, and on the socialization and identity formation of young Chinese citizens. Finally, Part 3 discusses various kinds of inequality, division and contention in the Chinese population, and looks at collective actions directed at overcoming perceived social injustices.

Three core themes run through the whole book. The first theme is *multiplicity, diversity and stratification*. In contrast to the common image of Chinese society as homogeneous, and of "Chineseness" as a singular identity, we highlight the enormous diversity of Chinese identities, cultures and experiences, and differences and inequalities between groups and individuals across the country. Although this book includes brief references to other Chinese societies, especially Taiwan, it is primarily concerned with society and social change in today's People's Republic of China (PRC). This can hardly be considered a narrow focus; the PRC covers a vast area, encompassing a wide range of different regional topographies, languages, cultures, economies and ways of life.

Some of these differences indicate divisions between ethnic groups. The Chinese population is categorized between the majority Han Chinese and 55 other minority ethnic groups, and we discuss this in depth in

Chapter 7. Differences between ethnic groups' family institutions and religion are further examined in chapters 1 and 6, respectively. We also consider the ethnic dimensions of inequality in education in Chapter 8 and of regional inequalities in Chapter 11.

Differentiated by ethnicity, Chinese society is also characterized by major variations between regions, rural and urban populations, social classes, and women and men. These axes of difference and inequality arise in several chapters and are the primary focus of chapters 3, 4, 10, 11 and 12, which deal respectively with household registration, community and citizenship; class and stratification; regional, rural–urban and within-community inequalities; and gender inequalities.

The second theme of the book is *historical and comparative perspectives*. We ask about the extent and direction of change over time in different aspects of Chinese society, and explore the most appropriate historical and comparative frameworks for understanding contemporary society. Although some see a sharp disjuncture between a static past and present, we emphasize both ongoing change and the presence of the past in Chinese society today. Our main focus is on society and social change in contemporary China, that is, what is commonly known as the "post-Mao period", which is conventionally understood as having begun with the 13th National Congress of the Chinese Communist Party (CCP) in 1978, following the death in 1976 of the founding leader of the PRC, Mao Zedong. However, we believe that Chinese society and the way in which it has changed during this period cannot be fully understood without a broader historical perspective.

The breadth of our historical perspective varies depending on the topic of each chapter. In most, we discuss the social changes that have resulted from the shift between the Maoist and post-Mao periods, as well as changes that have occurred during the post-Mao period. Many chapters also look much further back, referring to some of the main social institutions of imperial China, and to the momentous political, social, cultural and economic changes that began in the 19th century, a tumultuous period now understood as the beginning of "modern" China. Chapter 1, on families, kinship and relatedness, focuses strongly on historic institutions; in contrast, Chapter 2, on marriage, intimacy and sex, looks at the contemporary situation and the changes that have taken place over the past few decades. Other chapters give more or less weight to the social changes that have happened both between the Maoist and post-Mao periods and since the death of Mao.

We bring comparative perspectives to bear on contemporary Chinese society, examining the extent to which it shares features with other societies in East Asia, and asking, "Is it useful to group China with other (post)socialist societies, such as Vietnam and Russia, or does it make more sense, in the 21st century, to compare China with avowedly capitalist societies such as the United States?" Again, a framework is more or less useful depending on the particular aspect of society one examines. A dichotomy between eastern and western societies underpins some sociological and anthropological scholarship on China. A depiction of Chinese society as centered on the family and "collectively oriented", in contrast to the "individualist" west, is particularly prevalent. In this book we have largely sidestepped the east–west contrast because it is one of the least helpful frameworks for understanding Chinese society, understating as it does variations among Asian societies (and among western societies) and similarities between east and west. In Chapter 1, for example, rather than claiming a special status for the family in Chinese society, we begin by observing that the family is a basic institution and unit of human organization around the world. This chapter includes a brief discussion of the distinction (made in the 1930s by China's most famous sociologist and anthropologist, Fei Xiaotong) between Chinese and western societies, one characterized by overlapping family and social networks and *guanxi* (connections) and the other by individuals and the separate social groups into which they are organized. We also note, however, that many scholars today claim that Fei's 1930s formulation exaggerated differences between the east and west, and that it has become less valid as a result of rapid social changes in China and the rest of the world since then.

We do perceive some cultural affinities and social similarities between China and other societies in East Asia. In Chapter 8, for example, we draw attention to the similarities between China, Japan and other East Asian societies, in terms of the importance they attach to education and the intense competitiveness of their educational systems. This shared emphasis may be connected to Confucianism's emphasis on the link between education and social status (for men), but it might also indicate the value of education in the highly competitive job markets in these societies. In Chapter 9, we note that globalization has enabled the recent emergence of a youth identity and culture that is neither specific to China nor global but, rather, regional – that is, East Asian – in scope. This is evident in the popularity of East Asian, and especially Korean, popular culture in China. In Chapter 5, however, we show that, in the course of China's globalization, the conditions of Chinese workers have not kept pace with those of workers in other East Asian economies, and in Chapter 11, we point out that inequalities in China are noticeably greater than in Japan and Vietnam.

Aside from the east–west dichotomy, many studies of contemporary China are framed by a contrast between socialist and capitalist states and by the use of "postsocialist" China as a case study of the nature of the transition from socialism to capitalism. Each of the three parts of this book includes one or more chapters that discuss the influence of Marxism and the Soviet Union's model of socialist development on the formation of modern Chinese social institutions, organizations and patterns of social relations. Most chapters also explicitly discuss how market reforms and global capitalism have altered Chinese society. However, the complexity and interactive nature of changes in Chinese society, as well as in other postsocialist states over the past few decades, make it very hard to generalize about the social consequences of a transition from socialism to capitalism. Chapter 12, on gender inequalities, provides an illustration of the difficulties and limitations of a framework comparing socialism and capitalism.

Our third theme is *drivers of social change*. To what extent has change in different aspects of society resulted from direct or indirect state intervention or despite of, or in reaction to, state policy? How have the activities of non-state actors contributed to social change, if at all? And how far can social change in contemporary China be attributed to global trends characteristic of modernity and modernization, rather than to forces specific to China? These questions are addressed in various ways throughout this book. Chapter 3, for example, is primarily concerned with the changing impact of a state-imposed institution – household registration – on citizenship and inequality. However, this chapter also suggests that, in recent years, household registration has become less salient to the reproduction of social inequalities. Chapters 1, 2, 4, 5, 9 and 10 also refer to state policies, but focus more on literature concerning the relationship between changes in family forms and communities, work, and trends in youth identities, class and popular cultures on the one hand, and modernity and modernization on the other. Chapter 11 examines policies that have contributed to spatial inequalities. Chapter 13 looks at the potential for social change despite, or in reaction to, the state, this time focusing on the efforts of non-social actors, including non-governmental organizations (NGOs) and those involved in a variety of forms of collective protest, to resist the state and achieve social change.

The second part of this introduction provides background information about geography and modern history. First, though, we explain our usage of some key social science terminology in the text box below.

KEY TERMS

Social institution

The term "social institutions" is frequently used, and often contested, in the social sciences. For the sake of clarity and simplicity, we employ a broad sociological definition, understanding social institutions as the laws, rules, customs and norms that influence social roles and interactions. Examples include political and educational institutions and the institution of the family.

Discourse

Our understanding of the term "discourse" derives from the work of Michel Foucault. Discourses involve social institutions and bodies of knowledge, and the language that frames and communicates them. "Dominant discourses" are those that strongly influence social relations. An example of a dominant discourse discussed in this book is that of *suzhi* (quality), which has powerfully affected many aspects of social relations in contemporary China.

Ideology

We use the term "ideology" to refer to sets of beliefs, attitudes, opinions and practices that are represented rhetorically as coherent. Compared to the term "dominant discourse", "ideology" is more often used in a pejorative sense, to describe official propaganda. Reference to concepts or statements as "ideological" suggests that they are employed instrumentally, and casts doubt over their claims to truthfulness. In this book, we sometimes refer to Confucian, Maoist and post-Mao state ideologies.

Modernity and modernization

Like other social sciences scholars, we use the terms "modernity" and "modernization" as a shorthand way of referring to a raft of processes, including urbanization, industrialization, increasing mass education, commercialization and advances in technology that enable goods, values and people to travel further and more quickly. In line with conventional histories, we locate the start of the modern era in China in the 19th century. However, we note both that there were signs of modernization well before this and that the process has greatly accelerated since the late 20th century. We use the term "modernization" rather differently than Chinese state leaders, for whom the "four modernizations" (of agriculture, industry, science and technology, and defence) are a core component of the post-Mao goals of China's economic development and strengthened status as a nation.

People and places: population, administration, geography and regional diversity

China is the most populous nation on earth (although India is fast catching up): the 2010 population census recorded more than 1.33 billion people living on the mainland, and in the Special Autonomous Regions of Hong Kong and Macau, a further 7 million and approximately 500 000 people, respectively. Of the total Chinese population living on the mainland, about 92 percent are of Han ethnicity; just under 50 percent are women; and around 50 percent have a rural household registration (*hukou*).[1]

Administratively, as Map 0.1 shows, the PRC is divided into 22 provinces (not including Taiwan); five provincial-level "autonomous regions" (Tibet, Xinjiang, Inner Mongolia, Ningxia Hui and Guangxi Zhuang); and four municipalities, which have a political status equal to that of a province (Beijing, Shanghai, Tianjin and Chongqing). The two Special Autonomous Regions (Hong Kong and Macau) have much greater independence than provinces, but their foreign-policy and military affairs are under the control of the central government of the PRC.

Below the provincial level, the country is further divided into an administrative hierarchy. Branches of the ruling CCP and organs of government are located at the levels of province (*sheng*), city (*shi*) and county (*xian*) and, below these, in towns (*xiang*) and townships (*zhen*) and urban streets or wards (*jiedao*). At the grassroots level, villages (*cun*) and, in urban areas, residential communities (*shequ*), also have CCP branches and serve administrative functions, although they are not formal levels of state government.

THE CHINESE COMMUNIST PARTY (CCP)

Although China has nine political parties, it is often referred to as a "single-party authoritarian state". Why? It is authoritarian because political power in China is highly concentrated in the CCP and challenges to that concentration of power are prohibited and repressed. The CCP's power in both the state and society rests on the following pillars:

First, it directly controls the military and internal security apparatus. The 2.3 million strong People's Liberation Army (PLA) is headed by the top-ranked CCP leader, the Party General Secretary, not the President or the leader of China's legislature, the National People's Congress (NPC).

---

[1] Population Census Office 2012.

Second, the CCP maintains ideological control. The preamble to China's Constitution repeatedly affirms that the CCP led the Chinese nation in overthrowing imperialism and feudalism in the 20th century and will continue to lead the Chinese nation in the future. The eight other political parties in China must accept the leadership of the CCP; they play a consultative, not an oppositional, role. By the same token, although citizens may criticize policies, or the decisions or actions of particular individuals or agencies, they must not challenge CCP leadership. The CCP also rules on the content of national media, the arts and educational curricula.

Third, the CCP exercises organizational control. This is particularly evident in the relationship between the CCP and two other major state agencies, the government and NPC. At every level of the state hierarchy, there is a parallel Party committee, and the Party secretary at each level has the final say on major policy and budgetary decisions. For example, at the provincial level, decision-making power rests with the provincial Party secretary, not the provincial governor. Moreover, through the same type of *nomenklatura* system as that established by the Communist Party in the Soviet Union, China's CCP controls all appointments to senior positions in government, the judiciary and police force, and large organizations such as state-owned banks and enterprises, hospitals, universities, "civic" associations and the media. In this way, it acts as a gatekeeper to the most prominent positions in society. So, while the CCP is not the only political party in China, it is the only one that really counts.

Within the CCP, too, power is highly concentrated. In 2011, the CCP had more than 80 million members. Each Party member belongs to a branch or unit of the Party. Every five years, a few thousand branch delegates to the National Party Congress formally "elect" a new Party Central Committee, which in turn "elects" the Politburo. In practice, though, the outgoing Politburo approves a list of nominees for positions on the new Central Committee, the Politburo and the Standing Committee of the Politburo. Ultimate power rests in the hands of the seven or nine top-ranked CCP leaders who make up the Standing Committee of the Politburo. Although each of these leaders is responsible for a major portfolio, together they constitute a collective leadership that is intended to balance the interests and influence of contending party factions and constituencies.

China has a total area of 9 598 094 square kilometers, slightly less than that of the continental United States (including Alaska and excluding Hawaii). It is located in East Asia, with the Pacific Ocean to the east. It

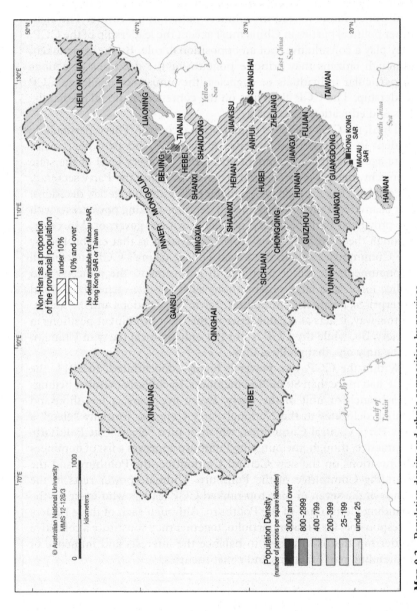

Map 0.2 Population density and ethnic composition by province.
Source: Australian National University (ANU) Cartography 2012. Data from Population Census Office 2012, p. 35.

has land borders with 14 countries: North Korea, Russia, Mongolia and Kazakhstan to the northeast and northwest; Kyrgyzstan, Tajikistan, Afghanistan and Pakistan to the west; and India, Nepal, Bhutan, Myanmar, Laos and Vietnam to the south. Historically, the Han Chinese population, who speak Mandarin (*putonghua*) or a related dialect, have been concentrated in the east of the country and have had closest cultural contact with Japan and Korea. China's other ethnic groups are now concentrated mostly in border regions, and many share languages, cultures and kinship ties with peoples in North, Central and Southeast Asia.

China's vast area is characterized by huge regional variations in topography, natural resources and climate, which in turn have contributed to marked variations in economies, cultures and lifestyles between different parts of the country. Geographically speaking, the territory of the PRC can be roughly divided between the eastern and western regions. Very high-altitude mountain ranges, plateaus, grasslands and deserts dominate the western two-thirds of the country. Those high altitudes, combined with inaccessibility, harsh terrain and low rainfalls, make much of this region less hospitable to human settlement and less suited to crop agriculture than the lower-lying eastern part of the country; all of these factors have contributed to patterns of cultural, social and economic development quite different from those found in the east.

As Map 0.2 shows, the western two-thirds of China are relatively sparsely populated.[2] However, as a proportion of the total local population, the largest concentrations of non-Han ethnic groups are found in western regions, especially in Xinjiang (the home of most Uyghurs and Kazaks) and Tibet (home to the majority of Tibetans, although many also live in what are today the neighboring provinces of Sichuan, Qinghai, Yunnan and elsewhere). Historically, an eclectic mix of Confucianism, Daoism and Buddhism has influenced culture in the east, while in the west, a large proportion of the population are either Muslim or (Tibetan) Buddhist. Many of the peoples of the west were traditionally nomadic herders, and the herding of livestock continues to be more important in the west's agricultural economy than it is in the east. The west has also been much less industrially developed than the east, in large part because its inaccessibility and remoteness from population centers has made it difficult and costly to bring in labor and material and to transport produced goods to key markets outside the region.

---

[2] In past centuries, the population of the western region was even smaller. Since the mid-20th century, Han migration from the east, much of it state-led, has greatly increased the population of the western provinces.

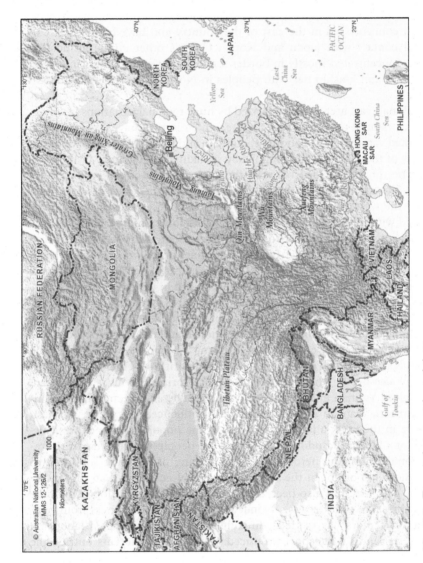

Map 0.3 Topography, mountains and rivers.
Source: ANU Cartography 2012.

About 90 percent of the Chinese population – most of whom are of Han ethnicity – live in the eastern third of the country, in an area of relatively low-lying land, bounded to the west by the Xuefeng, Wu, Taihang and Greater Xing'an mountain ranges. Most of the eastern region lies within the drainage basins of two great rivers: the Huang He (Yellow River) in the north, and in the south the Yangzi (Yangtse, or Changjiang – literally "Long River" – as most Chinese know it). As can be seen in Map 0.3, the sources of both rivers are on the Tibetan plateau.[3] Their fertile basin areas have been heavily crop-farmed for millennia. Historically, the east has also been the center of financial, industrial and commercial development.

In the eastern region, one can further draw a distinction between north and south, with the Qin mountain range and Huai River forming natural lines of demarcation between the two. The south has a much higher rainfall and the land is more fertile than in the north. To the south of the Huai River are China's main rice-growing (and rice-eating) regions; to its north are mainly wheat-growing regions, where the staple diet consists of wheat-based noodles, steamed bread, dumplings and unleavened pancakes of various kinds.

Images of peasants with conical hats in the lush green paddy fields of the southeast often feature in stereotypes of "traditional" Chinese society but in fact the origins of Han culture and identity lie in the settlement of an area to the north, in the Yellow River basin, where it is colder and drier. The kingdoms of the first Chinese dynasties, the Shang (16th–11th centuries BCE) and Zhou (770–221 BCE), were centered in northern Henan, and the philosopher Confucius (551–479 BCE), whose writings became so influential over Chinese statecraft and culture, was a native of what is now Shandong. The first capital of the Chinese empire, which the Qin dynasty (221–207 BCE) established, was in Xianyang, close to present-day Xi'an, the capital of Shaanxi province.[4]

The Yellow River – the country's second-longest river – is named for the vast amounts of silt it carries, which give it a distinctive yellow-brown color. It also is known as the Mother River and the "cradle of Chinese civilization", because its silt provided the foundations for the agricultural economies that nurtured the earliest Han settlements. But it also is sometimes referred to as "China's Sorrow", because over millennia

---

[3] In fact, the sources of all the major river systems of Asia, including the Indus, Ganga-Brahmaputra and Mekong, as well as the Yangzi and Yellow rivers, are on the Tibetan plateau. Climate scientists warn that, in the 21st century, global warming and the melting of glaciers on the Tibetan plateau threaten flooding of the rivers in the short term and their shrinkage in the long term. The social as well as environmental consequences across South Asia and China are potentially enormous.

[4] Dryburgh 2011, p. 10.

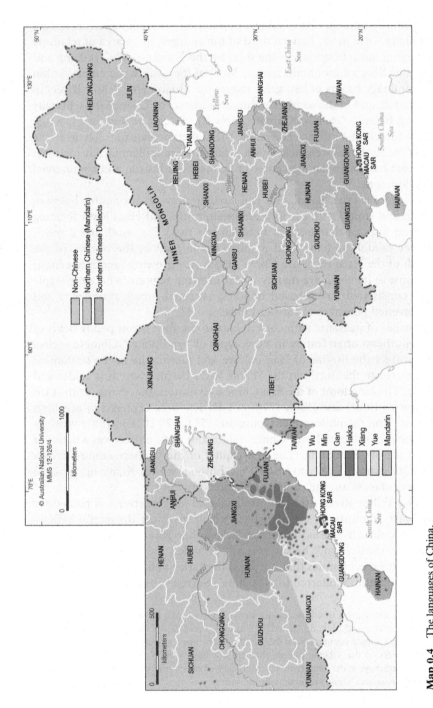

Map 0.4 The languages of China.

Source: ANU Cartography 2012. Adapted from Ramsey 1987, Fig. 5 and Fig. 6, pp. 16–17.

the build-up of silt has periodically caused the river to burst its banks and levees, flooding surrounding areas and causing huge loss of life and devastating social and economic effects.

To the south is the Yangzi River, China's largest and longest river. With a discharge rate 17 times that of the Yellow River, the Yangzi has been crucial to the irrigation of farmland, and has served as the country's main east–west transit route, for 3000 years.[5] In Yunnan, the deep gorges of the Upper Yangzi (Jinsha) and those of two other great rivers, the Nu (Salween) and the Lancang (Upper Mekong), form the Three Parallel Rivers of the Yunnan Protected Areas. This is one of the richest temperate regions in the world in terms of biodiversity, and home to a number of ethnic minority groups. The area was added to the United Nations Educational, Scientific and Cultural Organization (UNESCO) World Heritage List in 2003.[6]

In the middle reaches of the Yangzi is the Three Gorges Dam, the world's largest hydropower project. The project, which began in late 1994 and was fully functioning by mid-2012, displaced about 1.3 million people and, while important in the generation of "clean" energy and in flood control, has also caused a number of ecological problems. Nevertheless, it is being used as a model in the construction or planned construction of several more dams in China and overseas, including on the Jinsha, Lancang and Nu rivers. In addition, under the major new South–North Water Transfer Project, water from the Yangzi and its tributaries is being piped to the Yellow River basin. These massive projects have been the subjects of several collective protests in recent years.

More than 40 percent of China's population live in the Yangzi basin, especially in its middle and lower reaches. The Yangzi River Delta, which includes several major cities across three provinces, is the most densely populated area in China and is very highly urbanized and industrialized.

For centuries before the completion of the first bridge across the Yangzi in 1957, the middle and eastern reaches of the river were very difficult to cross and formed a natural physical barrier that was also of cultural, linguistic and political importance. This is partly reflected in Map 0.4 and inset, which show that, while Mandarin is the main language of the whole of the north and northeastern parts of China, of Sichuan and Guizhou provinces, and of most of Yunnan, people in the southeast region bounded by the middle and eastern sections of the Yangzi speak a variety of Chinese dialects, largely unintelligible to northerners.

China's third-longest river and the second largest by volume (after the Yangzi) is the Pearl River (Zhujiang), which runs through the

[5] Veeck et al. 2011, p. 28.
[6] UNESCO no date.

southeastern part of the country. Historically, this river has not been as important to China's cultural development as the Yellow or Yangzi rivers. However, in the economy of post-Mao China, the Pearl River Delta has played a significant role. Shenzhen and other cities in the Pearl River Delta have been at the forefront of economic reforms, and today this region is among the wealthiest and most highly industrialized and urbanized in China. This is due to a combination of political choice, geography and history. Post-Mao leaders initiated many market-oriented reforms in the Pearl River Delta, both because the region is close to Hong Kong (facilitating trade, foreign investment and the relocation of factories from Hong Kong, Taiwan and other parts of Asia), and because the fertile land of the Pearl River Delta, like that of the Yangzi River Delta, has enabled a prosperous agricultural economy and so, the necessary resources for industrialization and urbanization. Today, the majority of the population in the Pearl River Delta live in towns and cities. Most of the rural-registered population has moved out of agriculture, and entered relatively high-status positions in an economy that is dominated by large numbers of low-paid migrant laborers from other provinces, employed in foreign and local manufacturing industries.[7]

In the discussion so far, we have given a glimpse of the impact that geography has had in shaping variations between cultures, societies and economies across China.[8] Next, we look at some of the ways in which history has shaped society. Rather than trying to summarize a vibrant, centuries-long history into just a few pages, we confine ourselves to providing a skeleton outline of the modern period, from the 19th century to the present. Our focus is on the type of political and socioeconomic change that modernizing reformers, revolutionaries and state officials have aimed to achieve and on the policies they have introduced to realize their aims.

China from late-imperial to post-Mao periods

In imperial China, the writing of history was central to statecraft, as each successive dynasty summarized the history of its predecessor and documented its own. These records were framed by, and contributed to, a backward-looking but non-linear perspective that saw historical change as a cycle in which degeneration and decline from a past "golden age"

---

[7] Veeck et al. 2011, p. 280.

[8] Of course, geography is not the sole determinant of sociocultural and economic patterns. The complex relationship between geographical and other factors shaping societies and economies is discussed in relation to regional inequality in Chapter 11.

moved into regeneration and the restoration of social order and continuity with past ideals. In this cyclical view of history, dynasties that maintained social harmony and prosperity and kept the people satisfied were seen to hold the "Mandate of Heaven". This view of history, while conservative, did not rule out dynastic change, because dynasties that failed to maintain harmony and prosperity could lose the Mandate of Heaven. Such a situation, signalled by natural disasters and social disorder, could be viewed as justifying rebellion and the establishment of a new dynasty.[9]

However, from the 19th century onward, this model of history began to be replaced in elite discourse by historical narratives in which societies "progressed" in a linear fashion through different stages of development, toward more advanced, prosperous futures. Faced with serious economic problems and growing internal social strife, exacerbated by European and Japanese colonialist incursions, some members of the educated elite cast blame on the "foreign" Manchu Qing dynasty (1644–1912) and envisioned the transfer of the Mandate of Heaven to a new, ethnically Han dynasty. Others sought to revitalize the imperial system through modernizing reforms. However, increasing numbers became convinced that answers to the most pressing of questions – what was wrong with China? – were no longer to be found in the imperial system. Instead, many came to believe that a wholesale makeover of the Chinese national character, traditional culture, political institutions and ways of thinking was required for China to overcome its social and economic problems and maintain its sovereignty.[10]

In the early 20th century, young urban men, and some women, led efforts toward political reform and revolution. Their relatively privileged family backgrounds enabled them to receive an education and engage with ideas and discourses from Japan, Europe, Britain and the United States, in some cases through travel and study abroad. Many of these young people were motivated by personal frustration at the restrictions Confucian ideology and the traditional institution of the family imposed. They were driven, too, by their conviction that China's decline and weakness in the face of foreign incursion was a result of the inferiority of Confucianism as a system of morality and basis for governance, compared with more individualist ideologies, including liberalism, anarchism, feminism and socialism. Consequently, the central aims of reformers and revolutionaries included breaking the traditional institution of the family, in particular by denouncing ancestor worship, filial piety and arranged marriages, and improving the status of women. The reformers included

---

[9] Stockman 2000, pp. 24–5.
[10] Fitzgerald 1996, p. 108.

many who joined the Nationalist Party (formed in 1912) as well as the CCP (formed in 1921).

Until the CCP came to national power in 1949, however, these challenges to traditional institutions had little relevance for the vast majority of the population living in rural areas. It was far more important to the rural population that decades of political upheaval and war had resulted in what Judith Stacey refers to as "a 'realization crisis', an alarming decline in their capacity to realize proper Confucian family life, or any family life at all".[11] So, when the CCP later sought to gain power through revolution in the countryside, many peasants were motivated to support and join them, not by the CCP's efforts to destroy the traditional family order but by the hope they themselves could achieve a family life.

For many, the CCP did fulfil this hope after 1949, greatly reducing social strife and achieving enormous improvements in health and living standards, which made it easier for the majority of the population to form their own families. At the same time, though, it initiated radical changes in the organization of the economy and social life. And it introduced new ways of thinking about both the past and the future.

Communist leaders in both the Soviet Union and China, drawing on Karl Marx's writings, took a theory of history as a progression through a fixed sequence of modes of production: from primitive communal, to slave, feudal, capitalist and finally socialist modes.[12] They understood socialism to entail the abolition of private ownership of the means of production and a system of economic distribution based on the principle "to each according to his (or her) work". Beyond socialism lay the ideal of communism, under which everyone would be equal and resources would be distributed "to each according to his (or her) need". Marxist theory required that society should pass through a period of capitalism, during which the forces of production would be developed – in other words, the levels of productivity and economic growth would be boosted – and class antagonisms intensified, before socialism could be realized. Among Soviet and Chinese communists, debates ensued about the extent to which capitalism had already emerged and the best means to advance the forces of production, effect the transition to socialism and ultimately bring about communism.

There was also discussion about the role of different social groups in revolution and progress toward socialism. For orthodox Marxists, the most progressive group in society was the urban proletariat, that is, industrial workers. The achievement of socialism entailed advancing industrialization and urbanization and turning peasants into workers. However,

[11] Stacey 1983, p. 68.
[12] Stockman 2000, p. 26.

in China, the CCP's retreat to bases in the countryside during the 1930s encouraged it to develop a more positive view of peasants' revolutionary potential. Faced with a very small industrial proletariat, combined with Nationalist Party and Japanese dominance of China's cities, CCP members led by Mao focused on mobilizing poor peasants' support, by undertaking land reform in particular. This rurally oriented approach gained the upper hand in CCP ideology and, henceforth, Party leaders became known, both in China and abroad, as champions of the peasantry. After the CCP came to power in 1949, however, it introduced institutions, including a household registration system and central planning, with which it kept the rural population on the land and siphoned resources out of agriculture to fund industrialization and improvements in urban living standards. This had a significant effect, with the result that urban and industrial life developed rapidly while the relative disadvantage of the rural, agricultural population intensified.

Scholars have identified three approaches to socialism shaping the CCP's policy between the 1950s and the 1980s.[13] The first approach, which scholars nowadays term "Stalinist" because of its similarities with Joseph Stalin's approach in the Soviet Union, emphasized the need for central state planning of the economy, as well as the abolition of private ownership of the means of production, and the nationalization of industries. The second, "market socialist", approach resembled attempts undertaken in Yugoslavia in the 1960s to reform the Stalinist approach. Proponents of market socialism held that China was not ready for a full state takeover of the economy: first it needed to build up the forces of production by allowing private businesses to continue and using market mechanisms, as well as central planning, to ensure a rational distribution of resources and maintain incentives for improving labor productivity. The third, "Maoist", approach emphasized the need for the continual renewal of revolution and class struggle. This approach built on Mao's understanding that the socialization of productive property did not necessarily mean the end of class division and that, if the power of the CCP bureaucracy was unchecked, it could itself develop into a new ruling class, exploiting the masses.

In the 1950s, Chinese socialism combined all three approaches. A Stalinist approach was apparent in the nationalization of enterprises and central planning of all aspects of the economy. By the end of this decade, most industries and all urban land had been nationalized, and the majority of the urban working-age population were employed by state-run *danwei* (work units). And at the same time, the majority of the working-age

---

[13] Solinger 1984; Stockman 2000, pp. 26–7.

population in rural areas, together with land, livestock and equipment, had been mobilized into collective agricultural production.

In 1958, Mao launched the Great Leap Forward, an ambitious attempt to greatly speed up development of the productive forces and achieve the ideal of communism by rapidly expanding the scale of rural collectives, banning private plots, decentralizing administration and running political campaigns to mobilize people to work harder and make greater sacrifices for the revolution. This radical Maoist approach ended in early 1961, having resulted in widespread famine that caused tens of millions of deaths. Over the next few years, leaders who placed greater emphasis on central planning, but also allowed the re-emergence of small private plots and market activities, eclipsed Mao's influence over state policy. However, in 1966, Mao sought to make a political comeback by launching the Great Proletarian Cultural Revolution (henceforth, "Cultural Revolution"), calling on young people to serve as "red guards", to engage in vigorous class struggle to destroy "feudal" and bourgeois culture, attack politically suspect intellectuals and root out "capitalist roaders" from within the state bureaucracy. In the early years of the Cultural Revolution, university entrance examinations were abolished, many schools closed and the urban youth was encouraged to "go down to the countryside" to learn from the peasants. In later years, as conflicts escalated between "red guard" and "revolutionary rebel" groups with different social class backgrounds, and between politically favored worker-activists and resentful coworkers, Mao attempted to restore order by establishing revolutionary committees dominated by army members in all provinces, cities and factories, and redoubling efforts to send young urbanites to the countryside.

After the death of Mao in 1976, reactions against his vision of socialism strengthened. A faction of the CCP, led by Deng Xiaoping, gained power by discrediting the Cultural Revolution and the ultra-Maoist "Gang of Four", led by Mao's wife, Jiang Qing. In summing up its verdict on the years 1966 to 1976, the CCP declared that Mao's initiation and leadership of the Cultural Revolution was "responsible for the most severe setback and the heaviest losses suffered by the Party, the state and the people since the founding of the PRC".[14] The new leadership allowed urban youth sent down to the countryside to return to the cities, and rehabilitated officials and others who had been denounced during the Cultural Revolution. They also removed class struggle from the political agenda, promoted the premier Zhou Enlai's proposal that China should focus on "four modernizations" and "open up" to the outside world, and introduced far-reaching, market-oriented economic reforms.

[14] Chinese Communist Party [CCP] 1981.

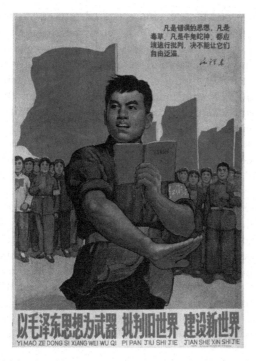

Image 0.1 "Criticize the old world and build a new world with Mao Zedong Thought as a weapon." Propaganda poster from the Cultural Revolution (produced in 1966 by the Propaganda Poster Group, Shanghai).
  The poster depicts red guards holding the little red book, a small book of quotations from Mao, which they were expected to memorize and carry with them at all times.
Source: Stephan Landsberger Collection, International Institute of Social History (Amsterdam).

Underpinning the new "post-Mao" approach was a shift in attitude toward history: a rejection of the Maoist notion that, by mobilizing the political will of the masses and engaging in class struggle, one could overcome the backwardness of China's productive forces and advance rapidly to a high level of socialism and then communism. The new leadership, under Deng, aimed to replace this vision with a more pragmatic approach that "sought truth from facts". China, it claimed, had only reached the first stage of socialism and needed to build the economy before it could attain a higher degree of socialism. The slogans "It does not matter whether the cat is black or white, so long as it catches mice" and "To get rich is glorious", supposedly coined by Deng, conveyed the idea that economic growth was to be achieved by whatever means possible and prioritized over direct efforts at social intervention aimed at overcoming class or other inequalities.

At first, the post-Mao reforms appeared to be a variant of the market socialist approach of the 1960s. However, by the time of Deng's death in 1997, it had become clear that China's new economic policies had taken it well beyond the kind of market-oriented reform previously envisioned in the socialist world. The reforms involved: a restructuring of first rural and then urban sectors of the economy; a series of measures aimed at attracting foreign investment, increasing trade and integrating the Chinese economy with the global capitalist order; changes to the banking sector; a new system for redistributing revenues and expenditure between the central state government and lower levels of government; and new models of funding and providing welfare.

Between the late 1970s and the mid-1980s, agriculture was largely decollectivized, as land-usage rights (though not ownership) and much of the control over production decision-making were devolved to households. At the same time, the state encouraged diversification and commodification in agricultural production and the development of private and collective non-agricultural ventures. This approach succeeded in stimulating growth in agricultural productivity and led to increases in rural incomes, which in turn provided the resources to enable a rapid growth in non-agricultural collective township and village enterprises (TVEs).[15]

In the mid-1980s, the state turned its attention to restructuring the urban industrial sector. The role of state planning was reduced with the introduction of a dual pricing system, under which the price of goods and services either continued to be fixed by the state or, in other cases, was determined by the market. In the state sector, reforms aimed at increasing enterprises' productivity and profitability were begun in the late 1980s and accelerated from the late 1990s onward. These reforms increased managers' autonomy and decision-making power and "smashed the iron rice bowl" of *danwei* welfare provision and jobs for life. State-run enterprises were also increasingly opened up to a wide variety of new forms of ownership and management, as growing numbers issued shares to be traded on the stock exchange. Restrictions were lifted on private enterprises, and growing numbers of Special Economic Zones (SEZs) were established to encourage foreign investment through tax breaks and other preferential policies. In the 1980s and 1990s, state enterprises faced increasing competition from collective enterprises (especially TVEs), the private sector and joint ventures and wholly foreign-owned companies. Consequently, the proportion of gross industrial output produced in the

---

[15] After the mid-1980s, however, growth in rural incomes slowed. In the late 1990s, many TVEs lost competitiveness and were either privatized or closed down.

Image 0.2   Shenzhen.
Source: © Shutterstock.com/Fuyu Liyu.

Shenzhen is located in the Pearl River Delta. Formerly a quiet fishing village, in 1979 it became one of the first four SEZs in China. Since then, it has become a center for manufacturing and services industries, and one of the fastest growing cities in the world. By 2010, its population was 11.1 million. In 2012, The Economist Intelligence Unit identified Shenzhen as one of 13 emerging megalopolises in China, and forecast that by 2020 its population would be 14.2 million, twice that of Hong Kong.[16]

state sector declined from about 70 percent at the end of the 1970s to 24 percent by the year 2000.[17]

By the end of the first decade of the 21st century, China was noteworthy for its combination of extraordinarily high levels of economic growth and the continued authoritarian rule of the CCP. However, when it

[16] Economist Intelligence Unit 2012.
[17] Tong & Wong 2008, p. 135.

came to economic institutions, observers struggled to identify the ways in which what the CCP termed "socialism with Chinese characteristics" was different from capitalism. The market now determined the price of almost all consumer goods and commodities, and the overall level of economic inequality in China was no lower than in most avowedly capitalist countries. On the contrary, China's Gini coefficient was higher than that of both wealthy capitalist countries (such as Australia, the United States and Norway) and poorer capitalist and postsocialist states (including India, Vietnam and Russia).[18]

However, some divergences between economic and social policy trends in China and avowedly capitalist states had begun to open. In many capitalist countries, social inequalities were exacerbated by economic downturn and financial crisis, followed by subsequent cuts in the state's welfare provision. In China, too, inequalities grew, but they were caused by growth rather than welfare cuts. Alarmed by rising social discontent and the threat this posed to their rule, the CCP's leaders introduced policies aimed at cultivating a "harmonious society" and "people-centered"' development. The central government funded a "western development strategy" and a program for the "construction of a new socialist country-side", which sought to ameliorate regional and rural–urban inequalities by investing in infrastructure. The state also sought to improve the economic conditions of the rural population by reducing fees and charges, removing agricultural taxes, subsidizing agriculture and rural education and removing state-school tuition fees. In addition, the state revised the Labor Law, improving protection and entitlements to insurance for all workers, including rural migrant laborers; extended minimum livelihood allowance (*dibao*) payments to the rural as well as urban poor; and introduced collective medical insurance and old-age insurance schemes in the countryside. Some state-owned enterprises retained government backing and continued to provide their employees with stable employment and relatively good benefits.

These new state policies have achieved mixed results. For example, the abolition of agricultural taxes removed one source of discontent fueling collective protests in the countryside. But a wide range of other sources of discontent has driven a growth in collective protest among both rural and urban citizens. In addition, while some citizens have clearly benefited from the state's redistributive policies and the expanded provision of state welfare, it is not clear that, overall, these policies have achieved a reduction in the inequalities that characterize Chinese society.

All these issues, and more, are explored in the pages ahead.

---

[18] The Gini coefficient is a commonly used measure of material inequality. We explain and critique this measure in Chapter 11.

Recommended reading

Bianco, Lucien 1971, *Origins of the Chinese Revolution, 1915–1949*. Stanford, CA: Stanford University Press.

Elvin, Mark 1973, *The Pattern of the Chinese Past: A Social and Economic Interpretation*. Stanford, CA: Stanford University Press.

Meisner, Maurice 1986 [first published 1977], *Mao's China and After: A History of the People's Republic [Mao's China]*, revised and expanded edition. New York: The Free Press.

Veeck, Gregory, Pannell, Clifton W, Smith, Christopher J & Huang, Youqin 2011, *China's Geography: Globalization and the Dynamics of Political, Economic, and Social Change*, 2nd edition. Lanham, MD: Rowman and Littlefield.

Zang, Xiaowei (ed.) 2011a, *Understanding Chinese Society*. London: Routledge.

Part 1

Social Institutions

1 Families, Kinship and Relatedness

The family is a basic social institution and unit of human organization around the world. Families nurture children as they grow into adults and learn, enact and sometimes resist norms of human behavior. Families are also among the sites where the affective aspects of human interaction are most intimately learned and most deeply felt. In all societies, though, there are gaps between the family as an institution, and actual families and family relationships, and ideals and practices vary among population subgroups and over time. In this chapter, we explain the main elements of the dominant institutions of kinship and family as they pertained in imperial China, and then look at how kinship norms were, and continue to be, extended to non-kin relationships and social interactions. We discuss some of the divergences between dominant family and kinship institutions and the realities of Chinese families, particularly in the late Qing dynasty of the late 19th and early 20th centuries. and explore the different ways in which Chinese family practices and understandings of what the family is and should be have varied among population subgroups. Finally, we examine how kinship and family institutions and practices have changed during the modern period, that is, since the late 19th century, and investigate the causes of those changes.

The model family: patrilineal kinship and virilocal marriage

Anthropologists describe dominant Chinese kinship patterns as *patrilineal* (meaning that descent is traced through the male line) and *patriarchal* (men have power over women, and the aged over the young); and marriages as *virilocal* or *patrilocal* (when women marry, they leave their natal family and the village in which they were born and move to their husband's home in another village). In imperial China, Confucianists took the harmonious patriarchal, patrilineal family as both the model for, and the most basic constitutive element of, the sociopolitical order, and identified filial piety (obedience to, and care and respect of, family elders) as the "foundation of virtue and the root of civilization".[1] Confucian norms concerning the "five human relationships" – between sovereign and subject, father and son, husband and wife, elder and younger brother, and friend and friend – were embodied in *li* (rituals and rules of social behavior). *Li* were disseminated through both the Confucian classics that formed the core of the elite male educational system (a thorough knowledge of which was a requirement for men's entry into public service[2]) and more popular stories and sayings. Over time, *li* were incorporated into imperial legal codes which stipulated different punishments for crimes, depending on whether the transgressor and victim were close family members, and the transgressor's subordinate or superior position in the family, in comparison to the victim. If the transgressor was a close relative, with a position in the family subordinate to that of the victim, the crime was considered particularly heinous.

Patrilineal descent, like matrilineal, is a form of unilineal descent. This means that, in tracing a family backwards in time, one need focus only on a single ancestor in each generation. In patrilineal descent, this key ancestor would be the father in the generation of one's parents, the father's father in the grandparent's generation, and so on. By having only one key ancestor in each generation, it is possible to remember the names of key ancestors going back many generations.

A common cultural feature of many unilineal societies is a deep-time depth in both historical memories and aspirations for the future. Individuals can imagine their lives as influenced by ancestors who lived many generations ago and can see that their own actions might affect their descendants many generations into the future. Unilineal societies also commonly feature great flexibility in the way the size of one's family is calculated. Depending on the context, one may include those related within a relatively small or large number of generations. Partially following Chinese usages, we use the term "family" (*jia*) flexibly, to refer to both relatively large and relatively small groupings of related individuals; we use the term "household" (*hu*) in a more precise way, to refer to groupings who live together, share meals, and have a common budget. In imperial China, people commonly aspired to an ideal, extended family household of "five generations under one roof", although, as we discuss below, poverty, social disorder and conflict within families often worked against the achievement of that ideal.

Lineages included people descended from a particular male ancestor. This key ancestor was often a man who first moved to, or opened up land in, a particular area, or who made a fortune that enabled him to

---

[1] The *Xiao jing* (*Hsiao ching*) [Classic of filial piety], cited in Stacey 1983, p. 30.
[2] Women were excluded from the formal education system and from official public service.

support a large family. Lineage members often built ancestral halls in honor of their founding ancestor. They held important family rituals and stored written genealogies there, listing all male descendants of the key ancestor. New branches of a lineage could be established if a man amassed the wealth to provide the material basis for many generations of descendants to thrive. In cases where lineage relations had been forgotten and records destroyed, family members from different households were able to combine to reinvent their lineage, tracing it back to a particular (often imagined) founder.[3]

Lineage members sometimes kept a list of characters to be used as the middle character in an individual's three-character name, to help keep track of complicated kin relations over a long period. These lists of characters often took the form of a poem, which made them easy to remember. Lineage members of the same generation (and sometimes of the same gender) would share the same middle name, known as a "generation name" (*beiming*). The fact that these poems needed to start with a particular character reinforced the fact that a particular lineage had to begin with a particular ancestor. Even families that were not part of formal lineages often used a generation name as the middle character for all children born to the same father or set of brothers. To give a concrete example, Mao Zedong, the founding leader of the PRC, had the family name *Mao*, generation name *Ze*, and personal name *Dong*. All of Mao's seven siblings also had the character *Ze* as the middle character in their three-character names. Generation names enabled lineage members to calculate easily how they were related to one another, even when their households were far apart. In China, lineages – codified in lineage halls, genealogies and poems of generation names – were imaginatively attached to ideas of the great glory of founding ancestors. Ambitious men, dreaming of such glory, could imagine themselves becoming a founding ancestor who would amass a fortune to allow future generations of his descendants to worship him after he died.

THE LI FAMILY GENEALOGY

During the 1980s, the elders of the Li family of rural Anhui province decided to update and reconstruct their lineage. They began with a written genealogy from 1930 that had been hidden away during the destructive political campaigns of the Maoist years. They required all living male lineage members traceable from that genealogy to pay 5 *mao* (50 Chinese cents) if they wanted to register on the new

[3] Hsu 1971.

genealogy and all whom they could contact eagerly did so. Because the original genealogy went back to 1369, by the early 1980s more than 50 000 male lineage members had been identified and registered. The elders obtained donations from lineage members of the six major lineage segments in six villages to build a new lineage hall. They also composed a new poem of generation names for the members of the next 20 generations of the Li family. The new poem read:

> The root is deep, and the branches and leaves are massive; the stream has a distant source and is endlessly long; thrift is the foundation on which our family can build; generation after generation will be prosperous (根深枝叶茂; 源远泉脉长; 勤俭为家本; 时代永荣昌).[4]

Efforts to maintain and extend patrilineages contributed to, and were shaped by, marriage patterns and practices relating specifically to the control and transmission of property, the most important of which was land. Marriage was considered to be a family, not an individual, matter and parents arranged the unions, sometimes with the help of a matchmaker or go-between. Patrilineages were maintained through virilocal marriage, combined with the practice of passing down land only to sons, not daughters. Families practiced partible inheritance, dividing land between all the sons rather than handing it down to just one of them.[5]

Patrilineal kinship and virilocal marriage should not be equated with patriarchy, although they are closely linked with it. According to imperial Confucian patriarchal ideology, a good woman was to be confined in the family home, and her interactions with non-kin, especially men, were kept to a minimum. Within the family, she was expected to adhere to the "three obediences": to her father when she was young and unmarried, to her husband after her marriage, and to the son who would become the head of the family should her husband die. A woman could not legally divorce her husband against his wishes, and the remarriage of widows was officially frowned upon. Chastity and devotion to a man and his family were so highly valued in the neo-Confucian ideology of the late imperial period that married women who committed suicide, either as a response to sexual molestation (by someone other than their husband) or in preference to remarrying after their husband had died, were officially recognised with the construction of commemorative arches.

Virilocal marriage and the significance attached to maintaining the male family line meant that women were sometimes treated as only

---

[4] Han 2001, p. 194.

[5] Partible inheritance can be contrasted with primogeniture, which was practiced in pre-modern Europe, in which a single son inherited property. Partible inheritance leads to the fragmentation of family property and hence contributes to a decline in socioeconomic status, and so societies that practice this form of inheritance tend to be characterized by higher levels of social mobility than those that practice primogeniture.

Image 1.1   Recently rebuilt lineage hall in southern Guangdong province. The banner across the top reads "Hu Lineage Ancestral Hall".
Source: Andrew Kipnis 2010.

temporary and marginal members of their natal family. Among poorer families, higher priority was placed on maintaining the patrilineal family than on nurturing its girls. In extreme cases, daughters might be considered such an unaffordable burden that they were killed at birth. Today, in the context of the birth-control policy discussed below, a minority of rural families want a son so badly that they practice sex-selective abortion. Virilocal marriage also meant that, after marriage, women were relatively more socially isolated than their husbands. In cases of domestic conflict, this probably made women more vulnerable to mistreatment by their husbands and in-laws. As we discuss in Chapter 12, virilocal marriage patterns still underpin the subordination of women in rural China today, despite several decades of state promotion of gender equality.

Conceptual extensions of patrilineal, patriarchal kinship

Today, Confucian *li* and the family norms they embodied no longer inform the law. However, some of the norms, practices and imaginative power of patrilineal kinship continue to apply in both familial and non-familial relationships. For example, in training situations where a student or apprentice learns skills from an individual "master" or "professor", the relationship between teacher and student can be likened to that of a father and son, the relationships between students of the same teacher is similar to those of relationships between siblings, and the entire grouping can be conceptualized as a lineage. Such forms of imagined lineage relationships can be found in the martial arts, where students learn a particular style of martial arts from a particular teacher; in academia, where graduate students are supervised by a particular scholar, often a specialist in a particular subfield of academia or style of scholarship; in factories, where skilled technicians train newcomers to the factory in particular skills; and even in mafia-like criminal groupings, where the "brothers" are expected to show unflinching loyalty to their leader.

Some norms of political hierarchy also have parallels to lineage hierarchies. The complex hierarchies of the CCP, which has 15 formal levels and many sublevels, are sometimes described and ritually expressed in a manner that parallels the relationship between members of different generations and siblings of different ages in a patrilineage. At the official funerals the CCP arranges for its leading officials, for example, details such as who attends, who stands where, and when each attendee should pay their respects to the deceased, are carefully orchestrated and carefully watched. In the same way, experts in lineage ritual manage these aspects of ritual functions at the funerals of lineage members. Just as lineage elders do not attend the funerals of those with younger generation names than themselves, so Party officials avoid the funerals of their subordinates. For example, in 1992, Deng Xiaoping, then the most important leader of the CCP, sent his condolences on the death of former president Li Xiannian but did not attend the funeral.

Throughout Chinese society, *guanxi* (relationships with people outside of the family) are often constructed through similar practices to those that form family relationships. People calibrate their manner of sharing food, exchanging gifts and addressing one another to make these relationships seem more like kinship relations than they really are. In some cases, individuals construct fictive kin relations with people outside their family and address and treat one another as if they were actually, brothers, sisters, fathers, mothers, daughters or sons.[6]

The father of modern Chinese sociology and anthropology, Fei Xiaotong, famously argued that, while western societies were characterized by individuals who joined well-bounded, discrete social groups, Chinese

---

[6] Kipnis 1997.

society was characterized by what he called a "differential mode of association" (*chaxu geju*). Fei used this term to describe a situation where each individual formed his or her own network, beginning with close relatives and spreading like the concentric circles that form when one throws a stone in a pond. Each individual's network was different from, but overlapped with, others and so there were few clearly delineated social groups.[7] Fei's work led to much research on the importance of *guanxi* in China: some sociologists argued that, in part because the rule of law is not well established in China, *guanxi* networks are much more important there than networks are in western countries. Others counter that either Fei exaggerated the contrast to begin with or that the situation in China is rapidly changing.[8]

Diversity within patrilineal, patriarchal kinship and virilocal marriage

Patrilineal models of the family are usually male-oriented.[9] For Chinese women, however, family has often meant something different. The anthropologists Margery Wolf and Ellen Judd have highlighted this in their discussions of women's efforts to maintain links with their natal family (i.e. their parents' family) after marriage and to form strong emotional bonds with their sons. Wolf has called the informal family unit of a woman and her sons the "uterine" family. Even though neither the uterine family nor women's connections with their natal family had any official place within the institutions of Chinese patrilineal, virilocal kinship in imperial China they all existed as sites of strong affective relationships and, if successfully nurtured, could be called upon to counter the more extreme forms of patriarchal subordination.[10] These female forms of relatedness are still very important to rural women in China today.

In imperial China, women and their affinal links (that is, the links a family established with another when a daughter married) provided families with a potentially valuable way to further their economic and political interests and to improve the status and well-being of their daughters. For this reason, most marriages were between families of roughly equal status, or were hypergamous (that is, the woman moved up the ladder of social status on her marriage). Some marriages were conceived as

[7] Fei 1992.
[8] Gold, Guthrie & Wank 2002.
[9] Stockman 2000, p. 99.
[10] Wolf 1972; Judd 1989.

the moment when a woman severed ties to her natal family and shifted once and for all to her marital family. In such marriages, the bride price (*caili*, money paid from the groom's family to the bride's before the wedding) was often quite high, and the wedding itself was a very sad occasion for the bride and her natal family. However, other marriages were used to build alliances between two families, in which case the woman could be thought of as occupying a key position between the two families. In these marriages, the bride price was either very low or was balanced by a large dowry that the woman's family provided for their daughter at the time of marriage. Such weddings were often joyous occasions for the elders in both families, if not necessarily for the bride and groom.

Aside from this, within the basic framework of patrilineal kinship and virilocal marriage in China, a wide range of practical arrangements have always existed. Some men took concubines, although scholars estimate that at the time of the late Qing dynasty, only a small percentage of men had concubines, while between 20 and 25 percent of men were unable to marry at all.[11] In periods of upheaval, such as those that characterized the late Qing (1644–1912) and Republican periods (1912–49), poor people's ability to achieve any kind of family life was further compromised by war and the breakdown of local economies and social order. Many households broke up as a result, as some family members died young through famine or warfare, and others traveled large distances in search of work and food.[12] Even in well-off families, the promise of partible inheritance, combined with conflicts between generations and among brothers and their wives, often led to early household division and hence smaller, simpler households. Urbanization also contributed to a rise in the number of nuclear households. It is estimated that, by 1900, nuclear households accounted for more than half of urban Chinese households. By the 1980s, this had grown to two-thirds.[13]

In southern China, before and during the first half of the 20th century, patrilineal families often held significant corporate property, especially land, and acted like local governments. Some built and ran schools, constructed temples and other facilities within villages, distributed income to individual households and provided care for widows, orphans and handicapped members. In other cases, lineages focused on ceremonial functions, on kinship-related services (conducting weddings and funerals, negotiating marriages and arranging adoptions) and on providing

---

[11] Ownby 2002, p. 242.

[12] For vivid accounts of the devastating human consequences of this, see Hershatter 2011, pp. 32–64.

[13] Zang 1993.

opportunities for alliance-building and networking among the lineage's households. These networking functions were more important in cases where lineages were spread over a wide geographical region rather than in one or two villages. In other cases, especially in northern China, lineages were less organized and undertook few, if any, formal activities, although here too the social norms of virilocal marriage, ancestor worship and an emphasis on the relationships between sons, fathers and brothers were important.

From the end of the 19th century until the late 1970s, the power of lineages and their role in social life decreased and many lineage halls were destroyed during the Cultural Revolution, in particular. In the post-Mao period, lineages have made a comeback in some places, especially in southeastern coastal regions, where both local and overseas lineage members have invested large sums in rebuilding lineage halls and other village facilities. In such places, lineages often play a major role in local politics as well as social life, and in the provision of public goods in the village. In much of northern China, however, lineages play a negligible role in village life.

In addition to these variations, many exceptions to patrilineal kinship and virilocal marriage have existed in China. The kinship practices of some minority ethnic groups were (and are) more matrilineal than patrilineal (see the text box below for an example), and even among the majority Han Chinese, alternative practices have always existed. In rural areas, a minority of marriages have always been uxorilocal (that is, the husband moves to his wife's village or even to her parents' house). As in all forms of marriage in China, a wide variety of motivations and arrangements exist within the framework of uxorilocal marriage. In many cases, parents who have only daughters seek to bring a man into the family through uxorilocal marriage, to insure against their abandonment in old age. Poor men may accept an uxorilocal marriage because they cannot otherwise afford to pay the bride price and get married.

In towns and cities, neolocal marriages, in which the newly wedded couple lives separately from the families of both wife and husband, became increasingly common from the early 20th century onward, and today are the dominant form. In some multi-surname rural villages, both the husband's and wife's family come from the same village. If they move into a separate home upon marriage, their marriage may also be described as neolocal.[14] Now, even in single-surname villages, newly married couples commonly live in a separate house and household than that of the groom's parents.

---

[14] See Chapter 7 of Chan, Madsen & Unger 2009.

MATRILINEAL KINSHIP AMONG THE NA

The Chinese anthropologist Cai Hua wrote a controversial book, *A Society without Fathers or Husbands: The Na of China*,[15] which depicted matrilineal kinship practices among a group of people living in the highland regions of Yunnan province. According to this book, among the Na, children belong to and live with their mother's extended family. Even as adults, men continue to live with their mothers, their mothers' brothers, and their sisters. Men's familial responsibilities are toward the children of their sisters rather than the children of their girlfriends. Of course, men and women have sexual relations, but men and women do not get married and do not live together. Because sexual relations are completely separated from questions of familial obligations, women may choose their sexual partners without considering their partner's ability to economically support a family. It is possible to remain loyal to a single partner or to have multiple partners either sequentially or at the same time. Critics of Cai say that he has portrayed an overly simplified and ahistorical picture of the Na, exaggerating the extent to which men do not provide support for their own children and ignoring forces of historical change and cases where men and women choose to legally marry. Nevertheless, Cai clearly demonstrates that alternatives to patrilineal, virilocal kinship have existed within the territory of what is today China for a long time.

Patterns of change and their causes

Patterns of marriage, familial residence, old-age care, childcare, and family size in China have all changed rapidly in the 20th and 21st centuries, but not always in a single direction. As China becomes wealthier and more urbanized, it is much more common for new households to reside neolocally rather than virilocally after marriage, although there are certainly exceptions to this trend in both rural and urban China. Sometimes this shift can be quite dramatic. In Shandong, where Andrew Kipnis has done research, rural parents in the 1980s saved their money primarily to build a house for their sons, as this made it easier to attract a bride to marry into their family. They gave less money to their daughters, as they assumed that their daughters would be able to demand a new house

---

[15] Cai, Hua 2001.

from the families into which they married.[16] Now, most rural parents' first savings goal is to amass the money necessary to send their children – both sons and daughters – to university. They assume that their children will find their own jobs and spouses in urban areas after graduation.[17] But reversals are possible as well. As parents age and become unable to care for themselves, particularly if one parent has died, their children (usually their sons and daughters-in-law, but sometimes their daughters as well) can take them into their homes or apartments. And in large urban areas like Shanghai, where housing is becoming astronomically expensive, fiancées and their families are increasingly demanding that the groom's family provide significant funding for the new apartment in which the couple will live. The fact that the new couple moves into their own apartment marks such marriages as neolocal, but the idea that the groom's family has more fiscal responsibility for the purchase of the apartment reflects patrilineal kinship. It suggests that the marriage, and the future production of children from it, are more important to the groom's than the bride's family.

The effect of birth-control policies

China has also undergone a classic, if somewhat uneven, demographic transition.[18] During the many periods of war and famine of 20th century China, mortality rates were quite high. although they dropped considerably after 1949, rising again during the Great Leap Forward famine (1959–62). For the first two-thirds of the 20th century, birth rates in China were also quite high, but have dropped since the 1970s, especially since the launch of a stringent birth-control policy in 1979. As a consequence of the timing of this transition, many parents who were of childbearing age between 1950 and the late 1970s had several children, and most children born in that era have several siblings, while many of those born after 1979 are only children (especially in urban areas) or have only one sibling.

The recent birth-control policy (sometimes misleadingly called the "one-child policy" because of how it has been implemented in urban areas) has evolved over time, varies across the country and has had multiple effects on Chinese families. In urban areas from 1979 to the present, most couples have only been allowed to have one child, but some have

---

[16] Kipnis 1997.

[17] Kipnis 2011b.

[18] The idea of a demographic transition stems from a pioneering article by Warren S Thompson (1929).

been exempted from this limitation. For example, in most provinces since the late 1990s, and in some since the mid-1980s, urban couples in which both partners are single children have been allowed to have two children.[19] In the 1980s and 1990s, few couples met this criterion, but of course, the success of the birth-control policy means that in the 21st century, many more do. In rural areas since the late 1980s, the policy has allowed a couple to have a second child if their first is a girl or a child with a disability, and in many rural areas today, the policy automatically allows two children. In many cases, where more than one child is allowed, the spacing between births also has been regulated, so that in many two-child families the elder sibling is significantly older than the younger sibling.[20]

The birth-control policy has had many intended and unintended effects on family relationships. The ratio of people in the older generation to those in the younger generation is growing rapidly. China's population in the 0–14 age category is expected to remain stable until the year 2020, at which point it will begin to decline. The working-age population (ages 15 to 64) will vary slightly until 2026, at which point it will decline rapidly. The elderly population (age 65 and older), however, is now growing rapidly and is projected to do so for the next 25 years. Consequently, while there have been relatively abundant resources for childcare and education for the past three decades, the burden of care for the elderly is increasing and will be high in the future. It is predicted that, between 2010 and 2050, the ratio of working-age to elderly population will drop from almost 10:1 to nearly as low as 2:1.

In urban areas, many families have had to get used to the idea of having a daughter but no son, which is leading to changing gender roles within the family and more equal treatment of daughters and sons.[21] The desire to have at least one son, in order to continue the patriline, is weaker but has not vanished completely. In rural areas where a second child is allowed if the first is a girl, almost all girls have one sibling, while boys are often only children; girls may be older sisters or younger sisters, but boys cannot have a younger sibling and so cannot experience the role of an older brother. In some places, a minority of parents wish so strongly to have a son that they practice fetal testing (although it is illegal) and sex-selective abortion, with the result that the national sex ratio at birth has increased from the natural ratio of about 105 (that is, 105 boys born for every 100 girls) to 118, according to 2010 census

---

[19] This information comes from Thomas Scharping's lengthy list (Scharping 2003, pp. 98–100) of the provincial birth-planning rules that allowed second births in the period 1979–99.

[20] For a review of recent books on the birth control policy, see Jacka 2007.

[21] Fong 2002.

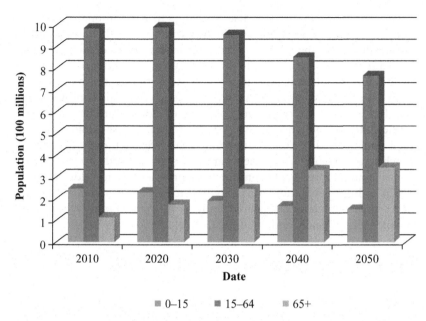

Figure 1.1 Population of different age groups.
Source: Data from Wei & Liu 2009, pp. 19–20.

data.[22] As a consequence, when these boys become men, many will not be able to marry. Finally, families who violate the birth-control policy often suffer enormous fines (usually six times the average annual income in a given area). To avoid these fines they sometimes hide their children from the authorities, with the result that China has an unknown number of unregistered children.[23] These children may suffer extreme disadvantage, unless their families are wealthy, both because the large fines cause poverty and because children who are not officially registered cannot access public schooling and other public goods.

The culture of Chinese kinship is becoming simpler because people born after 1980 tend to have fewer siblings. Children born now have many fewer aunts and uncles and cousins than those born just 20 years ago. Some only children complain of being lonely and wish for a brother or sister. The use of generation names is also declining, but not only because of the lack of siblings. Among urbanites, discrimination against rural residents and rural migrants is common. Urban parents often choose a two-character name, rather than three characters, to prevent the name being interpreted as a generation name, since this would mark the child as coming from a rural area where lineages are still important.

[22] Hudson 2012.
[23] Greenhalgh 2003.

Patterns of aged care are also evolving. In a traditional patrilineal, virilocal family, old parents would live with one of their sons and be physically taken care of by their daughter-in-law. Ideals of filial piety suggested that middle-aged people should focus on satisfying every whim of their aging parents and never argue with them (though this may not have been the actual experience). As family sizes have dropped and urbanization has increased, more diverse patterns of elderly care have emerged. Some older people end up living with or receiving at-home care from their daughters rather than daughters-in-law. Men sometimes provide as much financial support for their parents-in-law as for their own parents. Old-age homes are also becoming more prevalent. Some elderly people prefer to live in such homes as they find it easier to get along with their peers than with younger people; but, as in many societies, many old people feel physically and emotionally neglected.

THE WELFARE OF THE RURAL ELDERLY

Anthropologists doing research in Chinese villages in the early 2000s found that elderly people in rural areas were often unhappy with their living arrangements. Health-care costs were expensive; members of the younger generation were prioritizing financial support for their nuclear households over care for the elderly; poorer villages lacked the resources to build homes for the elderly or to force younger people to care for their parents; and some younger people migrated to urban areas and rarely returned home. In one village in Hubei province, the anthropologist Hong Zhang documented nine cases of elderly suicide between 1991 and 2000. In a 1991 case, an elderly widow did not get along well with her two daughters-in-law. When she fell ill, realizing that neither of her daughters-in-law would agree to pay for her medical treatment without a fight from her sons, she hanged herself.[24]

Since the early 2000s, the government has rolled out national schemes to provide the minimum livelihood allowance (*dibao*), medical insurance, medical relief funds and old-age pensions for the rural population. It is too early to gauge the full impact of the new schemes, but they are likely to contribute substantially to improvements in the welfare of the elderly and inter-family relations in rural areas. This may, in turn, lead to declines in elderly suicide rates.

---

[24] Zhang, Hong 2004, p. 80. Among two groups in China – young rural women and the rural elderly (women and men) – suicide rates are extremely high compared with those

Finally, intra-family power relations have shifted in the 20th and 21st centuries, with young adults gaining power and autonomy and increasingly carving out lives and identities independently from parents. This shift in power relations has both contributed to, and been bolstered by, a weakening in the premium placed on filial piety, ancestor worship and the maintenance of patrilineages, and in the growing strength of individualism and expectations for gender equality.

An important debate on the patterns of change that have affected Chinese families addresses the extent to which these changes are the result of either state policies or reactions to the processes of modernization. As we discussed in the introduction, modernization includes urbanization, industrialization, increasing mass education, commercialization and advances in technology that enable goods, values and people to travel further and more quickly. A realistic assessment would be that both state policies and reactions to modernization are important, and that the policies themselves have both shaped and been shaped by the processes of modernization. Nevertheless, heuristically separating the causes of change into these two categories is a useful starting point for discussion.

The effect of the Marriage Law

Many state policies affect family size and structure and relationships within the family, but the policies that have most directly affected them are the birth-control policy discussed above and the Marriage Law. In both cases, state policy reinforced trends that were occurring anyway to a certain extent. The Marriage Law, introduced in 1950, is discussed in more detail in Chapter 2. In brief, it had the potential to profoundly affect family formation and structure, because it raised the age of marriage; banned polygamy, arranged marriages and monetary transactions in marriage; and enshrined the principles of freedom of marriage and divorce, and equality between husband and wife.[25] In urban areas, the implementation of both the Marriage Law, and later, the birth-control policy, went relatively smoothly because the efforts of family reformers and revolutionaries, combined with the processes of modernization, had

---

of other countries. The causes of these high rates are poorly understood, but some attribute them to an exacerbation of family conflicts resulting from the rapid changes accompanying modernization. See, for example, Wu 2010.

[25] The fundamental elements of the 1950 Marriage Law already were included in the Civil Code proposed by the Nationalist Party in 1930, and the CCP's Marriage Law of 1934, implemented in the Jiangxi Soviet. The 1950 Marriage Law was substantially revised in 1980 and 2001. An excerpt from the 2001 Law is included in Chapter 2.

already resulted in a normalization of "love marriages", an increase in the average age of marriage, and declines in fertility and the size of families.

In the countryside, both the Marriage Law and the birth-control policy met with much more resistance. In the 1950s, many men and some women in villages responded with abuse and physical violence to officials' efforts to promote and implement freedom of marriage and divorce, fearing that such policies would both undermine their efforts to create stable families and also threaten patriarchal power. Increases in the autonomy and power of young women were also resisted by their mothers-in-law, who worried (with some justification) that the young women's new status would undermine their own hard-won position in the family structure. In response, the state backed off and to this day men and women do not enjoy equal rights in rural China.

In the 1980s, villagers were much more resistant to the birth-control policy than were urbanites, often responding to officials implementing the policy with levels of abuse and violence similar to those with which the older folk among them had greeted the Marriage Law in the 1950s. This was why the birth-control policy was revised in the late 1980s, to allow villagers to have a second child if the first was a girl. The main reason for the resistance was that, combined with the dominance of virilocal marriage, and given the lack of an old-age pension scheme in most rural areas, the one-child restriction on families posed a serious challenge to couples' efforts to secure their livelihood in old age, as it reduced their chances of having a son. Many researchers in rural China from the 1980s onward have noted that most parents say that their ideal family would include two children: one son and one daughter. The anthropologist Susan Greenhalgh has argued that a gentler, less dictatorial form of family-planning policy that always allowed two children might still have led to similar demographic results as the one-child policy as implemented, and that much of the reduction of birth rates during the 30 years of the policy has been a result of urbanization rather than of the policy.[26] State officials in rural areas, however, often argue that despite the ideal of two children, the preference of rural families for having a son would drive couples to keep having children until they had a son, leading to many families of more than two children.

The effect of modernization

How do processes of modernization lead to changes in family form? Many interrelated factors overlap. Patrilineal kinship and virilocal marriage are

[26] Greenhalgh 2008; Greenhalgh & Winckler 2005.

institutions that evolved in the context of life in an agricultural society in which the vast majority of people lived in villages, moved rarely and relied on farming to survive. As people have begun to move to urban areas, attend schools, work in factories and move more often from place to place, new possibilities have opened up, new desires have arisen and new problems have to be faced. For example, when young people attend school until the age of 20 or even older, they become less able to help their parents with labor at home or on the farm. The cost of raising children has also increased, and young people have had more opportunity to meet potential spouses away from home. Young people who have migrated to cities in search of work may also meet potential marriage partners without their parents' supervision. In the past, life in villages was relatively stable (at least during peaceful times). Young people were destined to be farmers, children were considered blessings who could labor at home and extend the patriline, and so, early marriage made much sense. Today, however, it is difficult for students and migrant workers to imagine what their future will hold and, partly for this reason, fewer people are willing to commit to marriage at a young age.

In the late 20th and early 21st centuries, life in urban areas has sometimes been very different from life in villages, but the extent and nature of these differences has varied over time and from one place to another. For example, from the 1960s to the mid-1990s, almost all retired workers in urban areas received pensions from the state. The existence of such pensions meant that older people did not need to rely on their children for financial assistance in their old age. In rural areas, however, old people depended more on their children to fund their retirement, and so feared the prospect of not having a son. In the later 1990s and into the 2000s, increasing numbers of retired urban workers found themselves without a pension, while some wealthy villages established new pension schemes for their retirees. Since then, the old-age pension schemes we discussed earlier have been developed across the country, for many rural and urban citizens. Modernization, then, does not always cause change for families in a single, linear direction.

Chapter 2 looks more closely at some of the sources of social change in marriage practices and intimate relationships in the post-Mao period. Later, Chapter 12 delves more deeply into changes that have occurred over this period in relation to gender inequalities and the status of women.

Summary

Until the late 20th century, Chinese kinship could be described as being predominately patrilineal, patriarchal and virilocal. Even in imperial times, though, there were always both alternative institutions of kinship and a great variety of concrete forms of affection, care and reciprocity, and power relations that took place within patrilineal, patriarchal, virilocal kinship.

The institutions of patrilineal kinship and virilocal marriage are still important in China today, especially in rural areas, and these institutions also provide cultural imaginaries of relatedness that are drawn upon in a wide variety of extra-familial relationships. However, Chinese society is changing rapidly and, especially in urban areas, forms of Chinese kinship that were dominant are becoming less visible. Most urban households, and many rural households, can now properly be called neolocal, and family relations are in many cases less patriarchal than before. China is also undergoing a rapid demographic transition and its population's age profile is transforming. This transformation has many implications for everyday practices of kinship and relatedness.

Discussion questions

1. What aspects of family change in modern China are most interesting to you? What are the most likely causes of these changes? How would you go about researching the changes and what information would you need to collect to analyze their causes?
2. Concepts such as patrilineal, patriarchal kinship and virilocal marriage can be considered abstractions that are somewhat distant from the actual practices of care and reciprocity, power relations, forms of conflict and feelings of affection or anger that can arise in actual families. What nuances of family life are missed when one sums up rural Chinese families with the terms *patrilineal*, *patriarchal* and *virilocal*? What about rural Chinese family life could not be explained without these terms?
3. Do you think that the family is a more important social institution in contemporary China than in the society in which you live? Explain your answer.
4. What sort of research would be needed to address the comparative questions raised by Fei Xiaotong's conception of a "differential mode of association"?

Recommended reading

Brandtstadter, Susanne & dos Santos, Goncalo (eds) 2009, *Chinese Kinship: Contemporary Anthropological Perspectives*. New York: Routledge.

Fei, Hsiao Tung [Fei, Xiaotong] 1992, *From the Soil: The Foundations of Chinese Society, A Translation of Fei Xiaotong's* Xiangtu Zhongguo (trans. Gary Hamilton and Wang Zheng). Berkeley: University of California Press.

Friedman, Sara L 2006, *Intimate Politics: Marriage, the Market, and State Power in Southeastern China.* Cambridge, MA: Harvard University Press.

Greenhalgh, Susan & Winckler, Edwin A 2005, *Governing China's Population: From Leninist to Neoliberal Politics.* Stanford, CA: Stanford University Press.

Hsu, Francis LK 1971 [1948], *Under the Ancestors' Shadow: Kinship, Personality, and Social Mobility in China.* Stanford, CA: Stanford University Press.

Ikels, Charlotte (ed.) 2004, *Filial Piety: Practice and Discourse in Contemporary East Asia.* Stanford, CA: Stanford University Press.

Kipnis, Andrew 1997, *Producing* Guanxi: *Sentiment, Self, and Subculture in a North China Village.* Durham, NC: Duke University Press.

Wolf, Margery 1972, *Women and the Family in Rural Taiwan.* Stanford, CA: Stanford University Press.

Yang, Mayfair Mei-hui 1994, *Gifts, Favors, and Banquets: The Art of Social Relationships in China.* Ithaca, NY: Cornell University Press.

2   Marriage, Intimacy and Sex

Many westerners visiting China between the 1970s and the mid-1980s reported that it seemed one of the most sexually conservative societies in the world. Whether or not those perceptions were accurate, few western visitors today would make a similar assessment. As in any society, sexually conservative attitudes often accompany, or respond to, public expressions of sexuality in whatever form. But, in contrast to the common perception of the 1970s and 1980s, it is easy to discern a huge range of sexual views and attitudes in China today. This development reflects a number of interrelated social changes, including a rapidly accelerating shift from arranged to chosen marriage; a gradual, but cumulatively large, extension in the number of years young people spend as single adults; changes to patterns of marriage and divorce; rapid urbanization; the explosive growth of consumerism and advertising, and the use of sexual imagery in advertising; the rise of the internet and other new communications' technologies and their use in finding romance, sharing pornography and discussing sexual issues; and the growth of a large and highly visible commercial sexual services sector. This chapter discusses each of these changes.

Marriage law, shifting marital practices and premarital sex

In rural China during the first half of the 20th century, it was common for parents and matchmakers to completely arrange a marriage. The couple would not even meet one another until the wedding itself and the wedding would occur when the couple was quite young. Often, the bride was two years older than the groom, because it was thought that the bride needed to make more of an adjustment than the groom (as she would move to a new family and village) and because given the young age of the new couple (often, the groom was about 12 years old while the bride was about 14), the bride's physical maturity, relative to her new husband's, would enable her to bear children more quickly. After coming

47

to power, the CCP enacted a new Marriage Law (1950), intended to end arranged marriages in China. The law required the new couple to register their marriage in person before the wedding (forcing the couple to meet each other and declare their wish to marry, without the presence of parents), and raised the minimum legal age for marriage (to 20 for men and 18 for women, since revised more than once). Today, almost all marriages in China involve the initiative and consent of those getting married, although matchmakers and members of the older generation may still be involved in the process, especially in rural areas. Even in urban areas, "matchmaking parks" exist where parents worried about the marital status of their children can meet up to identify socially appropriate potential partners. The parents then tell their children that they just happened to hear about "so and so's very eligible son or daughter" when chatting with friends. The average age at marriage has risen considerably (to the mid-20s and, often, the late 20s, depending on the part of China in question), and the average age for grooms is slightly older than that of brides (although, in some parts of rural northern China, a pattern of brides being two years older than grooms persists).

The shift from arranged to love matches has been gradual, and there are many possible stages between the two. Parents may arrange for a potential couple to meet each other once or twice before forcing the couple to decide on the marriage. The meetings may evolve into an extended courtship period; or, young people can initiate the entire process themselves and ask parents and matchmakers to get involved only after they have made up their own minds about the matter. As this shift has come about, at different speeds in different places, the criteria for ideal partners have also evolved, as have norms for appropriate decorum in public. While parents and matchmakers commonly emphasize considerations of household economy and political status when selecting a potential spouse, young people tend to place more emphasis on personal compatibility and physical attractiveness, as well as the individual's financial standing and security. Yunxiang Yan has depicted how, during the 1990s, young rural women desired young men with the ability to "talk", by which they meant both a general willingness to speak out in public and an ability to flirt and speak the language of romance in private; until then, parents and matchmakers had emphasized the virtues of the strong, silent type.[1] As late as the 1980s, young Chinese couples rarely displayed their affection for one another publicly. Even in relatively large cities, the act of holding hands in public (by people of the opposite sex) would elicit stares and laughter. Now, people often hold hands, kiss each other in public and cast affectionate glances to each other, even in small-town China. Moreover, as the vast majority of Chinese young people in their

[1] Yan 2003.

late teens and early 20s live outside villages, either studying at boarding schools and universities (located in urban areas) or laboring in cities as migrant workers, almost all young Chinese people come in contact with the culture of romance.

EXCERPT FROM THE PRC'S MARRIAGE LAW[2]

Chapter 1

Article 2

A marriage system based on the free choice of partners, on monogamy and on equality between man and woman shall be applied; the lawful rights of women, children and old people shall be protected; family planning shall be practiced.

Chapter 2

Article 6

No marriage may be contracted before the man has reached 22 years of age and the woman 20 years of age. Late marriage and late childbirth shall be encouraged.

Article 8

Both the man and the woman desiring to contract a marriage shall register in person with the marriage registration office.

Chapter 3

Article 16

Both husband and wife shall have the duty to practice family planning.

Article 17

The following property acquired by the husband and the wife during the period in which they are under contract of marriage shall be in their joint possession: (1) wages and bonuses; (2) proceeds of production and business operations; (3) earnings from intellectual property rights.

Article 18

The property in the following cases shall belong to one party of the couple: (1) the property that belongs to one party before marriage; . . . (3) the property to be in the possession of one party as determined by will or by an agreement on gifts.

---

[2] Excerpted from "Marriage Law of the People's Republic of China" 2001. As amended in 2001, this version of the law was current in 2012.

Chapter 4

Article 31

Divorce shall be granted if husband and wife both desire it.

Article 32

If one party alone desires a divorce...divorce shall be granted if mediation fails because mutual affection no longer exists.

The Marriage Law clearly supports the idea of romance. Not only does it stipulate that marriage should be based on free choice, but it also allows for divorce, even if only one party wants it, when "mutual affection no longer exists". The divorce rate in China has in fact been rising quite rapidly, from only four percent in 1979 to more than 21 percent in 2008. In addition, women initiated more than 70 percent of divorce cases between 2000 and 2010.[3] Even in rural areas, women are more likely to initiate divorce than men, with extramarital affairs being the most common reason for divorce; women are just as likely to conduct an extramarital affair as their husbands. After divorce, women in rural areas find new partners more often than rural men do. But in urban areas, the most common reasons for divorce are extramarital affairs conducted, and domestic violence committed, by men, and women are no more likely than men to find new partners.[4] The imbalance in remarriage reflects the fact that women attempt to marry men of higher social status (hypergamy), resulting in higher percentages of women living in urban areas than in rural areas. This imbalance will be exacerbated when the sex-selective abortion that began during the late 1990s and 2000s[5] leads to further skewing of sex ratios among people of marital age in rural areas.

The division of property after divorce is a contentious issue. In 2011, the Supreme Court made a judicial interpretation of Article 18 of the Marriage Law (see text box above), which implied that in cases of divorce where the man's family had provided the couple with a house or apartment, the apartment would remain the husband's property. This ruling shocked women who thought they had secured a safe life by demanding that their in-laws provide the couple an apartment before agreeing to

---

[3] Kleinman et al. 2011, p. 21.

[4] Ibid., pp. 21–3.

[5] Fetal sex-testing is illegal but occurs in China. In rural areas, son-preference and the restrictions of the birth-control policy lead some women to abort after learning that they are carrying a female fetus. This is the main reason for highly skewed sex ratios at birth in China today. See Chapter 1 for further discussion.

marriage, and set off a sharp-toned internet debate. Many women (or those posing as women on the internet) said that the ruling was a blow to marital equality and women's interests. Many men (or people posing as men on the internet) argued that, after the ruling, urban women would prefer to marry men who have the potential to earn a high income than those who have rich parents.[6] In rural areas, the financial outcomes for divorced women are often disastrous, as they not only lose their housing but can also lose all claims to land resources in their husband's villages.[7] This form of property division sheds new light on the rural divorce patterns mentioned above. Many rural women only dare to seek divorce if they have found a new partner who can provide land and property, which explains the fact that rural divorces often involve women who have had an extramarital affair. For rural women in unhappy marriages who do not have a relationship with another man, remaining married, even in cases of domestic violence, is often the only option.

Attitudes toward premarital sex are shifting, alongside marital and divorce practices. In the 1990s, Yunxiang Yan's research showed that premarital sex became increasingly common among engaged couples in rural China,[8] while James Farrer's research showed that, during the 1990s and early 2000s in urban Shanghai, premarital sex was common even among those who were not engaged, though most women emphasized the importance of a deep emotional attachment.[9] In the 1980s, even university students were not supposed to fall in love, while today, romance is tacitly accepted even in some secondary schools, although it remains against the rules at most schools. Børge Bakken has depicted how, in the 1980s, a perceived rise in the number of people having premarital sex led to a moral panic in which it was claimed that premarital sex led to disengagement from school, hooliganism and a life of crime, and was caused by "western influences" and increasing "disorder" in society at large.[10]

While conservative discourses (such as the one Bakken analyzed) persist, they are now only one voice among many in public discourse about sex. Some people publicly declare no-strings sex to be reasonable behavior, and many believe that sex is appropriate whenever there are true feelings (*ganqing*). Many men declare that the status of their wife's virginity at marriage does not matter to them, and others go to great lengths to have sex with a virgin. But much of the public discourse about sex – whether it sees premarital sex as good or evil, and female virginity as

[6] Some English translations of this debate may be found in Fauna 2011.
[7] Sargeson & Song 2010.
[8] Yan 2003.
[9] Farrer 2002.
[10] Bakken 2000.

unimportant or essential – mistakenly assumes that sexual behavior is becoming more and more liberated (or that sexual morality is declining). In fact, the increase in the average age of marriage has been central to the increasing rate of premarital sex. In China's largest urban areas, the average age of young women at their first marriage has now reached the late 20s, and it is still rising. Compare this situation to rural northern China in the 1930s and 1940s, when many teenagers were married before they reached the age of 15. Of course, girls who marry at the age of 14 are more likely to be virgins than are women who marry at 27. It is also safe to argue that teenagers in 1940s rural China had much more sex than their counterparts in contemporary urban China, but it was not premarital sex.

AGE OF FIRST MARRIAGE

Data on marriage age in China, especially before the 1950s, is difficult to come by. The sociologist Ansley Coale gives the average age of first marriage for all women in China as 17.5 during the 1930s.[11] The national average seems to rise gradually across the 1940s, 1950s, 1960s and 1970s to reach 23 by the early 1980s. In many urban areas, there was actually a decline in the average age of first marriage during the early 1980s, as policy during the late 1970s focused on reducing birth rates by promoting late marriage (after the age of 23 in rural areas, 25 in urban areas) while the 1980s saw birth rates controlled more directly through the birth-control policy, and a reduction in legal age for marriage to 20 for women, 22 for men. But the trend reversed after a few years of declining age at first marriage. According to data from the 2010 census in Shanghai, the average age of first marriage was 26.5 for women and 28.8 for men. This represented an increase of about 0.4 years from 2009.[12]

Commercialization, sex and romance

The post-Mao period in China has seen a gradual build-up of all aspects of market culture: a growth in marketing activity; the commercialization of a widening range of aspects of daily life; and the rise of a

---

[11] Coale 1989.
[12] On the 2010 marriage rates in Shanghai, see Chinese Women's Research Network 2011. For more demographic detail on marriage age in earlier periods, see Tien 1983.

consumer-oriented culture in which money grants its owner seemingly endless privilege. This market culture affects sexuality, intimacy and desire in a number of ways. Images of beautiful, mostly naked women (and much more rarely men) now adorn magazine covers, flash across television screens, and fill immense billboards at the busiest intersections in China's towns and cities. Various aspects of romance and sexuality are directly commercialized: businesses promoting elaborate wedding ceremonies and photography services and offering photo shoots of couples in expensive wedding outfits have sprung up all over China; many engaged or already married Chinese couples spend several months' income on large portraits of themselves in expensive outfits and romantic poses; Valentine's Day is promoted as a time for men to buy gifts for their girlfriends. A massive industry – extending into cosmetics, dietary plans and supplements, plastic surgery, and spa services – encourages and enables women to improve their physical appearance. Men can choose from a huge variety of lotions, supplements and medical services that supposedly enhance their virility. And clothes are sold to enhance the femininity of women and the masculinity of men, just as they are in most other countries around the world.

The pictures below depict large advertising billboards visible at a busy intersection in a small city in China. While there are certainly advertisements of fully dressed women, images of partially undressed women are quite common, and there are hardly any billboards of men in their underwear. In the 1990s, Dru Gladney observed that public images of undressed women were more likely to be of foreign women or ethnic minority women than ethnically Han women. Gladney interpreted this trend as reflecting the efforts of censors to discipline mainstream women into maintaining a prim and proper sexual demeanor by never showing provocative images of them in public.[13] However, since the early 2000s, images of undressed Han women have become increasingly prevalent.

The effects of all of this commercial activity are doubtlessly complex, but we can note a few general trends. First of all, the predominant forms of masculinity and femininity promoted in advertising are ones that equate masculinity with wealth, especially the ability to have both the money and the knowledge to consume the most elegant of products, and femininity with beauty and the consumption of products to enhance beauty. Advertisers play on the stereotype of a man who is crass and uneducated, a country bumpkin who has recently acquired money but who does not know how to spend it in a way that demonstrates his elegance and style. They suggest that, by buying certain types of products, men can demonstrate that they are worthy of their money.

---

[13] Gladney 2004a.

Image 2.1   Advertising billboards.
Source: Andrew Kipnis, Shandong 2008.

The lifestyles on offer are often depicted with the idea of "good taste" (*pinwei*), which connotes the ability to rank objects in terms of a distinctly graded social hierarchy.[14] Displays of women equate beauty with

[14] Song & Lee 2010.

wealth and status, suggesting that women's sexual attractiveness is their main path to power. A general equation between sexual desire and consumption is also made: advertisers suggest that consumers can satisfy their sexual and social desires if they buy the right products. The constant presence of sexually suggestive imagery in public also implies to the poor that the wealthy are able to satisfy all of their fantasies. Finally, the constant presence of sexual imagery suggests that sex itself is the ultimate form of human desire.

The impact of this latter suggestion can be seen in the growth of a medical services industry specializing in "men's health" since the beginning of the 1980s. Men's health is a euphemism for treatment for impotence and, while Chinese medicine has offered cures for impotence for thousands of years, it is only since the 1980s that specific clinics have arisen for the treatment of this problem and that hospitals have devoted space and doctors to it. These profit-seeking treatment centers can be said to have both responded to societal demand and spurred this demand with their incessant advertising. While it would be foolish to suggest that impotence did not exist before that time, the social and psychological importance of this problem for men (and perhaps their wives and girlfriends) has grown. The anthropologist Everett Zhang describes how, during the Maoist era, sexual desire was considered a form of selfishness and sexual crimes were forcefully treated as crimes against the state. While infertility was considered a problem, impotence was not (outside the context of reproduction). By the 1990s, patients at men's clinics began describing impotence as "the most shameful thing a man can experience".[15] A ditty circulated in men's clinics in the late 1990s, depicting the evolution in sexuality since the Maoist era:

In the past, I had the thieving heart [to indulge in sex], but not the thieving guts [to do it]. Later, I had both the thieving heart and the thieving guts, but not the dirty, thieving money. Now I have the thieving heart, the thieving guts and the thieving money, but the "thief" itself [i.e. my penis] doesn't work anymore [过去是有贼心没有贼胆. 后来是有贼心有贼胆没有贼钱. 现在是有贼心, 有贼胆, 有贼钱, 但是 "贼" 不行了].[16]

Prostitution and sexual services

Prostitution represents the ultimate commercialization of sex. While there are no reliable measures of the extent of prostitution in various

[15] Zhang 2007, pp. 491–508; p. 495.
[16] Ibid., p. 502.

countries, and we cannot say whether prostitution is more or less prevalent in China than in other countries, the visibility of sex work certainly increased from the mid-1980s to the late 2000s. As the ditty we quoted above suggests, money enables men to buy sex easily, as long as they are not impotent.

The growth of commercial sexual services in China has been tightly tied to the expansion of business entertaining. The need for this sort of entertaining relates to the debates about the lack of an established system of rule of law and the culture of *guanxi* we discussed in Chapter 1. Many laws concerning business transactions are either very loosely phrased, or phrased so tightly that almost everyone who does business can be accused of breaking the law, and so, businesspeople in many sectors need to have good relationships with the government officials who interpret the law. These officials have discretion to interpret the law favorably for, or award government contracts to, particular businesses. They can also ensure that the officials who work under them do not accuse certain businesses of violating the law. Businesspeople often go to great lengths to curry favor with the right officials because of their discretionary power. This may involve bribery, although offering bribes directly is very risky for all concerned, as higher levels of the government frequently launch anti-corruption campaigns and mete out extreme punishment (including the death penalty) to officials found guilty of accepting bribes and businesspeople found guilty of issuing bribes.

It is safer to entertain officials or provide them with favors that do not leave a direct monetary trace, and this may also be a way for a businessperson to build trust and encourage a particular official to accept a bribe. The most common methods of entertaining involve inviting officials to banquets and afterwards visiting a karaoke bar or a massage and sauna establishment, where women will serve the male businessmen and officials and may also offer sexual services. The prevalence of this sort of business entertaining is one factor that makes it difficult for women to get high-level positions in government and in certain industries, because it simply is not appropriate for women to visit such venues. The anthropologist Xin Liu has argued that, as a result of the extent of this sort of business entertaining, the triangular relationship between businessmen, officials and hostesses has become part of stock narratives – the stories people tell one another – about doing business in China.[17] Other anthropologists have described the evolution of business entertaining in China as a sequence, from arranging banquets of increasingly exotic and expensive dishes to setting up evenings with prostitutes to

[17] Liu 2002.

finding officials permanent mistresses, salaried and set up in their own apartments.[18]

Researchers who study the women involved in sexual services argue that the industry is closely tied to the phenomenon of rural-to-urban migration and discrimination against migrants of rural origins (we discuss this topic in Chapter 3). The anthropologist Tiantian Zheng depicts how women who worked in hostess bars in the northeastern city of Dalian between 1999 and 2002 said they were from large cities when in fact almost all of them were from rural areas. These women also went to great lengths to appear urbanized. They were very fashion-conscious, spending considerable amounts of money on clothes that marked them as having sophisticated urban tastes and disparaging other women – most likely those who actually were Dalian urbanites – as country bumpkins who lacked taste.[19] The women also used expensive skin-whitening creams and underwent other painful skin-whitening treatments; in China, dark skin is associated with working in the fields and so with rural origins. These social and psychological strategies speak to the insecurities attached to the women's profession in particular and to female migrant workers in urban China in general. As relatively uneducated women from rural areas, the women in Zheng's study had few options outside low-paying jobs in the service sector or factories. While few of them came to urban areas intending to become sex workers, those who stumbled into jobs in the service sector, such as waitresses or hotel workers, rapidly learned how relatively lucrative sex work was and how limited their other options were. The many levels of sex work – from women who are paid merely to flirt, to those who flirt and engage in limited forms of touching, to fully fledged sex work – enable a gradual transition for women who initially feel hesitant. Once they became sex workers, the women in the study encountered discrimination not only on account of their occupation but also because their work marked them as rural migrants. So, they adopted strategies to appear to be urban citizens.

Researchers in the Sichuan city of Chengdu discovered a related, but perhaps counterintuitive, phenomenon in the late 2000s. In Chengdu, the male clients liked to pursue – or at least to fantasize about pursuing – educated, urban, sexually inexperienced young women whom they labeled with the term "university students". As a result, many sex workers began dressing as prim-and-proper office workers (a style that to them indicated the status of a university student). At the same time, some female university students began wearing revealing, colorful and sexy outfits in public. A sexist joke circulated in Chengdu nightclubs: "How

[18] Osborg 2013.
[19] Zheng 2009.

do you tell the university students from the prostitutes? Young women dressed like prostitutes are all university students; those dressed like university students are prostitutes."[20] In short, the efforts of sex workers to disguise their rural origins reflects a form of social hierarchy that can be said to influence the types of discrimination migrant women workers face, the sexual fantasies of urban men and perhaps even the fashion tastes of college students (who, shielded from the discrimination migrant workers face, are more free to follow trends in alternative fashion).

Many women who undertake sex work follow quite conservative family values in other aspects of their lives. They hide their occupational identity from their friends and family in their rural villages. They suffer the humiliations of life as a sex worker – and sometimes violent attacks – so that they can send considerable amounts of money back to their parents to help pay family medical expenses or the education costs of their siblings or cousins. Most also dream of finding the right man, quitting sex work, marrying, settling down and raising a family. According to Zheng, many of them eventually achieve their goals.[21]

Men also work in the sex trade, engaging as their clients women and/or men. Like their female counterparts, these men are almost universally from rural areas. Although there are fewer of them than female sex workers, they also can suffer discrimination because they are presumed to have rural origins. Lisa Rofel describes how some gay men in China denounce "money boys" (an English term that is often used by Chinese speakers as slang for men who sell sex to other men) as rural migrants looking for easy money in the big city. In such discourse, the money boys are said not to deserve the label "gay", and not to understand the true meaning of love. The only "solution" is for money boys to either go home to their villages or get "real jobs".[22]

Mobility, urbanization and sexual culture

Two classic themes in the sociological literature on urbanization and mobility are relevant to cultures of sexuality and romance. First is the experience of leaving a rural home and living in an urban area. Rural-to-urban migration can involve escaping the parental (or other familial) supervision of one's behavior that stems from living in the same house or village with close relatives. Such patriarchal supervision can be especially strict in the cases of women and young people. A desire to avoid

[20] Osborg 2013, p. 65.
[21] Zheng 2009.
[22] Rofel 2010. Discrimination against rural people in the gay community is further discussed in Chapter 4.

such supervision may motivate a young person, especially a woman, to migrate to a city. Once a young migrant arrives in the city, however, she may experience loneliness. In addition, migrants are exposed to the incessant sexual imagery we have described above, and may have opportunities to go to nightclubs or other places of entertainment where it is possible to meet potential sexual partners. The combination of loneliness, lack of supervision and opportunities for socializing might seem ripe ground for the growth of a sexually liberal culture. Moderating these tendencies, however, is the fact that many migrant workers travel and live with friends and relatives from the same village, rendering them less lonely and still exposed to supervision from relatives who may report back to their parents.

One conservative discourse about sexuality links acceptable forms of romance to eligibility for marriage and stable employment. As marriage should be a match between social equals, it should ideally be delayed until one's position in life is known. Thus, secondary school or university students should not engage in romance because they do not yet know what their careers will be. When a student has graduated, settled down in a city and started a career, then the time for romance has suddenly arrived. Young women who work in relatively stable careers, such as teaching and nursing, report feeling pressure to find a husband quickly when they have started their first job, after a lifetime of hearing that dating was not proper behavior. Factories that offer stable jobs often arrange dance parties and other dating opportunities for their single workers. However, as employment opportunities for a wide variety of workers, especially migrant workers, become increasingly unstable, and as young people spend more time in formal education, hoping for good careers that may never emerge, this conservative ideal becomes difficult to live up to. The anthropologist Vanessa Fong has followed the lives of young people from the city of Dalian who travel the world in pursuit of higher education. Because these young people often have to improve their English skills before they embark on a course, and because they often work several jobs in order to be able to further their education, they often remain in formal education until their mid- or even late 20s. Living abroad and working hard may compound feelings of loneliness; many feel caught between the contradiction of the insecurities of an extremely precarious and unstable life and romantic ideals that link dating to a stage of life when one is prepared to settle down and get married.[23] In the same way, fictional discourse about the dating habits of young migrant workers depicts the contradictions between quite conservative sexual ideals and the unstable lives that make dating without firm commitment highly practical.

[23] Fong 2011.

The second theme in the classic sociology of urbanization is the manner in which the concentration of population in large urban areas allows the growth of diverse subcultures. Historically, in many countries, urbanization has helped to form social networks of gay men (and in some countries lesbian women). In large cities in China, gay subcultures for men (and, to a much lesser extent, women) have clearly formed. There is considerable debate, however, over how far China can be considered tolerant of homosexuality. On the one hand, in China the Christian tradition of labelling homosexuality a sin has much less strength than it does in many western countries (though there is now a large Christian population in China, Hong Kong and Taiwan, whose protests against homosexuality are increasingly visible). Literature depicting the sexual practices of elite men in imperial China often includes portrayals of sexual encounters between men, without taking a judgmental attitude. In contemporary China, one hears little about incidents of "gay-bashing", in which some men beat up others on a personal suspicion that they might be gay. On the other hand, both men and women in China often face considerable pressure to marry, and there are many stories of gays and lesbians arranging fake heterosexual marriages while really living with their same-sex partners. In contrast to the United States, where the politics of gay identity emerged as part of an oppositional political movement and has led to the formation of many formal and informal NGOs, in China authoritarian limits on public protest and restrictions on the formation of independent NGOs have severely limited efforts at political organizing among those who identify as gay or lesbian. While the term "comrade" (*tongzhi*) has been playfully borrowed from the political discourse of the Maoist era to refer to people who identify with their homosexual desires, "comrades" in contemporary China have little opportunity to organize themselves politically.

Intimacy and the internet

All over the world – at least, wherever people are wealthy enough to access it – the internet has revolutionized the way people interact with one another, including their sexual intimacy. People search for friends, lovers and spouses on the internet. They play games of virtual romance. They download, consume and share erotic or pornographic images, videos and stories. And they debate issues of what forms of sexual intimacy or relationship are moral or immoral, normal or perverse, exploitative or fair. In China, as we discuss in Chapter 9, internet use has soared, especially among young people. The state attempts to block access to pornographic sites and to close down blogs or debates that it views as being too controversial or detrimental to the interests of the Party-state. Nevertheless, great debate and discussion over sexual issues do occur on the internet and, through blogs and other methods, Chinese internet users do share erotica and pornography. There is no state interference in people's online search for lovers, nor in their games of virtual romance.

Among the most sociologically revealing forms of this internet activity are debates and discussions about what is proper or acceptable sexual behavior. While questions of who is willing and able to participate in such debates make it impossible to say what percentage of people in China support one particular view or another, the debates provide an overview of the range of positions people adopt and the ways in which even some opposing views can be said to share some common ground. Debates about sexual issues also shed light on attitudes toward a wide range of other issues, such as what comprises "human rights" or what "free speech" really means. For example, even the most conservative critics of Mu Zimei (see the text box below) agreed that single women had the right to pursue sexual affairs with men in private and agreed further that such a right would not have been considered to exist during the Maoist period. Sexual conservatives and liberals alike seem to agree that there is a right to express one's opinion in public, though conservatives think that this right ends if what one expresses is "pornographic" or involves "treason".

MU ZIMEI

Mu Zimei is the pen name of perhaps the most infamous female sex blogger in China's internet history. Her blog started in 2003 when she was 25, but did not attract a large following until she described her one-night stand with a rock star. By late 2004, there were more than 100 000 daily hits on her blog, and she became the most discussed internet topic in China. She was flooded with requests for interviews and was reported to have said that if a certain male reporter wanted to interview her, the interview would last as long as he lasted in bed. When she was 25, she claimed to have had sex with more than 80 men, although she had no sexual experience until she was 21. Although her writing focused on feelings, ironic conversations and cool urban settings, such as nightclubs and art galleries, more than sex acts, she was not very sentimental. She said: "I do not oppose love, but I oppose loyalty; if love has to be based on loyalty, I will not choose love."[24] She complained too that sex with male virgins was dreary because they

---

[24] Farrer 2007, pp. 1–36.

attached too much emotional significance to the experience. Her blog was eventually shut down by internet censors, and interviews with her were banned from publication, though later an internet company hired her to promote their website.

The internet debates over the Mu phenomenon raised a wide range of issues, such as whether she should be considered a pioneer of women's interests by asserting women's rights to sexual pleasure, or whether her separation of sex from emotional attachment and familial obligation harmed women's interests; whether various forms of sexuality should just be considered "natural" and thus that the human regulation of sexuality is simply interference in nature, or whether being "human" and thus being "above animals" means that we constrain our sexual desires within the framework of a civilized code of ethics. Views of social hierarchy and aesthetics also entered the debates over Mu and other female sex bloggers. Many criticized sex bloggers whose appearance was labeled ugly or unsophisticated (some bloggers post photos of themselves), whose stories about sex were not written in eloquent and beautiful language, or who did not include aesthetically pleasing discussions of ethically loaded terms such as "love", "feelings" and "beauty". Critics often used language that implied that lack of sophistication in these areas was evidence of rural origins.

Summary

The shifting practices of marriage, divorce, romance and sexuality are among the most significant aspects of social change in contemporary Chinese society. Arranged marriage is gradually disappearing, the average age of marriage is increasing, and divorce is becoming more common. As most young people remain single during their teenage years and well into their 20s, questions of how to handle premarital sexuality become more important to a greater number of people. At the same time, a highly visible sexual-services industry, the relationships between aspects of sexuality and processes of commercialization, the rise of the internet and increasing urbanization all create public discussion and debate over sexual issues. These debates can be used as a lens onto other aspects of social change in contemporary China.

Discussion questions

1. How have institutions and practices relating to marriage, intimacy and sex changed in China since the 1970s? What types of

data might be drawn upon to answer this question? What are the advantages and limitations of these types of data?

2. How would you compare the types of attitudes and behaviors depicted in this chapter with those in the society in which you live?

3. In so far as they are similar, to what would you attribute the similarities? Are they a matter of human nature, living in an industrialized society, living in a society with access to the internet, or other factors?

4. In so far as they are different, to what would you attribute the difference? Do the differences come from religious or other forms of moral tradition, kinship systems, aspects of the education system, the manner in which industrialization or urbanization occurs, or other factors?

Recommended reading

Evans, Harriet 1997, *Women and Sexuality in China: Dominant Discourses of Female Sexuality and Gender since 1949*. Cambridge, UK: Polity Press.

Farrer, James 2002, *Opening Up: Youth Sex Culture and Market Reform in Shanghai*. Chicago: University of Chicago Press.

Jeffreys, Elaine (ed.) 2006, *Sex and Sexuality in China*. London: Routledge.

Liu, Petrus & Rofel, Lisa (eds.) 2010, "Beyond the Strai(gh)ts: Transnationalism and Queer Chinese Politics", *positions: east asia cultures critique*, vol. 18, no. 2 [special issue].

Yan, Yunxiang 2003, *Private Life Under Socialism: Love, Intimacy and Family Change in a Chinese Village 1949–1999*. Stanford, CA: Stanford University Press.

Zheng, Tiantian 2009, *Red Lights: The Lives of Sex Workers in Postsocialist China*. Minneapolis: University of Minnesota Press.

3   Citizenship, Household Registration and Migration

Outside the family, some of the most significant institutions in societies are those that categorize people and establish principles of inclusion and exclusion and stratification between the categories. Among the most fundamental of such institutions in the modern world is citizenship, which draws sharp distinctions between citizens who enjoy rights and privileges by virtue of being legally recognized as permanent residents of a nation, and non-citizens who do not enjoy such rights because they are legally defined as foreigners or temporary residents.

In 1950, the sociologist TH Marshall wrote an influential paper about the historical evolution of citizenship in Britain.[1] In this, he argued that institutions of citizenship established, and partially fulfilled, a social expectation for the amelioration of the class inequalities between citizens that capitalism had created. Marshall wrote that this did not happen all at once, and in the 18th and 19th centuries, civil rights

gave legal powers whose use was drastically curtailed by class prejudice and lack of economic opportunity. Political rights gave potential power whose exercise demanded experience, organization and a change of ideas as to the proper functions of government... Social rights were at a minimum and were not woven into the fabric of citizenship.[2]

In the 20th century, however, state provision of social rights in the form of public education and a national welfare system acquired a new meaning. No longer merely "an attempt to abate the obvious nuisance of destitution in the lowest ranks of society", this provision began to reshape the whole structure of social inequalities and, Marshall predicted, "might even end by converting a skyscraper into a bungalow".[3] In other words, the gap between the wealthiest citizens at the top of the class structure and the poorest at the bottom might greatly reduce.

---

[1] Originally published in 1950 as "Citizenship and social class", the paper was reprinted in Marshall 1963, pp. 67–127.

[2] Ibid., p. 99.

[3] Ibid., pp. 100–1.

In the PRC, the relationship between (national) citizenship and intra-national class and other social inequalities has been radically different from how Marshall saw the situation in Britain.[4] The notion of citizenship "rights" is a modern import from the west and, some scholars argue, the concept of "political rights" remains undeveloped in China. All the same, the PRC's constitution sets out various political, as well as civil and social rights, and article 33 states that "all citizens of the People's Republic of China are equal before the law . . . Every citizen enjoys the rights and at the same time must perform the duties prescribed by the constitution and the law".[5] In practice, however, the Chinese population has been sharply divided in its enjoyment of both particular citizenship rights, and in citizenship defined as "the right to have rights".[6] Many of these divisions result from China's *hukou* (household registration) system.

Hukou was introduced by the state in the 1950s, and categorizes people according to place of residence and whether they belong to an "agricultural" or "non-agricultural" household. It has contributed to divisions between people in two ways. First, it has divided the "rural" population (those with agricultural registration, most of whom are registered in villages and townships) from the "urban" population (those with non-agricultural registration, most of whom are registered in larger towns and cities).[7] Second, it has separated "locals" (who have local registration) from "outsiders" (who do not). For most of its history, *hukou*'s most significant social consequence has been to contribute to a rural/urban divide in social status, entitlements and life chances. In the post-Mao period, however, the distinction between those who have a local *hukou* and those who do not has become increasingly important, relative to the rural/urban divide.

The *hukou* system bears some similarities to other forms of household registration and internal passport systems in the former Soviet Union,

---

[4] Several scholars have noted that, even as an examination of the relationship between citizenship and class in Britain, Marshall's paper is flawed. In particular, he neglected severe gender inequalities in citizenship. And, as we note below, his claim that citizenship ameliorates the class inequalities created by capitalism proved inaccurate in the second half of the 20th century, both in Britain and elsewhere. However, the points we make here about divergences between Marshall's account and the history of citizenship in the PRC go well beyond these critiques.

[5] "Constitution of the People's Republic of China" 1982 (amended 2004). Since it was first promulgated in 1954, the PRC's constitution has been amended several times, but each version includes articles on "citizens' basic rights and duties". The principle of equality between citizens is enunciated in all versions of the PRC constitution, except those of 1975 and 1978 (again revised in 1982).

[6] Yu 2002, p. 290.

[7] In our discussion of *hukou*, we will refer to those with non-agricultural registration as "urban" or "urban-registered" and those with agricultural registration as "rural" or "rural-registered".

apartheid-era South Africa, Vietnam, Japan and Taiwan, but unlike such systems, it continues to have a large impact on social relations. In combination with other institutions, the *hukou* system has led to a situation in which, well into the 21st century, the average social status, entitlements, living standards and life chances of rural citizens with agricultural registration, including local residents and rural migrants to the city, have been significantly inferior to those of urban citizens with non-agricultural registration.

In discussing the *hukou* system, scholars of China have likened it to an institution of citizenship.[8] Like national citizenship in the west between the 1950s and 1970s, urban (non-agricultural) *hukou* during the same period in China came with a raft of welfare entitlements, provided by the state, from which those with rural (agricultural) *hukou* were excluded. In this period, inequalities between the urban and rural populations were large, but within each subpopulation, inequalities were reduced, just as Marshall claimed they were among the citizens of Britain.

From about the mid-1980s onward, the relationship between *hukou* and social inequalities began to diverge from Marshall's account of the relationship between citizenship and social inequalities in Britain (but then, so too did the situation in Britain and other western countries). As Dorothy Solinger writes, post-Mao China's shift from a planned to a market economy resulted in an erosion of the entitlements of urban citizens, in the same way as the decline of the welfare state in the west led to the erosion of social rights:

Both transformations were departures from systems that had protected their recipients from the force of the free market. Just as the neoliberal "conservative project" in the west, with its dictate of social spending cuts . . . introduced rampant uncertainty and shocks to the expectations of old beneficiaries, triggering accusations and exclusionary initiatives against foreigners, so in China we find urbanites blaming peasants in their midst for the social ills induced by the market.[9]

Now, let us look in more detail at the history of *hukou*.

The origins of *hukou* and its operations in the Maoist period

Precedents for the contemporary *hukou* system can be traced as far back as the 5th century BCE, when the Qin kingdom adopted a system of

---

[8] See, for example, Solinger 1999; Kipnis 2004.
[9] Solinger 1999, p. 10.

household registration to record and monitor the population and restrict its movements, primarily for the purposes of taxation and labor and military conscription. This was coupled with a form of social control through a system of inter-household mutual responsibility known as *baojia*. Following the unification of China into a single empire in 221 BCE, successive dynasties adopted and modified household registration and mutual responsibility systems, and developed laws, records and administrative hierarchies to enforce them. In the modern period, the Nationalist Party implemented both household registration and *baojia* systems. Under *baojia*, family households were organized into groupings of 10 and 100. In each grouping, households monitored each other for signs of political and ideological deviance. The Nationalist Party government used the *baojia* system against the CCP to great effect. It also introduced a Household Registration Law in 1931 and a string of revisions and accompanying regulations from the early to mid-1940s.[10]

When the CCP built a new household registration system after 1949, it drew on both imperial and Nationalist precedents. However, the *baojia* system was not renewed and, under the new registration system, the household became little more than a unit of accounting. *Hukou* was transformed into a core element in the state's control and planning of labor deployment.

In this respect, the formation of the CCP's *hukou* system was influenced by the history of the registration and planning of labor and population movement in the Soviet Union. Russian Communist Party leaders adopted and modified a Tzarist system of registration similar to that of imperial China, to facilitate the planning of industrial production and limit the growth of urban centers by limiting rural-to-urban migration. From 1932, Soviet citizens residing in an urban center were required to have a *propiska* (residence permit) stamped in their passports, and a change of residence required a change of *propiska*. Rural residents, in contrast, were not issued passports and could not get a *propiska*, and rural-to-urban migration was limited to organized collective labor transfers, for which rural workers were given temporary permits.[11]

In the PRC, household registration evolved into a similar system. As in the Soviet Union, it was managed by the police forces under the organization of the Ministry of Public Security (MPS). Through the early to mid-1950s, the MPS established *hukou* files first for urban and then rural households, and set up a network of public security bureaus and police stations around the country to manage them. Households and their members were registered as either "agricultural" or "non-agricultural".

[10] Wang, Fei-Ling 2005, pp. 32–60.
[11] Dutton 1992, pp. 195–202.

The former were registered in rural collective entities (we will discuss this more in Chapter 4), and the latter in townships, towns and cities.

The support of the peasantry had been much more crucial to the success of communist revolution in China than in Russia. After 1949, however, the CCP used *hukou* and central planning to exploit the rural population in much the way of its Russian counterparts, siphoning resources out of agriculture and the rural sector and investing in heavy industrialization and subsidization of the urban population's living standards. So, during the Maoist period, "citizenship" meant something very different depending on whether one had urban or rural *hukou*. Most adults with urban *hukou* were given lifelong employment in a state-run *danwei* (work unit), which provided them (or their spouse) and their family with subsidized housing, a range of welfare entitlements, and free education for their children. Their urban *hukou* also entitled them to coupons for subsidized grain and other food. In contrast, those with rural *hukou* worked for a collective, which in turn was required to sell a large proportion of its produce cheaply to the state. Some welfare entitlements were provided, but most of these were inferior to those provided for urban citizens, and funded by the collective, not the state. The survival of those with rural *hukou* depended on the land, the weather, and the sweat and toil that they and other members of their collective put into tilling the fields.

At birth, people were assigned the same *hukou* as their mother and there were only a few possible ways to convert an agricultural into a non-agricultural registration. Joining the People's Liberation Army (PLA) was one method, gaining entry into a university another, but only a tiny proportion of the rural population was able to access either path. Even short-term migration to a city in a bid to escape poverty was extremely difficult for anyone with agricultural registration. In the absence of markets, and given that *danwei* controlled the allocation of housing and welfare and that, after 1958, the purchase of grain and other foodstuffs in the city required proof of local registration,[12] people without local registration could not survive for long in the city (unless they had been sent as part of a temporary work team). This contributed, on the one hand, to the maintenance and aggravation of serious rural disadvantage, not only in income but also in people's living standards, health and longevity, education and access to services. On the other hand, the *hukou* system and central planning had some benefits: until the 1980s, development in China did not produce uncontrolled migration, and nor did urban slums develop as they had elsewhere in the developing world.

However, the *hukou* system never completely prevented the temporary movement of rural people into urban areas and, indeed, that was not its

---

[12] Solinger 1999, p. 44.

purpose. On the contrary, the maintenance of rural disadvantage enabled the exploitation of rural workers as a reserve army of labor who could be pulled temporarily into urban production in times of high demand, at rates of pay lower than those received by permanent members of urban *danwei*, and with fewer, if any, welfare benefits.[13] In this respect, the logic of household registration was – and continues to be – similar to that of immigration policies of developed, western countries: to make use of migrant labor to advance economic growth, while keeping down the state's costs in providing full citizenship. In China, before market reforms were introduced into urban industry, temporary rural workers were hired in relatively small numbers. In 1980, a total of about 13 million temporary workers were employed in state industrial enterprises, of whom 9 million had rural registration.[14] However, as we will soon see, this set the scene for an explosion of growth in the exploitation of temporary rural migrant labor by both state and non-state enterprises when market-oriented industrial reforms took effect from the mid-1980s onward.

Aside from this, the *hukou* system has served one further purpose for the state: it has facilitated the control of people labeled as "bad class elements" and "targeted persons" (*zhongdian renkou*). Until the late 1970s, class categorization played an important role in the differential distribution of citizenship rights, and to be labeled a "bad class element" meant a serious diminution in one's life chances. Class labels were dropped in 1979, but lists of "targeted persons" remain. These lists, which are secret, include people deemed politically suspect, criminal or potentially criminal, or otherwise socially undesirable. Such people come under greater scrutiny and surveillance by those charged with monitoring *hukou* than do the rest of the population. The increased physical mobility of the population has made the task of surveillance of targeted people much more difficult in the post-Mao period, but such surveillance remains an important element in policing, including in identifying and apprehending members of outlawed groups such as the religious sect Falun Gong (see Chapter 6), and those suspected of terrorism.[15]

Patterns of change: *hukou* and migration in a market economy

From the early 1980s onward, a market in labor began to develop alongside the market for goods, and employers pushed the state for access to the cheap, flexible, unskilled labor that rural migrants offered. Meanwhile, a

---

[13] Ibid., pp. 38–42.
[14] Walder 1986, p. 48.
[15] Wang, Fei-Ling 2005, pp. 101–12.

Image 3.1 Construction workers in Beijing. The vast majority of construction workers are rural migrants.
Source: Tom Cliff 2003.

breakdown of rural collectives and a return to household farming, and the beginnings of a market economy, led to diversification in the rural economy and, for a time, higher rural incomes. After the mid-1980s, however, rural incomes stagnated and rural–urban income inequalities markedly increased. Consequently, rural people moved in vast numbers to urban centers in search of work. By the 1990s, rural migrant men dominated China's huge construction industry, and rural migrant women its textile industries. Urban street markets and stalls selling cheap clothes, kitchen appliances and fruit and vegetables were also run primarily by rural migrants, and migrant women comprised the vast majority of those hired as urban domestic workers, restaurant waitresses and kitchen hands, and (as we have seen in Chapter 2) as sex workers. In the export-oriented industrial zones of southeast China, whose factories produced most of the world's clothes, toys and electronic components, the workforce consisted largely of young migrant women from rural areas. China's rapidly growing status as an economic superpower was built almost literally on the backs of its rural migrant workers.

DATA ON INTERNAL MIGRANTS

The scale of migration in China since the 1980s is unprecedented in human history. According to the 2000 population census, the "floating population" or "temporary migrants" – that is, people who have lived for six months or more outside the place in which they are registered – numbered 144.4 million. By the time of the 2010 population census, that figure had reached 221 million, of whom 160 million (72.4 percent) were rural migrant workers.[16]

A survey conducted by the National Bureau of Statistics (NBS) found that in 2009, there were 145.3 million rural migrant workers (defined as having lived outside their registered home township for six months or more). Of these, 62.5 percent were to be found in the east of the country, including 22.6 percent in the Pearl River Delta in Guangdong and 19.4 percent in the Yangzi River Delta, which spans Shanghai, southern Jiangsu province and northern Zhejiang province. China's export-oriented manufacturing industries are concentrated in these two river delta areas. The majority of rural migrant workers worked in manufacturing (39.1 percent), construction (17.3 percent), services (11.8 percent) or catering and retail (7.8 percent). Almost 94 percent were employed as waged laborers; just over 6 percent were self-employed.[17]

Nationally, most rural migrants are male and relatively young, and their average level of education, higher than among the rural population as a whole, is nevertheless significantly lower than among the urban-registered population. The NBS survey found that 35 percent of rural migrant workers were women. Of the total rural migrant workforce, 61.6 percent were aged between 16 and 30, and roughly 65 percent had junior secondary school education.[18]

From villagers' perspectives, rural-to-urban migration in China from the mid-1980s to the early 21st century can be explained in terms similar to those most frequently employed in the literature on migration and rural "livelihood strategies" and "householding" in Southeast Asia.[19]

---

[16] Fan 2008, p. 23; "China's floating population exceeds 221 million" 2011. The 1990 census counted just 22.6 million temporary migrants. However, this earlier census used a different definition for temporary migration, including only those people who had moved from one county-level unit to another, and who had lived away from their registered place of residence for at least 12 months.

[17] NBS, Rural Office 2009.

[18] Ibid.

[19] Jacka 2012.

officials. They can also more easily afford to pay the standard fees charged by public schools or to "grease palms" to enable their children to attend schools from which other, poorer, migrants are barred.

In the early 21st century, local governments implemented some measures aimed at improving rural migrants' circumstances and citizenship rights. The most important of these related to migrant children's schooling, detention and repatriation, and the treatment of migrant workers. City governments passed regulations that prevented local public schools refusing entry to migrant children or charging them higher fees than those paid by locally registered students. Nevertheless, some schools continued such practices, primarily because local governments provided funds only for locally registered students. Meanwhile, local governments in some cities, including Beijing and Shanghai, continued to run campaigns to close down migrant-run schools.[24]

The picture is similar with respect to the detention and repatriation of migrants. In 2003, a university graduate and fashion designer, Sun Zhigang, was detained for not carrying the required temporary resident identification, and died in custody as a result of police brutality. Following a media outcry and pressure from legal activists, the law was changed to prevent the forced detention of migrants. From then on, it was claimed, "vagrants" could only be asked, but not forced, to go to a homeless shelter where they would receive a ticket home to the countryside. In 2009, however, Human Rights Watch reported that rural migrants continued to be detained in "black jails" set up soon after the 2003 legislation was announced.[25]

In 2007, the state introduced the Labor Contract Law and the Employment Promotion Law, emphasizing the protection of the rights of all workers, including migrants (see the discussion in Chapter 5). These new laws were an important advance on previous labor laws, but did not overcome problems of non-compliance among employers. Today, many rural migrant workers still receive wages below the legal minimum, work in poor conditions, and have no social insurance. In short, recent changes have produced only gradual and relatively small improvements in the circumstances and entitlements of rural migrants, despite their growing and increasingly vocal discontent.

The gap between their citizenship and that of local, urban residents has nevertheless narrowed. This is due in part to an increase in the number of rural migrants who settle in smaller towns and townships. Increasing numbers of rural citizens go out to work first in a larger urban center a long way from home, make as much money as they can as quickly as

[24] Buckingham & Chan 2008, p. 600; Jiang 2011.
[25] Human Rights Watch 2009, pp. 11–12.

possible (regardless of the hardships involved), and use their savings to buy an apartment in a county town much closer to home, where they settle with their families. In the county town, there is less money to be made and the quality of life is not as good as that enjoyed by well-off urbanites in the larger cities, but it is improving through economic development. In such towns, there is also less discrimination against those without local *hukou*, and migrants' access to resources is similar to locally registered people.

Even in the largest urban centers, there has been something of a convergence between the circumstances and entitlements of the majority of rural migrants and those with local, urban *hukou*. On the one hand, there has been an erosion of welfare entitlements enjoyed by urban workers in state-run *danwei*, as well as a growing number of people who are unemployed or can find only poorly paid, insecure employment. On the other hand, as we observed above, a minority of entrepreneurial migrants have become so successful in business that they are hardly affected by the restrictions associated with registration, being able to buy the privileges that local, urban registration affords, if not the registration itself.

Between these extremes, socioeconomic development across the country has improved overall living standards and average levels of education, including in rural areas, and has led to a freer labor market. Today, young rural migrants ("second-generation" migrants) have more opportunities and higher expectations for their life in the city than their parents did, and their goals are closer to those of urban youth, including urban migrants and even local urbanites.

At the beginning of this chapter, we noted that *hukou* has contributed to two key divisions: between urban and rural populations, and between locals and outsiders. In the 21st century, though, the relationship between *hukou* and these two divisions is more complicated and varied than it was at the beginning of the post-Mao period. For example, in some rapidly urbanizing regions in the Yangzi and Pearl River deltas, the urban-registered population no longer enjoys significantly higher average incomes and greater citizenship entitlements than the rural-registered population. Some wealthy villages have created shareholding cooperatives to manage collective assets, and these cooperatives have used rents from collective land and industries to fund miniature "welfare states" to provide locals with excellent social insurance schemes, schools and scholarships, pensions and other benefits. Village households also make money renting apartments to migrant workers. The emerging class divisions between many "local" people with agricultural *hukou* and "outside" people with agricultural *hukou* are extreme.[26] But not all "locals" are equal either, as new members of such villages (including children

---

[26] See Chan, Madsen & Unger 2009.

and women marrying in) do not tend to have shares in the village share-holding cooperatives, regardless of whether they have local *hukou*. It is often the case, too, that particular families or lineages dominate village economies, so that non-kin receive fewer benefits.

To give another example of changing patterns of citizenship, the local government in Chengdu set up a pilot scheme to foster "urban–rural harmonization", declaring that, from 2011, distinctions between agri-cultural and non-agricultural *hukou* would be abolished for all Chengdu-registered residents.[27] This reform gave all "locals" equal access to social insurance programs that were formerly available only to the local, non-agricultural population. However, migrants without Chengdu registra-tion, including those with non-agricultural as well as agricultural *hukou*, were not included in the scheme. Although they are entitled to some social insurance and welfare benefits, their entitlements remain inferior to those of "locals".

Aside from shifts in patterns of citizenship stratification such as these, and regardless of whether or not the *hukou* system will be reformed further – or even abolished – there are signs that it is becoming less and less relevant to people's citizenship, social status and life chances. The greatest inequalities are between poor urbanites, poor rural people and unskilled, rural migrants on the one hand, and wealthier urban-ites, shareholders in the collective income of wealthy urbanized villages, and migrant entrepreneurs on the other, and these inequalities are con-tinuing, from one generation to the next. Urban children from poor families, who fare poorly in the education system, tend to find them-selves alongside the children of rural migrants in vocational schools and in low-status, poorly paid, and insecure employment.[28] At the other end of the social scale, the children of wealthy urban residents with non-agricultural registration, wealthy villagers, and migrant entrepreneurs are more likely to enter higher education and to have strong employment prospects.

Meanwhile, state efforts to introduce rule by law have engendered a growing consciousness of the legal rights to which people, regardless of their *hukou*, are entitled by virtue of their status as Chinese citizens. As we discuss in Chapter 13, increasing numbers of people during the late 20th and early 21st century have participated in collective protests, often framing their grievances explicitly in terms of citizens' legal rights (*gong-min de hefa quanyi*).[29] Partly in response to this trend, and in order to

---

[27] Shi, Shih-Jiuan 2012.

[28] Woronov 2011.

[29] As Ching Kwan Lee notes, however, neither social rights nor political rights, which (along with civil rights) formed key elements in Marshall's definition of citizenship in Britain, have been important rallying points for collective protest in China in recent years (Lee 2010, pp. 57–8; p. 62).

achieve a "harmonious society" (a catchword for the Chinese regime in recent years), the state has sought both to strengthen citizens' civil rights and to develop institutions that will extend social rights and increase state-subsidized welfare provision to all citizens, including those with both urban and rural *hukou*. These include health insurance and old-age-pension schemes, basic unemployment benefits, a system of minimum livelihood allowances (*dibao*) and poverty alleviation programs. In addition, nine years of schooling have been made compulsory for all children and tuition fees for compulsory education in state schools have been removed. This means that, ironically, Marshall's account of the historical relationship between citizenship and the development of state welfare provision resonates more with trends in late 20th and early 21st century China than with contemporary trends in Britain.

However, there has been little sign to date that the extension of social rights in China is leading to the kind of amelioration of social inequalities that Marshall predicted elsewhere, and some evidence to suggest that state-subsidized welfare programs exacerbate certain inequalities. We will come back to this dilemma in Chapter 11.

Summary

In the 1980s, household registration was key to the state's efforts to limit migration and to restrict the citizenship rights of rural migrants. Perhaps even more significantly, the hierarchical division between rural and urban populations – so effectively produced during the Maoist period with the help of the *hukou* system – meant that, as capitalism began to take hold in the 1980s, employers had at hand a subaltern group of rural workers who could be exploited with relative impunity. The *hukou* system, in other words, set the scene both for huge economic growth in the post-Mao period and for the creation of intra-urban inequalities between local, urban-registered citizens and rural migrants entering urban areas. New regulations then maintained these inequalities, imposing limitations on the citizenship entitlements of people without local, urban *hukou,* and so contributing to their poverty, disadvantage, discrimination, exploitation and vulnerability to abuse.

By the start of the 21st century, however, *hukou* itself had become less directly salient to patterns of inequality. This is not to say that inequalities among urban citizens or between rural and urban citizens were disappearing but, rather, it began to look increasingly as if the persistence of these inequalities resulted from interactions between *hukou* and class, rather than *hukou* in itself.[30]

---

[30] Class and class inequalities are discussed in Chapter 10.

Discussion questions

1. What are the main continuities and discontinuities in the operation and social effects of household registration in China? How do you explain these?
2. How has the *hukou* system contributed to, and hindered, development in contemporary China?
3. Why are rural migrant workers' citizenship and their average working and living conditions inferior to those of the urban-registered population?
4. If, or when, the *hukou* system is abolished, how and to what extent will this change patterns of inequality in citizenship in China?

Recommended reading

Chan, Anita 2001, *China's Workers Under Assault: The Exploitation of Labor in a Globalizing Economy*. Armonk, NY: ME Sharpe.

Dutton, Michael 1998, *Streetlife China*. Cambridge, UK: Cambridge University Press.

Fan, Cindy 2008, *China on the Move: Migration, the State, and the Household*. London: Routledge.

Gaetano, Arianne & Jacka, Tamara (eds) 2004, *On the Move: Women and Rural-to-Urban Migration in Contemporary China*. New York: Columbia University Press.

Jacka, Tamara 2006, *Rural Women in Urban China: Gender, Migration, and Social Change*. Armonk, NY: ME Sharpe.

Pun, Ngai 2005, *Made in China: Women Factory Workers in a Global Workplace*. Durham, NC: Duke University Press.

Solinger, Dorothy J 1999, *Contesting Citizenship in Urban China: Peasant Migrants, the State, and the Logic of the Market*. Berkeley: University of California Press.

Wang, Fei-Ling 2005, *Organizing through Division and Exclusion: China's Hukou System*. Stanford, CA: Stanford University Press.

4   Community Institutions

What is a "community"? Sociologists offer many different answers to this question. The 19th-century German sociologist Ferdinand Tönnies, for example, treated community (*gemeinschaft*) as an organic collection of people, knit together by territory, kinship, labor, shared customs, and a sense of belonging.[1] Tönnies contrasted community, exemplified by what he imagined to be the unchanging kinship and neighborly relations of agricultural village life, with the new, artificial forms of association created in urban industrial societies. Scholars later criticized this view, arguing that communities have always occurred along a rural–urban continuum and exhibited varying levels of interdependence, internal differentiation and dynamism. More recent research highlights non-territorial social, symbolic and political constructions of community, and its normative force.

Each of these arguments has been applied to explain rules, norms and ways of being a community in China. Fei Xiaotong wrote that connections between villages illustrated the "interdependence of territorial groups, especially in economic life",[2] while William Skinner argued that historically, villages were not closed territorial groups and that the openness of village communities and their interdependence with other social entities correlated with cycles of dynastic overthrow and consolidation, and with changes of government.[3] In the 1950s, the state's organization of a centrally planned economy and efforts to revolutionize property and work created what Vivienne Shue has described as a "cellular" political and economic structure, like a honeycomb.[4] In settlements across the country, the rural or urban definition and functions of the community rendered members' obligations, entitlements and relations with the state unequal; the *hukou* (household registration) system we discussed in Chapter 3 ascribed these definitions and functions to households. By the

[1] Tönnies 1955.
[2] Fei 1983, p. 16.
[3] Skinner 1971.
[4] Shue 1988, pp. 2–3.

end of the 20th century, sociologists were showing how rapid marketization, urbanization and migration, and new modes of local governance and globalization, were fostering heterogeneous forms of community in both territorial and non-territorial social spaces. In this chapter, we examine how forms of community in both rural and urban areas have altered in response to recent political and economic change in China.

Rural communities in China's recent history

In the early 20th century, around 80 percent of China's population lived in small, nucleated settlements that, over generations of virilocal marriage and patrilineal inheritance, had become populated predominantly by agnatically related males (males who share patrilineal bonds). Aside from kinship bonds, complex relations of land ownership, tenancy, sharecropping, seasonal labor, and money-lending linked households economically. In wealthy, densely populated areas with strong lineages, lineage corporate estates were established to counter the fragmenting effects of the custom of partible patrilineal inheritance families practiced. Rent from these corporate estates and from temple lands, together with donations from local gentry, funded schools for boys and charitable organizations to help integrate disparate kin groups in the community.

Temple fairs and periodic markets provided opportunities for entertainment, as well as marriage negotiations, trade in commodities and livestock, and sharing of news, which connected villages to wider regional networks. Headmen, elected by male villagers and lineage elders, liaised with government authorities, demanded corvee labor and taxes, and oversaw the administration of justice. They also organized village militia and watchmen, irrigation and conflict mediation. Few farmers would have traveled beyond their nearest market town. However, villages were linked with a vast network of other communities through a steady traffic in commodities; through villagers' recruitment into the military, craft associations, contract labor gangs or, for a lucky few, higher education and the civil service; and through residents' pilgrimages and emigration and the incursion of roving beggars, bandits and armies.

When the CCP came to power in 1949, it set about transforming the political and economic foundations of rural communities. Between 1950 and 1953, land reform teams were dispatched to the countryside to destroy "feudal" property relations by encouraging villagers to "speak bitterness" against those who, the teams told villagers, had been exploiting them for generations. In a method of campaign implementation that subsequently became a standard approach to both economic and political planning, the teams were allocated quotas of landlords to dispossess.

As the following exchange from William Hinton's classic ethnography, *Fanshen*, illustrates, "speaking bitterness" also was intended to turn villagers into class-conscious political activists, willing and able to critically analyze appeals to "community" sentiment:

"In the famine year he gave us nothing. He even drove beggars away from his door, but now he suddenly weeps for our hard life – now we are 'people of one village'", said one.

"It is clear he only wants to buy off the leaders and undermine our ranks. We should never be taken in by such tricks", added another.

"This should be a lesson to all of us", said T'ien-ming. "Never trust a landlord; never protect a landlord. There is only one road and that is to struggle against them."[5]

The often bloody events in which villagers categorized each other as landlords, rich, middle and poor peasants, and landless laborers – class labels that, as we will explain in Chapter 10, were later inherited – resulted in the redistribution of land from wealthy families or lineage and temple estates to poor and landless villagers, as well as land reform activists and former Red Army soldiers. Middle-class households retained their landholdings, but even these better-off households still only held just over half an acre per capita, on average.[6] So, although land reform reconfigured property and power in rural communities, little surplus produce became available for reinvestment.

Yet, as we noted in Chapter 3, one of the CCP's key objectives was to create a modern industrial economy. Following the strategy recommended by Soviet experts, the CCP planned to finance the industrialization process by extracting surplus from the agricultural sector. Other than the *hukou* system, three policies facilitated this extraction: the collectivization of agricultural production; the creation of artificial "price scissors" between the rural and urban economies, which allowed the state to procure agricultural output at below-market prices and sell industrial goods to farmers at above-market prices; and the territorial compartmentalization of all expenditure on public goods. Rural collectives were expected to fund their own infrastructure, education and welfare, while the state would finance public goods in urban areas.

Within a few years, CCP branches had formed in the villages, and urged villagers to pool their land and tools and farm cooperatively to overcome the constraints of small peasant agriculture. The CCP's repeated

[5] Hinton 1966, p. 159.
[6] Selden 1993, p. 86.

denunciations of private plots and rural markets as "sprouts of capitalism", and its emphasis on local self-sufficiency, reduced villagers' opportunities to trade outside the scope of state procurement. State planners made decisions about planting, labor allocation and prices that farmers had formerly made in response to household needs and market prices. In 1956, the land titles handed out during land reform were revoked, and all rural land was transferred to collective ownership.

Despite farmers' resistance to collectivization, national campaigns promoted the creation of even larger-scale collectives and then, in 1958, the formation of "people's communes". In the communes, dozens of villages containing up to 15 000 people were organized to meet the state's compulsory procurement quotas. Symbolized, most controversially, by the opening of public canteens to reduce the time farmers spent preparing meals, communes also controlled distribution and socialization in almost every sector of rural life, including ideological propaganda, education, training, sanitation and health. During the Great Leap Forward of 1958, the commune system produced an unsustainable dynamic. In a "wind of exaggeration", commune leaders competed to win political favor by ignoring local conditions and inflating reports on the size of the harvest. State planners responded to the inflated figures by constantly increasing the procurement quotas that stripped villages of food. The mass mobilization of labor and militarization of production, intended to break down parochial boundaries and concentrate huge squads to work in different "theatres of operation" (for example, canal building, or reclaiming forests for agricultural use and cooking-pots for their steel), wasted resources and lowered morale. Institutional failures caused a famine in which tens of millions of people died.

In response to the continuing famine, in 1960 the control of agricultural production was transferred from communes to smaller "brigades" and then to "production teams". This decentralization of production enabled farmers to better defend themselves against excessive state procurement. As brigades typically comprised either a large village or two neighboring hamlets, and teams were made up of a few dozen adjacent households, their elected leaders were well motivated to protect the interests of kin and community. They did this by bargaining with commune leaders to set lower quotas, and colluding to hide part of the harvest for people to consume in their homes. Production teams allocated farming tasks to their members on the basis of their age, sex, health and skill. For each task, members received work points that were converted into a cash payment at the end of each year, after the team had calculated its income from the state and set aside a portion to purchase livestock or machinery and to finance welfare for poorer households.

The impact of collectivization on community in rural China is still debated today. Whereas some scholars argue that villagers' economic initiative was stifled by egalitarianism, others assert that between the 1960s and the liberalization of agriculture after 1978 the collectives laid the economic foundations for rural industrialization and entrepreneurship.[7] Li Huaiyin concludes that villagers' experience of collective organization trained them in basic accounting and administration, and so gave them skills that would be called upon in later experiments with land contracting, business and rural community "self-government".[8] Moreover, although most villagers led a life of "shared poverty", collective agriculture managed to absorb a fast-growing workforce, while still achieving significant improvements in rural health services, sanitation, transport, communications and literacy. Chinese statistics indicate that the average rural life expectancy rose from about 35 years in 1952 to more than 60 years in 1978.

Another point of debate is whether, contrary to the predictions of community modernization theorists such as Tönnies, rural insularity strengthened during the collective era. As the quality of villagers' nutritional intake relied heavily on the success of the collective harvest and output from household plots, their interdependence and loyalty to community and kin certainly intensified. Cross-community trade and geographical mobility declined, and marriage within villages may have become more common. The emphasis on rural self-sufficiency also produced great disparities in consumption and welfare between villages in fertile, densely populated areas and those in harsh environments. Even greater disparities, however, emerged between villagers and the residents of urban communities who received state-subsidized grain and welfare.

Decollectivization of agricultural production began spontaneously. Based on localized experiments with land contracting conducted in the mid-1950s and early 1960s, the village of Xiaogang, in Anhui province, began covertly subcontracting land to households in 1978. After meeting their quotas for compulsory crop sales to the state, households were allowed to sell their surplus. Despite conservative opposition, by 1982 Deng had approved the "household contract responsibility system" (*jiating lianchan chengbao zeren zhi*), and it was being implemented nationwide. At the same time, the government was dismantling the other foundations of the planned economy. State prices for agricultural produce were raised, the scope of state compulsory procurement was reduced, and controls on markets were relaxed. Farmers responded to rising prices

---

[7] See, for example, Zweig 1989; Bramall 2008.
[8] Li, Huaiyin 2009.

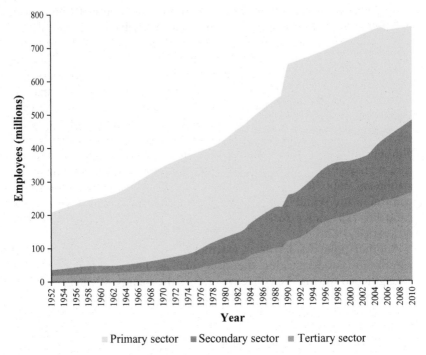

Figure 4.1 Changes in the size and sectoral distribution of China's workforce, 1954–2009.
Source: National Bureau of Statistics (NBS) 2011.

by diversifying production and raising productivity. Rural incomes more than quadrupled during the 1980s. With more opportunities and income to invest, collectively owned township and village enterprises (TVEs) flourished. By the mid-1990s, more than 120 million rural residents were employed in TVEs, and a similar number had migrated to urban areas. From 2000, for the first time in China's modern history, there was a sustained downward trend in the number of people working in the primary (agricultural) sector (see Figure 4.1).

Decollectivization profoundly altered the economic foundations and the built landscape of rural communities. In much of the countryside, collectively owned enterprises were sold or subcontracted to villagers, and the income from these transfers was distributed among village households. Rather than being channelled into infrastructure, however, villagers' growing private incomes were invested in competitive consumption. Officials cautioned that a "rural house-building craze"[9] was

---

[9] Sargeson 2002.

destroying China's scarce cultivable land and risking national food security. Parents with unmarried sons helped them woo brides by building new "European-style" villas; extended families that, forced to share cramped, dilapidated homes for want of construction materials during the collective era, now split into separate households comprised only of nuclear family. Deprived of collective revenue and investment, village infrastructure deteriorated. Irrigation networks collapsed, and professional staff fled rural schools and clinics in search of better paid urban positions. But in some coastal areas, most notably in the single-lineage villages of the southeast, collective assets (including land and factories) were transferred to shareholding cooperatives that were jointly owned by, and paid dividends to, all community members. As we have discussed in Chapter 3, these shareholding institutions simultaneously strengthened community solidarity and produced striking inequalities between the residents who originally lived in the communities and the immigrant workers who now staffed their factories.

From 2003, in an attempt to reverse the deterioration of rural community infrastructure and reduce rural–urban disparities, China's government intervened directly to improve the situation of the "three rurals": villagers, villages and agriculture. It abolished the agricultural tax, and committed increased funds to the "construction of a new socialist countryside", with a rural cooperative medical insurance scheme, *dibao* (minimum livelihood allowance) for all rural households whose income fell below locally determined poverty lines, and upgraded sanitation, living conditions and cultural and sports facilities. However, as social-security funds were accumulated at the county level, villagers could only access their welfare entitlements in the areas in which they were registered as residents. Territorial fragmentation of social security systems thus disadvantaged migrant workers and their families. Moreover, because many new funding initiatives required co-payments from local government and villages, only wealthy villages were able to afford improvements in their facilities and services. Inequalities between rural communities increased dramatically.

Decollectivization also precipitated the transformation of rural governance institutions. As communes and brigades were dismantled, newly formed township governments and villages, respectively, assumed their administrative functions. Although the state intended to retain control over village affairs through their CCP branches, in the face of declining collective revenue from villages and the availability of more lucrative jobs in business, many Party branches had collapsed. Rural protests spread, fuelled by perceptions that Party members and local officials were embezzling collective assets, and by a rapid increase in the fees and levies that local authorities arbitrarily charged.

Image 4.1 and **Image 4.2**   Two village libraries established to comply with quotas for "construction of a new socialist countryside" projects. The poor village on the left moved an old bookcase into its meeting room and filled the shelves with outdated political works and farming manuals. The wealthy village on the right built a new, well-resourced library. *Source:* Sally Sargeson, Zhejiang 2012.

In an effort to restore rural government and curb social unrest, China's leaders drew on long-standing village electoral practices, Maoist models of mass supervision of officials, and contemporary global theories of participatory development, to institutionalize self-government in villages. The Organic Law of Village Committees was passed in 1987 (and later revised in 1998 and 2010), setting out procedures for all eligible adult village members to vote for their village committee heads and committee members in a secret ballot, and for villagers to create their own citizenship charters. Direct, multi-candidate elections have gradually become standardized and, in most areas, important issues such as major investments in roads and readjustments of contract land are now discussed in village-wide assemblies.

However, the democratic quality of village self-government varies greatly. There is no doubt that self-government has educated villagers politically and provided channels through which they can act collectively to defend their citizenship rights. Elected village committees also have the potential to counterbalance the influence of both local Party branches and hierarchical, gender-exclusive lineages. Critics point out, though, that the

nationwide rebuilding of rural CCP branches in the early 2000s and the proviso in the Organic Law that the local Party branch would "lead" village government mean that the Party secretary, elected only by Party branch members, and not the popularly elected village committee head, usually wields true decision-making power. Besides, both the village committee head and Party secretary are pressured to serve as the agents of township governments, rather than as villagers' representatives, and so it is questionable whether elections are democratizing rural government, or simply making authoritarian rule more effective. A second problem, identified by Sally Sargeson and Song Yu, is that men's predominance in village leadership positions and decision-making fora has allowed them to enshrine the norms of virilocal marriage in gender-exclusive village citizenship charters. Under these charters, women who marry men from another rural community are often excluded from their natal community and, if they later divorce, they are also excluded from the community into which they married. In both instances, the village charters deny women the rights to vote, contract collective land and receive welfare.[10] Androcentric territorial principles have been reproduced in practices of village self-government.

[10] Sargeson & Song 2010.

Modern conceptual extensions of the "rural community"

Modernization and urbanization have led to much variation in the ways villages are temporally and spatially conceptualized as communities. In contrast to the above account of the economic and political institutional foundations of territorially bounded rural communities, local annals present an emic, or indigenous, perspective on community as a temporal–cultural continuum. Local annals trace a narrative of original settlement; list the achievements of former "native sons"; describe local scenic sites, historic monuments, unique products, customs, cuisines and recent advances in residents' livelihoods; and negotiate connections between past, present and an imagined glorious future. In doing so, the annals construct a community with which all people whose ancestors hail from the place can identify, and in which they can feel proud. They are also useful from a practical point of view as they may be cited in applications for the state's capital-improvement grants for the "construction of a new socialist countryside"; to attract investment and tourism; and to claim recognition of villagers' material and intangible heritage. So, local annals discursively link a historicized, cultural conception of the rural community and the desires of diasporic and migrant populations to trace their "roots" with contemporary nationalist modernization projects.

EXTRACT FROM THE CHASHAN LOCAL ANNALS

Chashan is one of the well-known districts in Dongguan city, from which many talented people have hailed, generation after generation... Legend has it that Chashan has never yielded to power. For instance, in the past there was Ye Zhiqing, a national hero against invasion in the Yuan dynasty; He Zhen, one of the heroic founders of the Ming dynasty; Lin Guang, a well-known philosopher; Yuan Guansha and Deng Ting, historian and writer; Zhong Huangshan, an official... Since the [establishment of the People's] Republic of China, there have been Chen Yiyuan and Yuan Qinhui, military officers; Liu Naixun, an eminent official; Yuan Zhenyue, an economist; Chen Yuzhou, a traditional Chinese doctor; Liu Junren, a painter; and Fan Wei who participated in the Long March and dedicated his life to communism. Their achievements not only compare with those of their ancestors, but also set good examples for later generations.[11]

---

[11] Quoted in Qing, Deqing 2006, pp. 87–8.

"Villages-in-cities" (*chengzhongcun*) illustrate how community can be consolidated through contesting normative images of "rural" and "urban" societies. Villages-in-cities are the result of low-cost urban growth, and are created when cities and towns encompass villages but transform neither collectively owned land to state ownership nor residents' rural *hukou* into urban residential registration. These places become residual rural enclaves (or, as He Xuefeng puts it, "tumors") in the expanding urban landscape.[12] Some scholars have argued that because such villages remain self-governing, property-owning entities they constitute comparatively autonomous enclaves in an otherwise regulated urban society. Villagers' rental incomes afford them a leisurely lifestyle that contrasts with that of both their hardworking migrant tenants and their middle-class urban neighbors. Community spirit is reinforced by collectively funded welfare provisions and shared tales of the residents' resistance to government efforts to expropriate their land and turn them into urbanites. In turn, many urban residents view villages-in-cities as islands of rural "backwardness" in the modern city, seeing them as poorly incorporated into urban design and function; lacking the civilizing influence of formal, modern bureaucratic institutions and transport and sewerage infrastructure; populated by an unsavory mix of "slum landlords", the unemployed and outsiders; and riddled with crime. Villages-in-cities are viewed as literally being "out of control". The mirror image of this representation of villages-in-cities, as a territorial deviation from the norms of city life, shows urban communities as sites of productivity, order and civility.

Another conceptual extension of the rural community occurs in coastal provinces, where rapid industrialization and urbanization have increased demand for land. In response to the central government's requirement that, in order to ensure national food security, about 85 percent of the country's scarce farmland must be conserved, local governments are demolishing remote villages and relocating their inhabitants into either new, purpose-built, high-density rural settlements or suburban apartments. The original village site is then "rehabilitated" as farmland, allowing farmland closer to cities and towns to be expropriated for construction. In areas where this strategy of land development has been followed, such as the lower Yangzi River Delta, both the institutional foundations of community and the class composition of rural society are transforming. Villagers remain the joint owners of collective assets, which are governed by the village collective organization, but their residential registration is converted to an urban one, and their daily lives are managed by urban community committees. Because only wealthy villagers can afford

[12] He, Xuefeng 2010, p. 71.

to purchase the expensive villas built in the new rural settlements, the countryside is becoming gentrified. Conversely, poor farming households moved into apartment blocks must commute to work in the fields. As members of the original economic collective, all households receive contributions from the collective towards their health insurance and pension funds, as well as annual dividend payments from the collective's income. Through institutional disaggregation and spatial dispersion, "community" is thus reconceptualized primarily as a joint property relationship. While maintenance of the rural–urban boundary produces community consolidation in villages-in-cities, here the dissolution of that boundary attenuates community.

Urban work units and residential and non-territorial communities

Shortly after the Communist occupation of Beijing in 1949, Mao wrote: "Only when production in the cities is restored and developed, when consumer-cities are transformed into producer-cities, can the peoples' political power be consolidated."[13] This succinctly conveys the twin roles he envisioned for cities, of industrial production and political socialization. By 1956, the new regime had replaced the "anarchic", urban, economic landscape of ownership of private enterprise, labor markets and production, with a Soviet-style planning system that allocated finance, resources, labor and even consumer goods among publicly owned, spatially defined, self-contained *danwei* (work units).

Today, the term *danwei* might be loosely applied to any employer organization, but in the Maoist era the *danwei* was conceived as an ideal type of socialist community. First and foremost a publicly owned enterprise, it also fulfilled political, moral and social-reproductive functions. *Danwei* administered their employees' household registration and the personnel files that recorded their work history, class background and political attitudes, liaised on their behalf with police and courts, and approved or rejected their applications to marry, divorce, travel and – after birth controls were introduced – reproduce. The *danwei* also hosted CCP branches that educated employees in politics, mobilized them to participate in national campaigns, and advised them on promotions and demotions. Hence, employees' rewards and punishments reflected not only their productivity but also their compliance with state policies and displays of loyalty to the nation, the Party, the working class and the *danwei*.

[13] Mao 1979b, p. 181.

Throughout the 1960s and 70s, *danwei* employed most of the urban workforce (see Table 4.1). When assigned to a large state-owned *danwei*, workers entered a comprehensive cradle-to-grave employment and social security system, colloquially known as the "iron rice bowl". In the walled compound of the *danwei*, they enjoyed subsidized housing, canteens, clinics, schools and bathhouses. Indeed, virtually all their needs, from old-age pensions, to snack foods and entertainment tickets, to marriage-mediation services, were provided for. These *danwei* compounds thus comprised comparatively self-contained, homogeneous communities. However, not all *danwei* were alike. As few of the smaller collectively owned *danwei* could afford to provide the same pay and benefits as large state firms, enterprise ownership quickly became a measure of urban workers' standard of living and status. In the absence of a labor market, and with rigid administrative barriers to changing jobs, competition among school leavers to join large state *danwei* led parents to retire early and bequeath their own jobs to their children; to frantic searches for a "back door" in the local labor bureaus, which would tweak job assignments in return for favors; and to fervent demonstrations of political activism on the part of young people. Young men fared better in this competition than young women, producing a male-dominated workforce in the privileged state *danwei*, and a female workforce in the collective sector.

A considerable body of literature suggests that state *danwei* resembled the "total institutions" described by the sociologist Erving Goffman in his book *Asylums*.[14] The all-encompassing nature of "total institutions", argued Goffman, is symbolized by walls that impede social interaction between inmates and outsiders. Internally, the main axis of inequality and conflict is between inmates, working, living and socializing together in a contained, functional space, and staff, who supervise inmates' activities, reward their compliance, and penalize infringements of rules, and who are not confined to the institution. "Total institutions" provide all inmates' needs, maintain comprehensive surveillance and disciplinary systems, and use exclusive, highly stylized communications to strip inmates of their wider social identity. Like "total institutions", the *danwei* of the 1960s and 1970s were self-contained, often existing in walled compounds that bounded employees' life chances and social horizons and which, through an elaborate system of rewards and penalties, taught them to adopt conformist expressions and politically quiescent behavior.

It is analytically illuminating to draw parallels between *danwei* and "total institutions", but these parallels are empirically limited. Whereas

[14] Goffman 1961.

	Total urban employees	1 State *danwei* (millions)	2 Collective *danwei* (millions)	3 Private firms (millions)	4 Cooperatives, shareholding & limited liability companies (millions)	5 Foreign-owned firms (millions)	6 Self-employed (millions)	*Danwei* (1 & 2) as a percentage of total urban employees
1978	95.1	74.5	20.4	–	–	–	0.1	99.7
1998	216.1	90.5	28.8	9.7	10.6	5.8	22.5	55.2
2010	346.8	65.1	5.9	60.7	38.9	18.2	44.6	20.4

Table 4.1 Changes in the distribution of the urban workforce among ownership categories

Source: NBS 2011.

there is an unbridgeable split between inmates and staff in "total institutions", Andrew Walder has written that in *danwei* the Party and management incorporated and controlled workers through a dual set of relationships, described as "organized dependence" and "principled particularism".[15] Workers became organizationally dependent because, in the absence of a market economy, they were immobilized in the *danwei* to which the government assigned them, and the *danwei* supplied all the goods and services they required. Through principled particularism, Party leaders and managers built up networks of loyal activists who followed their directives in return for preferential treatment. This description of how workers were integrated into *danwei* relationships, though, is called into question by research showing that *danwei* also were riven by bullying, factional conflict, shirking and strikes.[16] The *danwei* workforce was also divided between the politically, economically and socially advantaged permanent employees and the temporary workers who had no "iron rice bowl".

Even at the height of the planned economy, not all urban residents worked and lived in *danwei*. This residual population was administered by "residents' committees" (*jumin weiyuanhui*) under the jurisdiction of the street government (*jiedao*), the lowest level of the state bureaucracy in urban areas. Staffed predominantly by retirees, residents' committee members were disparagingly referred to as "old snoops" and "mothers-in-law". This language reflected the nature of the committees' functions, some of which harked back to the ancient *baojia* system we discussed in Chapter 3. They managed public security – often reporting on residents' visitors, drunkenness and marital infidelities – propagated government policies and mediated conflicts. In other respects, however, the residents' committees were a precursor to the types of grassroots organizations that were created to manage the far more diverse communities that formed in the post-Mao market economy.

Since the 1980s, sectoral transformation of the economy and the shedding of workers and administrative and social welfare responsibilities by *danwei* (see Table 4.1), together with migration and urbanization, have transformed urban communities from places dedicated to public production and political socialization, to sites of private accumulation and consumption. In contrast to the old *danwei* compounds, which housed a comprehensive range of activities, the function of space in the city changed. And, with the emergence of an urban real estate market and rapidly growing levels of home ownership, residential suburbs became

[15] Walder 1986.
[16] Perry 1993.

increasingly socially stratified. Vast sums were invested in the construction of gated communities of luxurious villas and condominiums for wealthy businesspeople and globally nomadic expatriate professionals. The emergent middle class sought out "civilized" places where the standards of public safety, civic pride and education would guarantee that their neighbors would be of similarly high *suzhi* (quality). Laid-off workers, rural immigrants and a growing population of urban poor concentrated in the dilapidated remnants of public housing, low-rent apartments, factory dormitories and villages-in-cities. At the junction of these social enclaves, citizenship claims based on lifelong urban residence or public service rubbed up against the demands of different categories of migrants, the new logic of private property rights, and a neoliberal ethos in which wealth, entrepreneurship and individual autonomy figure as virtues.

These changes challenged the state to replace the functions that had been served by *danwei* and residents' committees with new institutions and organizations that could better manage the diverse, mobile population. In 1994, the Ministry of Civil Affairs began promoting the construction of "community residents' committees" (*shequ jumin weiyuanhui*). Now, while appointment to these committees is determined by street-level governments' pre-selection of candidates and election by residents, there is little electoral competition because of the low salary and heavy responsibility a committee role entails. Each *shequ* committee receives a budget from the city government to administer a demarcated area that contains up to several thousand households, as well as enterprises, schools and hospitals. The committee's responsibilities include implementing state policies; monitoring *hukou* and birth control; collecting statistical information; keeping an eye on "targeted persons" and reporting deviant and criminal behavior; and administering applications for social assistance such as the *dibao*, medical subsidies, care for the elderly and disabled, and low-rent public housing. In addition, the committee is expected to build community spirit. To this end, it organizes dance groups, book clubs and hobby classes, and mobilizes volunteers to beautify the neighborhood. In 2006, in an attempt to "civilize" villages-in-cities and settlements around the urban fringes, the state also began to promote the replacement of elected village committees with urban community committees.

However, in the face of increasing social differentiation, divergent patterns of urban community governance have emerged. Owing to their welfare and surveillance roles, community committees loom large in the lives of the poor, the disabled, rural migrants living in the midst of urban areas and people whom the authorities consider dangerous. Community committees are of less significance, though, to wealthy businesspeople

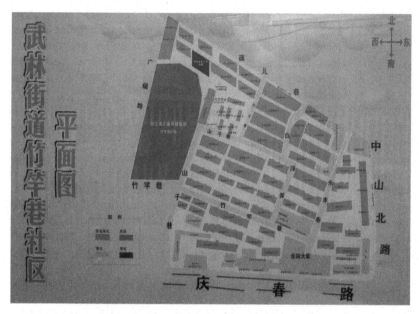

Image 4.3 Public billboard mapping the area governed by an urban community (*shequ*) committee in Hangzhou.

The map shows residential blocks (red), *danwei* enterprises (pink), a hospital (blue) and a school (maroon).

Source: Sally Sargeson, Hangzhou 2012.

and professionals living in middle-class gated communities, and to rural migrants and former villagers living in settlements on the urban fringes. In these areas, commercial property-management companies, homeowners' associations, or former villagers' shareholding cooperatives often provide administration, maintenance, services and security. To some extent, then, social class mediates the types of governance institutions found in different suburbs. While poor and "vulnerable" groups are subjected to direct, paternalistic government, economically independent people tend to be trusted to manage their own lives.

Generally, the stated goals of the new non-state urban governing agencies have mirrored those of the community committees: they aim to mould law-abiding, responsible citizens and stable, harmonious communities; improve civility and patriotism; and contribute to China's modernization. However, the privatization of governance functions also foregrounds, and creates channels for the defence of, conflicting interests. For example, in some locations where community committees subcontracted certain tasks such as birth-control monitoring to property-management companies or shareholding associations, governments have had less ability to intervene to influence residents' reproductive decisions and their lifestyles. Property developers and management companies also come into conflict with homeowners' associations over residents' consumer rights. In cities across China, disgruntled apartment owners have acted collectively to protest against property-management companies' price gouging and shoddy maintenance. In some cases, apartment owners have even demolished roads, car parks and shopping centers that developers had not included in their original plans. At the other end of the spectrum, homeowners' associations, divided over issues such as home extensions or pet ownership, have placed increasingly restrictive caveats on what can be done in their neighborhoods. So, rather than interpreting the new urban community governance arrangements as either tools of the state or as opportunities to expand residents' autonomy from the state, we can view them as institutions that urban residents can draw on when they need to act as a community to deal with a range of problems.

The formation of non-territorial urban communities

The institutions that gave rise to both the old socialist *danwei* and the contemporary urban community are territorially bounded. But what of urban residents who are mobile, or those whose community identities and ways of life these institutions ignore? Here, we highlight two alternative experiences of community, examining how expatriates and lesbian, gay, bisexual and transgender (LGBT) activists negotiate community boundaries established by national political and economic institutions and normative sexuality.

China's economic rise is transforming it from a country of net emigration into a major destination for international immigrants. The 2010 census indicated that the foreign population had grown to more than 1 million people, primarily comprising students, businesspeople, Chinese returning home after acquiring foreign nationality, Hong Kong residents and Taiwanese, and cross-border migrants.

Frank Pieke has investigated why foreigners tend to concentrate in particular municipalities with, for example, hundreds of thousands of Taiwanese living in the lower Yangzi and Pearl River deltas, around 30 000 traders from Africa in Guangzhou, Indian textile merchants in Shaoxing and large clusters of Russians and Kazaks in Beijing, Urumqi and Harbin.[17] Chain migration, and foreigners' efforts to deal with the familiar challenges of living as expatriates by establishing shops, schools and hospitals that cater for their particular needs, partly explain these

[17] Pieke 2012.

concentrations. Expatriates form communities around corporate head-quarters, foreign-language media, clubs, gyms and bars, and where religion and styles of socializing provide common ground. At the same time, China's municipal governments are competing with one another to attract and retain global talent and trade by selectively relaxing community regulations. While students, petty traders and cross-border migrants tend to be kept under surveillance, many cities provide preferential services to foreign professionals and wealthy businesspeople. Pieke writes that large cities have established foreign affairs service centers to provide "one-stop" access to police, utilities and real estate and property management companies. And in Zhejiang, the small apparel-manufacturing center of Yiwu has sought to attract foreign businesspeople by streamlining the application process for visas and residence permits, and allowing them to conduct business and financial transactions on the same basis as Chinese nationals; observe and offer suggestions to the city's People's Congress; participate in local community administration; and attend local schools. For foreigners differentiated by their market linkages, languages, kinship networks, homelands and religious beliefs, national de-territorialization and the terms of their interaction with China's state and society are intrinsic to the experience of community.

The dilemma facing China's LGBT activists highlights a second, cross-cultural challenge faced by non-territorial communities. In a society in which sexual orientation is presumed to conform with a starkly gendered binary and many regard even homosexuality as an aberration, how do LGBT people attempt to create and organize, and gain respect for, their communities? Mistrustful of both non-normative sexuality and the political implications of their appropriation of the term *tongzhi* (comrade; homosexual), the state proscribed groups that labeled themselves *tongzhi* until the turn of the 21st century.[18] Since then, however, sexual activists have opened clubs, bars, media sites, hotlines and representative organizations, including the Beijing Lesbian, Gay, Bisexual, Transgender Center and the Queer Film and Culture Festival, to cater to their diverse needs and speak for their concerns. Since 2001, activists have repeatedly lobbied China's legislature, the NPC, to amend the Marriage Law to allow same-sex marriage. Over the same period, the globalization of gay popular culture online, the formation of "netizen" networks with LGBT activists in Taiwan and Hong Kong, and the proliferation of government-sponsored and international projects focusing on sexual health, particularly HIV/AIDS, provided new sources of recognition and funding for these groups, especially those speaking for gays in China. Because of their

---

[18] Until 1997, China's legal system designated homosexuality "hooliganism", and it was only in 2001 that it was removed from China's classification of mental illnesses.

formation of these cross-border alliances, Lisa Rofel suggests that much of this activism resembles "homo internationalism".[19]

At the same time, sexual activists in China have been challenged to overcome popular perceptions that non-normative sexuality is associated with foreign funding for the prevention and treatment of HIV/AIDS. Particular concerns have been raised that foreign interference might exacerbate domestic discrimination against non-normative sexualities, and that foreigners fail to understand the familial and social pressures under which LGBT people in China live. Not surprisingly, therefore, some activists use nationalist rhetoric to advance their causes. The activist Li Yinhe, for example, has argued that China's approval of same-sex marriage would enhance its international standing, by demonstrating its support for spiritual values and human rights.[20] Others publicly represent the gay community as a "high-quality", modern citizenry committed to promoting responsible, healthy sexual practices. As comments by one of Loretta Ho's interviewees suggest, these representations can implicate same-sex activists in class stratification and stigmatization, particularly of rural gays:

I think, in some way, the *suzhi* [quality] of the Chinese (same-sex) community is lowered by rural people. The low *suzhi* of the rural population makes it extremely hard for us to promote the legitimacy of gay rights in China.[21]

This aptly illustrates how the old rural–urban boundary drawn in modernist discourses and Soviet strategies of accumulation can be referenced to distance China's urban LGBT communities from the country's "peasant" past, and align them with an imagined globalized modernity.

Summary

The rural and urban categories have been central in shaping many different forms of community in China. In the Maoist era, self-contained, unequal rural and urban communities were organized by the state to serve its goals of rapid industrialization and political socialization. The dismantling of the planned economy, greater state investment in rural development, and withdrawal of subsidies for urban residents, together with the "democratization" of grassroots governance, have reduced material differences between rural and urban communities. However, they have not eliminated these categories as normative stereotypes, signifying disorder and backwardness on the one hand, and order, civility and modernity on the other.

[19] Rofel 2013, p. 159.
[20] Chase 2012.
[21] Ho 2010, p. 91.

Recent community-building efforts align with broader global trends, in which communities are mobilized administratively and through state–civic partnerships and voluntary activism to address multiple aims and express different ways of being in a mobile, socially differentiated, globally integrated society. Nevertheless, as the discursive construction of China's LGBT community and the extension of freedoms to de-territorialized, expatriate expert communities suggest, territoriality remains an important aspect of community institutions, identities and relations in contemporary China.

Discussion questions

1. How might the different types of community governance institutions exacerbate or ameliorate social inequalities between rural and urban people in China today?
2. How, and with what specific consequences, have post-Mao changes in rural community institutions changed patterns of interdependence and solidarity among village families?
3. What is distinctive about contemporary processes of rural and urban community formation in China, compared to communities in the country in which you live?

Recommended reading

Bray, David 2005, *Social Space and Governance in Urban China: The* Danwei *from Origins to Reform*. Stanford, CA: Stanford University Press.

Chan, Anita, Madsen, Richard & Unger, Jonathan 2009, *Chen Village: From Revolution to Globalization*. Berkeley: University of California Press.

Hinton, William 1966, *Fanshen: A Documentary of Revolution in a Chinese Village*. Harmondsworth, UK: Penguin.

Li, Huaiyin 2009, *Village China Under Socialism and Reform: A Micro-History, 1948–2008*. Stanford, CA: Stanford University Press.

Lü, Xiaobo & Perry, Elizabeth (eds) 1997, Danwei: *The Changing Chinese Workplace in Historical and Comparative Perspectives*. New York: ME Sharpe.

Potter, Sulamith Heins & Potter, Jack 1990, *China's Peasants: The Anthropology of a Revolution*. Cambridge, UK: Cambridge University Press.

Read, Benjamin 2012, *Roots of the State: Neighborhood Organization and Social Networks in Beijing and Taipei*. Stanford, CA: Stanford University Press.

Shue, Vivienne 1988, *The Reach of the State: Sketches of the Chinese Body Politic*. Stanford, CA: Stanford University Press.

Walder, Andrew G 1986, *Communist Neo-Traditionalism: Work and Authority in Chinese Industry*. Berkeley: University of California Press.

5   Work

Work is the subject of a great deal of research in China. Yet it is fair to say that most of this research is quite narrowly focused and overlooks many forms of work. Three terms in Chinese are commonly used to refer to work: *laodong, dagong* and *gongzuo*. First, there is labor, work or toil (*laodong*), which refers to the action of transforming nature, creating products or performing services. The term can therefore be used to describe many things, from activities that involve coercion to the growing of food for personal consumption, cooking, cleaning and caring for others in a home, to volunteering, self-employment or paid employment. Second, temporary or seasonal employment (*dagong*) may involve physical effort. Third, if a person has a "proper job" (*gongzuo*) they are typically employees (*zhigong*, literally "staff and workers") within enterprises, professions or the civil service. The bulk of research into work in China has focused on *gongzuo* and *dagong* in enterprises. Less attention has been paid to the work done in China's huge civil service, the armed forces and the media, and nor has much research been conducted on the many activities referred to as *laodong*, including bonded and child labor, sex work, farmwork, volunteer community service and unpaid domestic work.[1] Owing to the scarcity of evidence, this chapter also says little about these latter forms of work.

Why are some types of work considered to be "proper jobs" (*gongzuo*), while others are not? To some extent, the distinction reflects linguistic, cultural and institutional practices that arise during the course of industrialization, which differentiate economic activities from political, social, religious and family life, purpose-built places of production and commerce from the "domestic" sphere of women, and work that generates monetary income from both non-commodified labor and leisure. It also is a consequence of concurrent struggles by states to secure taxes and limit social security expenditure, and by workers to regulate their

---

[1] See, however, China Labour Bulletin 2007; Zheng 2009; Huang, Yuan & Peng 2012; Rolandsen 2010; Cook & Dong 2011; Huang, Yuqing 2011.

working hours, remuneration, safety standards and rights to access welfare and organize as a collective.

In China, distinctions between "proper jobs" and other work sharpened under the centrally planned economy, when *gongzuo* became associated with the bureaucratic assignment of urban residents to tenured positions in state and collectively owned industries. Since the 1980s, however, such distinctions have become less clear-cut. This divergence has been associated with two historic trends mentioned in previous chapters: the structural transformation of the economy, involving the movement of a growing proportion of the workforce out of agriculture, and the contractualization, casualization and "outsourcing" of labor, driven by regulatory reforms.

The second of these trends has proceeded at varying rates in different economic sectors and categories of enterprise ownership. Eli Friedman and Ching Kwan Lee note that the rising employment of workers on short-term contracts or without contracts has coincided with the growth of the services sector.[2] But the once-strong association between ownership categories and work institutions in China also has weakened. Certainly, the state retains majority ownership of large firms in economic monopoly and national security areas such as telecommunications and power generation, and regular employees of these firms enjoy better job security, pay and conditions than most workers. To varying degrees, though, most state enterprises now incorporate some private and foreign investment, and hold shares in subsidiaries that are predominantly privately owned. This can be seen in the Yangzi River Delta's industrial sector, which comprises a vast network of enterprises in which Chinese and foreign companies, various levels of government, village collectives and individuals hold ownership shares. These firms source labor and materials globally. Foreigners and staff from all regions of China engineer high-value goods such as software, vehicles, pharmaceuticals and surgical instruments; less capital- and knowledge-intensive goods, such as photovoltaic cells; and labor-intensive processed foods and furniture, using materials from massive state firms such as Shanghai Petrochemical Corporation, local family farms and imported components.[3] In fact, between 2000 and 2010, Chinese businesses operating in this manner were trading more than eight percent of all intermediate goods used in global production chains and more than 30 percent in the Asian region.[4] So, domestic sectoral changes and ownership diversification have combined with the globalization of production and supply to fragment

---

[2] Friedman & Lee 2010.

[3] Ross 2007.

[4] Whittaker et al. 2010, p. 449; United Nations Trade and Development Board 2011.

and disperse work, workforces and production processes across, as well as within, China's borders. In this chapter, we survey the ideological and institutional reforms of work that have also contributed to these changes.

From socialist social compact to market competition and labor contracts

The introduction of a labor market and contractual employment involved fundamental ideological and institutional transformations in Chinese society. In the 1980s, confronted with growing competition from foreign and private firms and in international markets, China's government sought to improve the competitiveness of state-owned firms by granting managers more freedom in hiring, retrenchments and performance-based remuneration, and offering them stock-ownership and profit-sharing incentives. Public honors were bestowed on star entrepreneurs who boosted enterprise profits, exported Chinese goods and attracted international investments. But these "carrots" were counterbalanced by the "stick" of tighter budget constraints: public enterprises were told to either generate profits or declare bankruptcy, as the state would no longer cover their debt.

The guaranteed job tenure and generous benefits that state employees enjoyed, formerly offered as evidence of the superiority of the socialist social compact, were depicted increasingly in China's press as a brake on national competitiveness and an insupportable burden on enterprises. Readers were told that, for the sake of efficiency and fairness, work should be rewarded on the basis of expertise and productivity, rather than on seniority or need. Until then, in line with socialist ideology, *danwei* (work units) and communes had distributed common product to their masters and owners in the form of welfare. In contrast, and consistent with the new market ideology, welfare was now represented as a commodity funded by employers and employees as part of a negotiated remuneration package, and supplied through unemployment, medical and pension insurance schemes.

Urban workers were promised that labor markets would offer opportunities to increase job options and income. Like their bosses, though, they were threatened with a stick: vast numbers of migrants from the countryside might be willing to work harder, for less money. At the same time, rural youth were encouraged by predictions that the labor market would reward merit in the form of qualifications, skills and productivity, rather than *guanxi* (social and political networks) and urban residence.

Economists' calculations that competition would reduce production costs underpinned the promotion of a labor market ideology. As one research group put it:

We must utilize our unlimited supply of labor, by prudently and gradually breaking down barriers to job mobility, encouraging a flow of workers between ownership systems and between the cities and rural areas and, in general, allowing the surplus labor force to enter into market competition. Forming a labor market and labor mobility will not only create a direct check on wage increases through employment competition, but will also help lower people's expectations and self-evaluation, thus indirectly checking wage increases.[5]

Since the 1980s, the language of labor-market competition has permeated a wide variety of discursive and physical sites: media statements by government spokespeople, television dramas, advertising, billboards, education curricula, gatherings of migrant workers newly arrived at urban railway and bus stations and, of course, recruitment centers and workplaces.

Regulatory reforms have institutionalized labor-market competition, contractual employment relations and market-based remuneration and welfare schemes. The most significant of these reforms occurred in the following sequence:

- *1986:* State enterprises were instructed to employ all new recruits on fixed-term contracts. Nevertheless, a distinction was made between contract-system workers, who had urban *hukou* and received the same wages, holidays and welfare as tenured employees, and contract workers, predominantly rural migrants who were ineligible for the pay and conditions of tenured and contract-system workers.
- *1988:* The state declared that it was ending the bureaucratic assignment of urban graduates and school leavers to jobs, though this change actually took place at different times in different provinces. Moreover, some scholarships for higher education still obliged recipients to accept job assignments given to them after graduation. In the main, however, job seekers were urged to find work through "talent fairs", employment agencies and media advertisements.
- *1995:* China's first national Labor Law required all enterprises to sign a contract with employees, to specify the duration of workers' employment, remuneration, welfare, conditions for termination, duties and rights. There could be no discrimination against

[5] Reynolds 1987, pp. 19–20.

employees on the basis of their race, ethnicity, sex or religious belief. The law introduced a 40-hour week, limited overtime to 36 hours per month, and pegged the minimum wage to the average urban wage and the basic cost of living in each locality.

- *2001:* The Trade Union Law reiterated that the All China Federation of Trade Unions (ACFTU) is the peak union body in China, and prohibited autonomous trade unions. Under the ACFTU umbrella, enterprise-level unions were to be created in all firms with 25 or more employees. Enterprise union committees were to be democratically elected by the union membership. The union's role was to represent the legitimate rights and interests of all staff and workers, irrespective of their nationality, *hukou* type or occupation; investigate infringements of labor rights and industrial accidents; and, during work stoppages and strikes, represent the workers in negotiations with their employers and dispute arbitration bodies.

- *2007:* Three laws introduced reforms to work-related institutions. The Labor Contract Law required all aspects of employment relations, including social insurance provision, to be formalized in a written contract between employer and employee within one month of recruitment. Contracts could be open-ended (for employees who have been employed for 10 consecutive years), fixed term, or task-specific. To improve employees' job mobility, employers were prohibited from retaining employees' ID cards and other documents, and from demanding bonds or other security from them. Longer term workers were given stronger protection against unfair dismissal, and rights to severance pay. Temporary, part-time and dispatch workers could be employed only for limited periods, and were entitled to the same remuneration, conditions and trade union membership as longer term employees. Trade unions were allowed to sign collective contracts with employers, stipulating wage-adjustment procedures and protections relating to health and safety and female employees' rights. Workers were allowed to turn down overtime and work to be carried out in unsafe conditions, and to initiate arbitration in the event of unpaid wages and abuses in the workplace.

- *2007:* The Employment Promotion Law required employers to provide all workers with equal employment opportunities and working conditions, and prohibited them from refusing work to people with disabilities or communicable diseases such as HIV/AIDs and hepatitis, which were not a workplace risk. Tax breaks were granted to enterprises that employed people with disabilities and the unemployed. Rural residents were granted equal labor rights and conditions, and could not be subjected to discriminatory restrictions. Workers experiencing discrimination were allowed to file a lawsuit in court.

- *2007:* The Labor Dispute Mediation and Arbitration Law stream-lined, and gave workers better access to, dispute-resolution and arbitration processes.
- *2010:* The Social Insurance Law mandated that all citizens, including rural residents, would be eligible to join, and enjoy equal benefits from, nationally pooled pension, medical, work-ers' compensation and maternity-insurance funds. To facilitate workers' geographical and job mobility, individuals' entitlements would be transferrable between provinces and between cities.

There are widely differing views about the impacts of these regulatory reforms. Some have argued that they have eroded workers' job security and suppressed wages while also granting them rights that would chan-nel their complaints and attempts to improve their situation into state-controlled administrative and legal arenas, away from forms of activism that threatened the state's power. Others see the reforms as a major con-tributor not only to national economic growth, but also to improvements in people's standards of living and personal freedoms.

Another debate centers on the segmentation of the labor market, and the questions of whether people now compete for jobs on the basis of "merit" or their *guanxi,* and how personal attributes such as gender, age, *hukou* type and ethnicity affect recruitment and workplace organization.

Others have asked why, despite the state's stress on the formaliza-tion of contracts between employers and employees, a large proportion of employment is informal and handled under subcontracting arrange-ments. Researchers have also studied trends in wage levels. Despite the setting of a minimum wage level, and notwithstanding complaints from both domestic and foreign employers that this favors workers over businesses, there is widespread agreement that China's semi-skilled and unskilled workers have suffered from a global "race to the bottom". Relatedly, there is debate about the reasons for the apparent failure of the unions to improve the wages and conditions of much of the workforce. These issues are examined below.

Labor markets and workplace organization

One of the main consequences of the regulatory reforms listed above was that, as economists had predicted, mass rural migration, combined with the laying-off of more than 60 million workers from the state sector in the 1990s, intensified labor-market competition, allowing China to compete internationally on the basis of low production costs. In the mid-2000s, some economists began to caution that because of population aging and the simultaneous restructuring of the economy and growing percentage of young people receiving higher education, the country might soon reach the limit of what had been thought of as its unlimited supply of labor. But underemployment and low profit margins in the agricultural sector were still driving millions of rural people to look for work away from the farm, and when China's exports slowed in the wake of the 2008 global financial crisis, more than 49 million rural workers lost their jobs.[6] By 2010, China's labor force comprised 784 million people, and many more millions of children and elderly people engaged in unreported work.[7] Competition among this vast population influences the strategies used by both job seekers and employers.

Worldwide, social networks play an important role in providing job seekers with information and referrals. Particularly in societies with unreliable accreditation and legal systems, networks can create a basis for trust between employers and potential recruits. Employers may interpret the quality of an individual's social network as an indicator of their sociability, reliability and human capital. Networked workforces might also be more stable and less contentious.

Guanxi plays a similar role in China's labor market. When Yanjie Bian studied urban state employment at the beginning of the 1990s, he found that social networks and associations with people in the CCP were important determinants of employment outcomes.[8] Some sociologists assumed that *guanxi*'s significance would wane as labor-market competition increased. Recent research has indicated the opposite: as competition for jobs has intensified, *guanxi* has assumed greater importance for both job seekers and employers.[9] Self-employed people have also made more use of their networks to get information about profitable opportunities, and secure business licenses, bank loans and sales orders.

However, the importance of *guanxi* in employment varies across different employer types and their economic activities. Xianbi Huang's qualitative research, for example, found that connections influence the recruitment and promotion decisions of state agencies and enterprises only if the positions being filled do not require specific skills and quantifiable outcomes.[10] Large private firms more consistently stress qualifications

---

[6] Huang, Jikun et al. 2011, p. 805.
[7] NBS 2011. The International Labor Organization's definition of "labor force" includes all people above the minimum legal working age of 16 who provide labor to supply goods and services, including those who currently are unemployed and employees. See International Labor Organization 2010.
[8] Bian 1994.
[9] Knight & Yueh 2008.
[10] Huang, Xianbi 2008.

and market-based productivity measures, in comparison to the state sector, and use standardized recruitment and performance evaluation procedures. Although differences between social networks and professional associations may be exaggerated, professionals such as doctors, accountants and teachers do appear to rely less upon *guanxi* to find work, when compared to people working in fields such as management and marketing. In many industries and services, including in the massive construction sector, semi-skilled and unskilled people seek work though recruitment agencies, public notices and word of mouth. In the agricultural sector, too, the great majority of hired labor is sourced through word of mouth. Much of this work is performed by middle-aged local farmers who seek these jobs to supplement their income from their farms and the remittances migrant members of their households send home, and to reciprocate their own occasional hiring of day-labor.[11] On commercial farms with constant labor requirements, such as dairies and egg farms, a larger proportion of the workforce comprises male "skilled hands" recommended by local officials or agricultural colleges.

In the same way as businesspeople who curry favor with officials, job seekers' cultivation of *guanxi* with employers and intermediaries sometimes turns into gift-giving or even outright bribery. For example, in 2010, a court found the deputy mayor of the city of Dengzhou, in Henan province, guilty of many corrupt acts, including accepting bribes in exchange for approving the promotion of an official in the city's planning bureau; finding a job in the healthier environment of the city's roads bureau for a district official's sister who had been working in a fertilizer factory; and arranging the transfer of a teacher from a town middle school to one located closer to the city.[12]

HOW OFFICIALS ARE PROMOTED

The following rhyme, heard by Sally Sargeson in 2008, illustrates popular cynicism about the extent to which appointments in government are "meritocratic":

Central leaders fight their way up;	中央领导是斗出来的
Provincial leaders follow their way up;	省内领导是跟出来的
City leaders boast their way up;	市内领导是吹出来的
County leaders buy their way up;	县内领导是买出来的
Village leaders drink their way up.	村内领导是喝出来的

---

[11] Huang, Yuan & Peng 2012, p. 155.
[12] Tanghe County People's Procuratorate 2011.

In a practice that synthesizes *guanxi* and brokerage, some firms pay existing employees a bonus if they bring in new recruits who stay for a minimum period. On the one hand, this recruitment strategy reduces the firm's costs in finding, training and assimilating new recruits. On the other hand, large firms who use the strategy risk creating concentrations of workers who, because they share a place of origin or social network, might find it easier to mobilize collective actions. For workers, too, there is a potential risk: those who have been recommended to their employer by a relative, friend or person from the same village might feel obliged to remain in an unsatisfactory job so their contact does not lose face.

The scope and intensity of labor-market competition has also opened up opportunities for a range of organizations to operate as employment brokers. Lower level government labor bureaus and commercial recruitment agencies offer an array of employment services, including vocational training, certification of job seekers' health and skills, the direct recruitment and transport of large batches of migrant workers, and the subcontracting of labor. The extent to which these brokerage organizations have assisted in commodifying and outsourcing Chinese labor is shown in the fact that, by 2008, almost 270 million workers were employed by specialist recruitment and subcontracting agencies that "dispatched" their employees to temporary, substitute and hourly jobs in all areas of the economy.[13] In inland towns, governments compete to attract and retain business investments in their jurisdictions by offering not only cheap land, transport infrastructure and utilities but also free training and recruitment services and lists of local residents willing to perform home-based assembly work. Large enterprises that have high staff-turnover rates and fluctuating labor demands have established agreements with local government education departments and vocational colleges to supply them with cohorts of student interns during peak production periods, and have even subcontracted their production processes to schools and colleges in poor areas. In 2012, the Hong Kong–based NGO China Labor Watch found that, during school vacations, student interns comprised 80 percent of the workforce in one large electronics firm based in Guangdong.[14] In such an environment, people who work for a firm will have found their jobs through different routes, and they will answer to disparate employers, who employ them on unequal terms.

Employers capitalize on labor-market segmentation and demographics to manage their workforce. This is less likely to affect university graduates, whose qualifications entitle them to urban *hukou* and who compete for positions in which knowledge and skills are highly valued.

[13] Friedman & Lee 2010, p. 512.
[14] China Labor Watch 2012.

But notwithstanding the promulgation of equal opportunities legislation, semi-skilled and unskilled rural migrants are employed on unequal terms, often under the supervision of local residents.

Gender and ethnicity also influence recruitment strategies and work-place organization. New university graduates and middle-aged laid-off workers who are female, for example, have weaker employment prospects than their male counterparts, while the vast majority of assembly-line workers recruited in Guangdong's labor-intensive industries are young women whose work is supervised by male technicians.[15] Mirroring the hierarchical and functional separation of male and female workers, the employment of workers from different ethnicities and provinces in enter-prises, and their allocation to separate workshops, canteens and dormi-tories, is a common strategy to divide large workforces both symbolically and spatially, and so to gain greater control over them.[16]

Contracts, casualization and outsourcing

Some people were employed on short-term contracts and in tempo-rary positions by state enterprises even during the Maoist era. In the post-Mao period, however, institutional reforms allowed employers to split their workforces into two groups: first, a core of regular employees with valued managerial, marketing and technical expertise protected, to varying degrees, from market competition; and second, a cohort of flex-ible, temporary workers employed according to demand. In the 1990s and early 2000s, only lucrative state-monopoly industries offered open-ended employment to the majority of their staff. In labor-intensive enter-prises and services, such as entertainment, retail, catering and commu-nity services, vast numbers of people were employed in undocumented casual positions. According to one report presented to the NPC in 2007, only about 50 percent of all enterprises provided employees with valid contracts. The figure among non-state firms was even lower, at only 20 percent.[17] More than half of all contracts were for less than one year's duration. During this period, the incidence of undocumented employ-ment varied between segments of the workforce. Most urban entrants to the workforce signed contracts, but in 2004 the Ministry of Labor and Social Security found that only 12.5 percent of rural migrant workers had an employment contract.[18]

---

[15] Hurst 2009a; Xue 2008, p. 91.
[16] Hess 2010.
[17] Friedman & Lee 2010, p. 509.
[18] Lee & Shen 2009.

Resistance to the signing of contracts comes mainly from two sources. Obviously, some employers' business models are predicated on the employment of a flexible, low-cost workforce. Undocumented workers can be sacked without compensation and, because they are ineligible for employer co-contributions into social insurance funds, are cheaper to employ. It is perhaps more surprising that many workers also are reluctant to sign contracts because they do not wish to be obliged to pay those co-contributions, and this is a condition of contract employment. Until 2011, these funds only paid benefits to people living in the municipality, an obvious deterrent both to migrant workers and to locals who aspired to find jobs elsewhere. Today, in breach of national legislation, some employers still retain contract workers' personnel dossier or identity card, or withhold part of their wages, to ensure they comply with workplace rules and complete their contract terms; such actions, understandably, deter workers from quitting an unsatisfactory position. Yet without an employment contract, workers not only lack job security but also have no basis on which to appeal to the state and courts should they be unpaid or abused in the workplace.

The raft of labor and social insurance laws passed between 2007 and 2010 was intended to strengthen the legal framework governing labor relations, to reduce the incidence of undocumented and dispatch work, and to put in place the foundations of a nationwide social security system that would facilitate, rather than inhibit, labor mobility. Some firms sought to evade the new laws by shifting from low-cost export-oriented manufacturing centers in Guangdong to even lower cost production sites in Burma and Bangladesh. Other corporations evaded the new legal requirement to provide open-ended contracts and severance pay by laying off their long-term staff and telling them to either reapply for a new, short-term contract or sign up with the employers' preferred recruitment agency. Contrary to the intent of the laws, therefore, some enterprises increased their reliance on subcontractors and dispatch workers. For example, at the end of 2008, in a large European conglomerate's Guangdong plant, the researcher Bill Taylor found that loading work had been subcontracted to a businessman who, in turn, had subcontracted the work to a gang boss from Sichuan, who employed seven laborers.[19] Seventy percent of the workforce in another Guangdong firm, which China Labor Watch investigated in 2011, comprised dispatch workers.[20] The more subcontracting relationships there are between the parent corporation and worker, the less the parent corporation's obligation (and ability) to ensure satisfactory pay and conditions for workers.

[19] Taylor 2012.
[20] Li, Qiang 2012; China Labor Watch 2012, p. 11.

On the other side of the coin, after the 2007 laws came into effect, a larger proportion of workers were issued with contracts. A 2009 survey by the National Bureau of Statistics (NBS) found, for example, that 42.8 percent of migrant workers had signed a labor contract – an increase of 30 percent on the figure five years earlier.[21] Moreover, workers proactively referred to their contract terms and used the appeal avenues set out in the new laws to try to defend their rights. This resulted in an upsurge in labor protests and a dramatic increase in the number of labor disputes going before arbitration and the courts.[22]

KEEPING IT CASUAL: HUAWEI TECHNOLOGIES COMPANY, SHENZHEN

Shenzhen's Huawei Technologies Company became notorious in late 2007 when, before the implementation of the Labor Contract Law, its management instructed all employees who had worked for Huawei for eight or more years to resign. According to one mid-level manager, Xiao, "My director called me into his office and told me that I would have to submit my resignation as soon as possible. 'Don't worry. We're just going through a certain process,' the director gave me a pat on the back. 'You know, Mr Ren has already resigned earlier this week, and me too. Actually all the old employees will do the same thing within the following two months. You'll need to reapply for your post. But I think you will get a new contract from the company very soon. And of course,' the director added, 'we will have a very generous compensation package for you.'"[23]

Xiao, like 7000 other long-term employees of Huawei, was re-employed on a new three-year contract and given a compensation package equivalent to two-thirds of his annual income. However, 500 employees were not re-employed, and Huawei did not have to pay them the severance pay mandated for unilateral firings of long-term employees in the new Labor Contract Law.

Wages and working conditions: a race to the bottom?

Throughout the 2000s, governments and enterprise owners took a growing share of China's total national income. There were significant gains for those earning the highest salaries, especially in large private

[21] "Swimming against the tide" 2010.
[22] Wang et al. 2009; Friedman & Lee 2010, pp. 518–19.
[23] Quoted in Wang et al. 2009, p. 493.

enterprises and state-monopoly sectors. The urban minimum wage increased and the national poverty line rose. And yet the share of wage income in total national income actually declined, from 54 percent in 1998 to 39 percent in 2008.[24] One of the key reasons for this decline was that wages rose at a slower rate than productivity growth. Another reason was that the wages of blue-collar and semi-skilled service workers did not keep pace with the salaries of high-income earners. For many years, the average wage for unskilled workers was little more than the minimum wage. And, according to Jane Golley and Xin Meng, relative to the cost of living, the "real wages of migrant workers may not have increased at all during the period 2000 to 2009".[25]

International comparisons offer another perspective on this story: as a proportion of average wages in the United States, between 1975 and 2000, manufacturing wages in Korea and Taiwan increased from eight percent to over 30 percent. But between 1980 and 2005, manufacturing wages in China stayed at between two and three percent.[26] In other words, the income of the proletariat in the PRC was falling further behind that of workers in other "Asian tiger" economies. Why?

Before the 1980s, China's state enterprises operated a unified grade-wage system, in which regular employees' rate of pay was pegged to official seniority grades. From the 1990s onward, state employees' remuneration comprised three components: a base wage (which reflected seniority rather than individual productivity), performance-linked rewards (such as bonus payments or profit shares) and non-cash benefits and allowances (such as employer contributions to housing). Non-monetary benefits, such as insurance and the subsidization of employees' purchase of housing, represented a large proportion of the remuneration packages of regular staff in state-monopoly sectors. Although the new remuneration system incorporated performance incentives, entitlements to agreed working hours, annual leave and social insurance, and the health and safety standards under which state employees worked, generally complied with national legislation.

Much more differentiated remuneration systems emerged in the private sector. Base wages were spread across a wider band, and most total remuneration packages included incentive rewards such as share dividends for managers or piece payments for blue-collar and semi-skilled service workers. Fewer non-cash benefits were provided than before. There also was a much greater variation in hours worked, employers' provision of rest days and holidays, contributions toward social insurance, and workplace safety.

[24] Lu & Gao 2011, p. 118.
[25] Golley & Meng 2011, p. 570.
[26] Hung 2008, pp. 161–2.

At the upper end of the occupational spectrum, today's remuneration systems reward entrepreneurship, qualifications, skills and cultural qualities that are expensive to acquire, and elite *guanxi*. At the other end of the spectrum, though, a crude calculus of supply and demand allows managers to squeeze unskilled and semi-skilled workers' wages. First, as we saw earlier, much production is subcontracted to second- and third-tier supplier firms that compete for the custom of global giants like Walmart on the basis of low production costs.[27] These competitive pressures are transferred to workers, who are constantly reminded that they, too, are competing against workers paid even lower wages in China's hinterland and in other countries. In 2010, researchers observed banners on the walls of Foxconn's Chengdu plant, warning workers: "Work hard on the job today or work hard to find a job tomorrow!"[28] Between 2010 and 2012, Foxconn responded to media stories of the draconian conditions that led to a spate of suicides in their Shenzhen plants by raising wages and transferring all dispatch workers there onto direct-hire contracts. Yet Foxconn's employees continued to labor under the ever-present threat that businesses would move to cheaper sites.

Second, subcontracting and "just-in-time management" practices have been combined with Tayloristic "scientific management" approaches from the 19th century, involving the disaggregation and standardization of tasks, detailed auditing of production times, and payment by piece-rates rather than time. Hong Xue studied electronics supplier factories in Guangdong and found that "engineers have accurately calculated how many seconds are required for each action on assembly lines and have recorded the data in computers beforehand. On each assembly line, the computers not only record the yield and failure rate for products but also trace mistakes down to a certain work station and the individual operator by the barcodes".[29]

A third, and related, reason for manufacturing workers' low wages is that the legal minimum wage in China is pegged to a monthly average wage rather than a minimum hourly wage. When employers decrease the payment per piece, workers are forced to work excessive hours simply to earn a living wage. In 2006, Anita Chan and Kaxton Siu found that each month more than 55 percent of the piece-rate workers in Walmart garment suppliers in Guangdong worked more than 300 hours, and more than 60 percent had only one, or no, rest days.[30] The longer their work hours, the less they were paid per hour. On average, these skilled

[27] Chan, Anita 2011b, p. 4.
[28] Duhigg & Barboza 2012.
[29] Xue 2008, p. 91.
[30] Chan & Siu 2010, pp. 174–7.

garment workers received around four *yuan* per hour.[31] Similarly, in 2012, China Labor Watch reported that workers in Foxconn electronics suppliers in Shenzhen frequently worked 150 to 180 hours' overtime per month. With an average hourly income of 10 *yuan*,[32] they needed to work approximately twice the legally defined standard working hours each month to earn just three-quarters of the average urban wage.[33]

Fourth, more use is made of dispatch and home-based piece-workers and interns, who are paid considerably less than regular workers. Live-in domestic maids contracted to recruitment agencies often are required to be on call 24 hours a day, in return for which they get a minimum wage, less a fee for their board. Such exploitation is quite widely accepted. Following a China Central Television (CCTV) documentary on the topic of domestic maids in 2005, viewers were invited to answer a set of questions. More than half of the 5000 who responded said maids should not expect to have one rest day each week, and 83 percent thought that maids' employers should not be expected to contribute to their health insurance.[34] The treatment of student "interns" is even worse. Unlike dispatch workers who are employed by agencies, students are not legally defined as "employees". So, while they are working, none of the provisions of the labor laws apply to them; they are not entitled to social insurance; and they cannot join a union. In many cases, the students are not paid until they have completed the internship and returned to their studies. Then, their colleges pay them a below–minimum wage amount, from which they have deducted what they term "introduction fees", and the students' travel expenses and board.

Finally, non-payment and late payment of wages, insurance and pensions are widespread. China's construction firms are notorious for their multi-layered subcontracting relations that facilitate the embezzlement and non-payment of wages, while in manufacturing, some employers capitalize on the complex methods they use to calculate overtime and piece rates to steal wages.[35]

Some of the massive new manufacturing compounds in China – containing dormitories, canteens, post offices and clinics as well as multiple workshops – superficially resemble the "total institutions" of the old socialist *danwei*. But whereas surveillance in *danwei* monitored political conformity, in the new plants surveillance and disciplinary systems are designed to maximize productivity, in the interests of which they control every aspect of workers' lives on and off the shop floor. Workers pass

[31] US$0.50 at 2006 exchange rate.
[32] US$1.50 at 2012 exchange rate.
[33] Li 2012; "China: migrants" 2012.
[34] Sun 2013, p. 38.
[35] Pun & Lu 2010.

through a series of electronic security gates when they enter the plant compound, and again when they arrive at the workshop. In many plants, workers must not chat on the production line, may only have a drink and visit restrooms during scheduled breaks, and are not permitted to return to their dormitories or leave the plant compound during breaks. Fines are deducted from their wages if they fail to meet production quotas, produce substandard items, are a few minutes late for work, or have a mobile phone, camera or USB drive on the shop floor. Each shift has a curfew, after which workers are restricted to their dormitory. People working on a mobile-phone assembly line at a Foxconn plant told Pun Ngai and Jenny Chan that working in their plant was like being

trapped in a 'concentration camp' of labor discipline – Foxconn manages us through the principle of 'obedience, obedience, and absolute obedience!' Must we sacrifice our dignity as people for production efficiency?[36]

Research conducted in the agricultural sector, although there has been a limited amount of it, suggests that remuneration systems there also are designed to intensify productivity pressures. The simplest, least draconian remuneration scheme, which Sargeson observed on a large organic fruit and vegetable farm in the lower Yangzi River Delta in 2012, paid laborers a fixed amount per day that, if received each day for 28 days, was equivalent to the local monthly minimum wage. The laborers were closely supervised, and expected to pay for their own medical and old-age insurance. In plantation agriculture, share-farming, base wages and incentive schemes are more common. For example, on coffee plantations in Yunnan province, some companies split the harvest with workers according to a 6:4 ratio and allow them to build their own housing on plantation land. As "live-in" labor, they provide round-the-clock care for the plantation's coffee trees. Others employ salaried staff to supervise laborers who are paid according to the area of land they cultivate and each kilogram of beans harvested on that area, plus a daily wage for picking beans.[37]

Unions and the representation of workers' rights and interests

The regulatory reforms introduced in China since the 1980s guarantee workers' rights to a regulated minimum wage, safe working conditions, rest days, welfare and union representation. Why, then, are so many workers' pay and conditions substandard, labor rights so frequently violated,

---

[36] Pun & Chan 2012, p. 398.
[37] Zhang & Donaldson 2010.

and worker discontent so widespread? The argument scholars generally give to answer these questions is that upholding labor rights depends on local governments and workers' nominated representative organization, the union. Local governments are unwilling to enforce workers' rights, and unions are unable to represent their interests.

China's Ministry of Human Resources and Social Security is responsible for administering workers and monitoring and enforcing employers' compliance with regulations. The ministry has departments, bureaus and offices at each succeeding level of the government hierarchy. However, local-government bureaucracies also are responsible for fostering economic growth and employment, and for collecting the business, company and land development taxes that are their main sources of revenue. To succeed in these tasks, they must compete against governments in other localities to attract and retain investment. Moreover, as explained above, many governments own shares in large enterprises in their jurisdictions and consequently have vested interests in enterprises' profitability and share price. So, the lower levels of the Chinese state tend to be strongly pro-capital and they set the bar low when it comes to determining the minimum wage for the locality. In fact, it is not uncommon for local governments to collude with employers to cheat workers out of the pay and welfare benefits to which they are legally entitled, to suborn enterprise union leaders, to intimidate dissatisfied workers and to suppress strikes. Some governments have also quashed NGOs that have attempted to educate workers about their legal rights, health and safety standards or offered advice and representation to workers bringing a lawsuit.

Local communities might also have vested interests in suppressing workers. For example, in Guangdong, many shareholding corporations in villages have rented land and factories to corporations whose comparative advantage lies in low-cost manufacturing. As Anita Chan writes, this creates an "unspoken alliance between the local village governments (and the levels of government immediately above them), and foreign invested enterprises with regard to keeping the migrant production-line workers in line".[38]

As we noted above, the ACFTU's role is to represent the rights and interests of staff and workers.[39] Representation, though, is a slippery concept: it can mean formal delegation and accountability, as in a principal-agent relationship such as the one between the owner and manager of a business; or it can imply the substantive act of responding to, promoting and defending someone's preferences. According to these definitions, the

[38] Chan, 2012, p. 41.
[39] There is no mass organization representing farmers and hired agricultural workers in China.

ACFTU, China's peak trade union body, acts as an agent – but not as an agent of workers. Instead, following its formation as a mass organization under the leadership of the CCP, it became an agent and transmission belt for the CCP and government. Some scholars have gone so far as to describe the ACFTU not as a union but rather as a part of the state. Certainly, the career paths of CCP and ACFTU leaders are intertwined, and a substantial part of the ACFTU's budget comes from the state.[40]

In the 1990s, the ACFTU faced a crisis that forced it to try to adjust its organizational scope and representative activities. As enterprise ownership and labor-market reforms progressed in the largely unionised state sector, lay-offs and pension arrears became more common. In the rapidly expanding non-unionised private sector and among the migrant workforce, disputes and strikes were larger, more frequent, and often violent. In many instances these protests were organized without the knowledge of the union. Even more worrying for the CCP – in view of the role the independent labor movement Solidarity played in the fall of communism in Poland – some workers were creating their own groups to advocate and represent their interests against employers and local governments. All this, when the ACFTU was experiencing declining union membership: between 1995 and 1999, membership dropped from 103 million to 87 million.[41]

The state and ACFTU embarked on a campaign to restore the union's strength by increasing its membership, recruiting migrant workers, establishing enterprise-level unions in the private sector, and protecting workers' legal rights and interests more effectively. They succeeded in achieving all but the last of these aims. By 2005, membership had risen to 150 million, migrants were included in the membership, and more than half a million enterprise-level unions had been established in private businesses.[42] Even the huge US-owned firm Walmart finally bowed to pressure from the state and allowed unions to be established in its Chinese stores in 2006. By 2009, total national union membership had grown to 230 million, apparently the largest in the world.[43]

That figure, though huge, may be misleading because, in many foreign and private firms, enterprise unions exist in name only. The great majority of new enterprise unions have been established in a top-down manner, through negotiations between provincial or county ACFTU branches, local governments and the management of individual enterprises. In this process, few union leaders are elected by the members. Instead, the

---

[40] Taylor & Li 2007, pp. 701–2.
[41] Cheng, Ngok & Huang 2012, p. 385.
[42] Ibid., p. 385.
[43] Zhu, Warner & Feng 2011, p. 131.

union leaders typically are mid-level managers whom the firm's management appoint, and workers are co-opted into the union as nominal members. The principal tasks of the union are to communicate between management and workers, pre-empt disputes, and maintain production and "social harmony" in cooperation with employers, government labor departments and the police. They also provide what Feng Chen refers to as "service responsiveness", by organizing social activities for workers, assisting individuals to access welfare services, and providing them with legal advice.[44] When there is an indisputable violation of workers' legal rights, unions mediate with management, provided that local government is not implicated in the violation. If their mediation fails, they direct workers into state-sanctioned administrative or juridical channels. The union only rarely assists workers in mobilizing protests or formulating collective demands to improve their pay and conditions. China Labour Bulletin examined 553 labor protests and strikes between 2000 and 2010, and found that none had been union-led.[45] In fact, workers do not even expect this of their union. Because it is widely viewed as weak or, worse, as a tool of management, in most collective disputes workers approach their employers directly, and then the local government, to demand their rights. Sometimes, striking workers have even regarded the union as an antagonist, and come to blows with union leaders whom managers have sent to talk them back to work.

Summary

Until the 1980s, there was a clear divergence between the security, remuneration and social prestige attached to the *gongzuo* or "proper work" of most urban workers and the *laodong* labor rural people did. In the succeeding years, regulatory reforms produced an intensely competitive labor market, and the contractualization, casualization and outsourcing of labor. Now, Chinese people working alongside one another, and performing exactly the same task in an enterprise or on a farm, could be employed through different routes and by different employers, and be entitled to different wages, bonuses, non-wage benefits, insurance protections and union representation. The institutions of China's workforce continue to fragment and, at the same time, workers continue in their efforts to defend their legal rights. The ACFTU, in response to the demands of this more variegated and restive workforce, has increased its membership and gained a foothold in foreign and privately owned firms.

---

[44] Chen, Feng 2003, p. 1026.
[45] "Swimming against the tide" 2010, p. 17.

Constrained by its dual role as CCP transmission belt and workers' representative, however, the union is still unable to act effectively on behalf of its own members, much less the hundreds of millions of non-unionised workers in China. For these reasons, workers are at the forefront of most of the collective actions we examine in Chapter 13.

Discussion questions

1. Which aspects of the fragmentation of Chinese labor have occurred as a result of domestic institutional reforms, and which aspects would you attribute to the globalization of production and supply processes? If you were to research the answer to this question, what types of data and what case studies would you draw on?
2. Compare the roles and actions of the ACFTU, and unions in the society in which you live. What are the similarities and differences? On the basis of your comparison, draw up a list of definitive features of a truly "representative" trade union.
3. Is the use of *guanxi* complementary, or inimical, to merit-based competition in China's labor market?

Recommended reading

Chan, Anita (ed.) 2011a, *Walmart in China*. Ithaca, NY: ILR Press.
Chen, Calvin 2008, *Some Assembly Required: Work, Community and Politics in China's Rural Enterprises*. Cambridge, MA: Harvard University Press.
Entwisle, Barbara & Henderson, Gail E (eds) 2000, *Re-drawing Boundaries: Work, Households, and Gender in China*. Berkeley: University of California Press.
Eyferth, Jacob 2006, *How China Works: Perspectives on the Twentieth-Century Industrial Workplace*. Milton Park, UK: Routledge.
Hurst, William 2009a, *The Chinese Worker After Socialism*. New York: Cambridge University Press.
Lee, Ching Kwan (ed.) 2007a, *Working in China: Ethnographies of Labor and Workplace Transformation*. Milton Park, UK: Routledge.
Sargeson, Sally 1999, *Reworking China's Proletariat*. Houndmills, UK: Macmillan.

Part 2

Cultures, Socialization and
the Formation of Identities

6   Religion, Ritual and Religiosity

In contemporary China, there are a huge variety of ideals, activities, people, practices, networks and buildings that could be depicted as either religious or quasi-religious. These include Christian churches, Islamic mosques, Buddhist, Daoist and local temples, ancestral shrines, fortune tellers, geomancers, *qigong* practitioners (those who manipulate *qi*, the vital energy of life), Confucian ritualists, teachers of Confucian, Daoist or Buddhist philosophy, and even the purveyors of state ideologies and rituals, who often draw on broadly religious sensibilities. To grasp this huge array of discourses, activities, people and things, we must begin by examining why some are classified as "religious" while others are not, and how Chinese historical experience has affected this classificatory logic.

Defining and regulating religious activity in China

In western countries, over the latter half of the second millennium, the category of religion took shape through the gradual emergence of secular modes of governing and scientific reasoning in societies that were formerly ruled in the name of Christianity. Because Christianity emphasized inner belief, and because the power of religious leaders was diminished by the separation of the church from both state rule and the scientific depiction of nature, the category of religion came to refer to relatively powerless institutions of belief, clearly separate from both government and science. Freedom of religion became a freedom of "belief" that was not to impinge on either state rule or scientific reason. Individuals or groups who wished to impose their religion on the state, or who ignored scientific findings because of their religious beliefs, were dismissed respectively as zealots or cults.[1]

---

[1] For more on the development of the category of religion in Europe, see Asad 1993. For application of this idea to China see Kipnis 2001.

Before the late Qing dynasty, there was no category of religion in China. What we today call Buddhism was known as "the teachings of Buddha"; what we call Daoism was known as "Daoist teachings"; and Confucianism was termed "Confucian teachings". The imperial Chinese state ruled through various combinations of these teachings. A huge variety of local temples (often seen as sites of "popular religion") borrowed lore and imagery from them, and various forms of traditional Chinese science (including Chinese medicine, geomancy, *qigong*, fortune-telling, ship-building, agriculture and astrology) drew from these teachings.

Western imperialism in China made a deep impression on the Chinese intellectuals of the late 19th and early 20th centuries. Arguments emerged about what China needed to adopt from the west to become strong again and what in Chinese tradition would need to be abandoned. Most, including future CCP leaders, agreed that science and secular government were to be adopted, that proper religions (those that resembled Christianity with upright moral teachings and a trained clergy) were to be given a limited role similar to that of Christianity in western societies, and that what they saw as superstitions were to be ruthlessly stamped out. In the 20th century, this consensus resulted in different fates for different forms of religiosity. Buddhism and Daoism became formal religions. Various forms of Chinese medicine, acupuncture, and *qigong* (derived mostly from Daoist teachings) were labeled as sciences. Confucianism became a secular philosophy, and many forms of local religion, fortune-telling and geomancy were forced underground as illegal superstitions. The Nationalist regime converted many local temples to schools, and more were destroyed during the CCP's land reforms. To get away from the state categories that officially define what is and is not a religion, many scholars use the term "religiosity" when discussing the wide range of activities that relate to systems of belief or reasoning in China.[2]

It is important to acknowledge the state's categories, however, if we want to understand how state regulation affects religious activities in China. There have been five official religions for most of the 20th and early 21st centuries, including since the founding of the PRC. These are (Protestant) Christianity, Catholicism, Buddhism, Islam and Daoism. All places of worship in China must be recognized as one of these five religions by the Religious Affairs Bureau (RAB)[3] or they become at least technically illegal. In addition, some adherents of these five

---

[2] Goossaert & Palmer 2011.

[3] In 1998, the national level of the RAB was renamed SARA (State Administration of Religious Affairs). As many of the actions depicted in this chapter either take place at the local level or took place before 1998, we will use the name RAB in this chapter.

religions refuse to register with the RAB and so their activities are therefore illegal and sometimes pushed underground. The RAB appoints or
approves clergy members in official places of worship and is supposed
to prevent "superstitious" activities from occurring there. Forms of Chinese religiosities that are not categorized as religions are also often state-
regulated. For example, *qigong* has been regulated by agencies in charge
of Chinese medicine as a form of healing, by the National Association
of Science and Technology as a topic for scientific research, by various
national sport associations as a form of fitness activity, and, when certain forms of *qigong* have been declared illegal, by the Ministry of Public
Security (MPS) as a form of superstition.

Almost all forms of religiosity (other than various forms of Mao-
worship) were forbidden during the Maoist era. Many temples were
destroyed and little openly religious activity took place. Since the 1980s,
scope for religious activity has greatly expanded. Alhough the CCP still
forbids its members from formally joining religious organizations and
officially views religions as false, and although crackdowns and suppression have occurred, there is greater room for legal religious activity.
In the past few years, a new legal space for conducting quasi-religious
activity has opened up under the name of "intangible cultural heritage"
(*feiwuzhi wenhua yichan*). This category, taken from UNESCO movements to preserve oral tradition, has become an excuse for local
governments to support a great variety of temples, temple festivals, quasi-
religious performing arts, and other local traditions that previously might
have been linked to "superstition".

Popular and organized religion

Popular religion in China has several distinguishing characteristics. First,
it is polytheistic. For practitioners of popular religion, it is quite appropriate to worship at a temple or shrine or holy place devoted to one god,
spirit or ancestor and then go straight to another location to worship
a different one. The spiritual world is understood to be inhabited by a
wide variety of supernatural beings, and it makes sense to direct prayers
to more than one. Analysts of Chinese popular religion have pointed out
how the range of spiritual beings – gods, ghosts and ancestors – mirrors
the traditional Chinese social worlds of officials, strangers and relatives,[4]
and how the pantheon of gods was often imagined as a bureaucratic
organisation parallel to the imperial state.[5] In popular religion, notions

---

[4] Wolf 1974b.
[5] Feuchtwang 2001.

of efficacy and reciprocity are important. Efficacious spirits are those who answer one's prayers, and reciprocity involves sincere and loyal religious practice. Loyal worshippers return regularly to particular places of worship (though not exclusively to one place) and are sincere in their offerings. The particular manner of making an offering is fairly standard in a wide range of Chinese temples. One should burn incense in the large cauldron in front of the temple, place money in the donation box, and kowtow to the image of the god.

The polytheism of popular religion is anathema to the large, monotheistic religious traditions, and contemporary Chinese Christians, Catholics and Muslims often come into conflict with friends and relatives who pray at popular temples. Many Christians even debate whether burning incense for ancestors constitutes a form of idol-worship or whether it can be respected as a type of secular custom.[6]

Before 1949, popular Chinese temples were understood to be temples of a particular village or neighborhood, and in some places this is still the case. Ritual occasions for consolidating village or neighborhood solidarity can be held there, and almost all worshippers at such temples are locals. In the past, while there were often networks of such temples, and pilgrimage routes that would take worshippers far away, popular religious activity remained linked to particular places. In this way, it contrasted with a religion such as Islam, in which practitioners should face Mecca and pray to God five times a day, no matter where they are. As China urbanizes and tourism develops, religious activity has less and less of a local character. Many temples become sites of pilgrimage and tourism, and religious morality often directs itself to doing good and performing charity on a global rather than a local scale.[7] In the practice of forming global or national charities, non-local forms of religious organization often emerge.

Despite the differences and potential conflicts, popular and organized religions often overlap in interesting ways. The rest of this chapter examines several contemporary examples of Chinese religiosity with an eye to understanding the forms of this overlap, the ways in which this religiosity entwines with various levels of politics (international, national, local and even household) and how the lines between activities that fall into the categories of "science", "superstition" and "religion" are continually redrawn.[8]

---

[6] Kipnis 2002.

[7] Huang, Chien-Yu Julia & Weller 1998.

[8] The following case studies touch on aspects of Daoism, Christianity and (Tibetan) Buddhism, as well as other forms of religiosity. For studies of Islam in China, see Gillette 2000; Gladney 2004b; and Zang 2011c.

Image 6.1   Burning incense in front of Dong Yue Temple on the Mount Tai pilgrimage route, Shandong province.
Source: Andrew Kipnis 2008.

A local temple becomes "Daoist"

The northern part of Shaanxi province is poor and drought-prone. For centuries, one of the most worshipped gods there has been the Black Dragon King (*Hei Long Wang*), who controls rainfall and other things. One of the largest temples devoted to him in this region is located next to a spring where the dragon king is said to live and whose water is said to have magical curative properties. The temple was torn down during the Cultural Revolution, but a group of men from six local villages rebuilt it in 1982. Adam Chau describes how this temple that originally was not officially recognized was able to flourish and eventually secure classification as a proper "Daoist" temple.[9] This case illustrates the complexity of the relationship between religion and politics at local level.

Like most Chinese temples, the Black Dragon King Temple has figures of various gods (including the dragon king), incense pots and donation boxes. Visitors who have a request for the dragon king place burning incense for him in the incense pot, put money in the donation box and

[9] Chau 2006.

kowtow in front of his figure. The temple has thus had a stream of monetary income, amounting to millions of *yuan* each year since the 1990s, which the temple committee has used to expand the temple, build an opera stage near the temple (the Black Dragon King is said to enjoy traditional forms of local opera), construct a primary school for local villagers and beautify the surrounding landscape.

Local officials made no attempt to close the temple, despite its lack of an official affiliation. Because they had to enact other unpopular policies, such as birth control and tax collection, the officials did not want to further anger the local population by closing the temple. For their part, the temple officers went out of their way to cultivate good relationships with local officials, bribing the members of the bureaus responsible for the regulation of religious activity. Finally, it was said that many local officials themselves believed in the Black Dragon King and did not want to incur his wrath.

The head of the temple committee, Boss Wang, worked hard to establish the reputation of the temple among both officials and the local population. During the 1990s, he attracted funding for a reforestation project from a Japanese NGO. Local people donated their labor to plant trees around the temple, and the dragon king was consulted about where exactly to plant. Boss Wang also managed to get an archway that had survived the destruction of the Cultural Revolution officially declared to be a "cultural relic". Both of these actions brought positive recognition to local officials. But the final grace came in 1998, when he convinced the RAB to declare the temple Daoist, despite the fact that it had no Daoist clergy and that most of the activity at the temple appeared to fall under the heading of "superstition".

The temple's organisers scheduled its celebration of this recognition to coincide with the Black Dragon King's birthday. They gave the local police numerous gifts and invited them to maintain order at the festival, also giving presents to the Electricity Bureau to ensure adequate electricity supplies. They also invited an opera troop to perform the dragon king's favorite opera and a wide range of state officials attended a ceremony and banquet held on the temple grounds.

More than 100 000 visitors attended the six-day festival. The valley around the temple was packed with food stalls, circus acts, freak shows, firecracker stands, makeshift gambling dens and brothels, and all manner of fortune-tellers and diviners. At the ceremony itself, officials, including the head of the county RAB, who was a Daoist priest from a relatively staid official temple, gave speeches in which they reiterated the need to uphold proper religious values and avoid superstitious activity. They then hung the official plaque declaring the temple Daoist, and the opera and banquet (attended by Boss Wang, all of the officials, and seemingly, though invisibly to non-believers, by the dragon king himself) were held. Despite its contradictory messages, politically the festival was a huge success. All the participants were allowed to do their jobs. The words spoken by the officials explicitly corresponded to Chinese law and policy, but their actions implicitly allowed them to be seen as socializing with the Black Dragon King and thus as both recognizing and being recognized by the god. The festival has become an annual event and (at the time of writing), images of the 2009 festival by the professional photographer Cao Changjin are available online.[10]

Tibetan Buddhism

Ethno-religious conflict between Tibetans and the Chinese state (and the majority Han Chinese population) is one of the most explosive issues in China today. Exploring this case illuminates how religiosity infuses ethnic and international politics. In 1951, the CCP came to an agreement with the 14th Dalai Lama that recognized Chinese sovereignty over Tibet and allowed the People's Liberation Army (PLA) into Tibet, while guaranteeing the preservation of Tibetan politico-religious structures, including the leadership of the Dalai Lama and the landed estates that supported a system of monasteries with tens of thousands of monks. However, during the 1950s, conflict between China and Tibet arose because of pressures to enact land reform on the estates, undermining the economic basis of the monasteries, and because of attempts to impose religious restrictions on monks. On 10 March 1959, the PLA invited the Dalai Lama to watch a performance in their camp. As rumors started that the PLA was intending to kidnap him, thousands of supporters amassed, riots began and armed conflict followed. The Dalai Lama and 80 000 of his supporters (mostly from other religious elites) fled to Dharamsala, India, where they set up a government in exile. The PRC declared the earlier agreement void and moved aggressively to close monasteries and redistribute their land, an act that the PRC's government claims liberated the common Tibetan serfs. Despite this "liberation", private forms of worship among ordinary Tibetans continued.

The Cultural Revolution hit Tibet especially hard. Seen locally by many as an assault on Tibetan Buddhism by Han Chinese, it led to the bloody Nyemo Revolt of 1968–69. In the revolt, a young nun declared herself possessed by a local deity and claimed to be bulletproof. Her followers killed many CCP officials, until the rebels were violently

[10] Cao Changjin's website can be found at: <http://caochangjin.blshe.com>.

suppressed and the leaders publicly executed.[11] During the 1980s, post-Mao relaxations on religious activity have led to a renewal of signs of religiosity, including pilgrimage, temple-building and more religious teaching. Still, restrictions on support and training for monks have meant that, although the number of temples now exceeds pre-1949 levels, the number of monks is drastically lower.

The PRC has made a few attempts to reach out to the Dalai Lama and the government in exile during the post-Mao period but has not been able to reach a compromise with them. The government, still exiled in Dharamsala, desires more independence for Tibet than the PRC is willing to allow. Since 1990, the PRC has generally denounced the Dalai Lama and tried to increase its popularity among Tibetans by promoting economic development and allowing, but regulating, religious practice. The promotion of development has resulted in some economic gains for average Tibetans, though many complain that most of the gain has been captured by in-migrating Han Chinese. Central to the regulation of religion has been control over the appointment of monks and the institution of reincarnation.

In Buddhism, all life may be reincarnated as higher or lower forms, and especially enlightened individuals may leave this world and the cycle of reincarnation altogether. Some enlightened individuals, however, choose to return to this world to help others move toward enlightenment. Especially charismatic masters are often seen as the reincarnates of past, enlightened, religious leaders. Lines of reincarnation are institutionalized in different monasteries. The RAB has limited reincarnates to one per monastery and requires that they be approved by the RAB. The Dalai Lama has been completely eliminated from the process of selecting reincarnated lamas, leading to a widespread view among Tibetans that the officially selected lamas lack legitimacy. In addition, a large number of reincarnated "lines" ended with monks who were killed during the Cultural Revolution. Tension is running high around attitudes toward the Dalai Lama. The RAB attempts to force monks to disparage the Dalai Lama as a "splittist" (*fenliezhuyifenzi*), in other words a traitor who wishes to split up the country. Monks who do not make this declaration will not be approved as reincarnates, and they often suffer other sanctions as well. Dissatisfaction with such arrangements has been one of the factors behind continuing Tibetan hostility toward the PRC, as well as the severe ethnic rioting of 2008.

In the meantime, the Dalai Lama and Tibetan Buddhism have gained a worldwide following, which further complicates the relationship between

[11] For differing perspectives on how to analyze this incident, see Makley 2009; Goldstein, Jiao & Lhundrup 2009.

Beijing and Dharamsala. To the great aggravation of the Chinese state, the Dalai Lama was awarded the Nobel Peace Prize in 1989, and hundreds of Tibetan Dharma centers have been established around the world. Many Han, from Taiwan and western countries as well as the PRC, have also shown an interest in Tibetan Buddhism. During the 1990s, hundreds of Han joined several thousand Tibetans to study at an unofficial Tibetan teaching center in northwest Sichuan province, only to be expelled by a work team from the RAB in 2001.[12]

Falun Gong

The example of Falun Gong demonstrates that major politico-religious conflict does not only occur in cases of ethnic division. In the late 1980s and early 1990s, toward the end of the period of "*qigong* fever"[13] during which many forms of *qigong* became popular, Li Hongzhi developed his own distinctive form of *qigong* practice, which combined physical movement with meditation to promote health and spiritual attainment. He called this practice Falun Gong (Buddhist Law Qigong), and wrote a book called *Zhuan Falun* ("Spinning the Wheel of Buddhist Law"), which combined pieces of Buddhist and Daoist philosophy and moral injunction with traditional Chinese exercise and meditation principles. Li moved to New York City and has profited from the sale of his books, audiotapes and videotapes, which have been translated into 10 languages. Many websites promote his writings and introduce his philosophy under the slogan "truthfulness, benevolence and forbearance".

When pressed, especially in the Chinese context, Li has argued that Falun Gong is not a religion, cult or movement, and that it is not anti-science or anti-medicine, but rather a form of spiritual cultivation and health-training based on principles that are not against (although possibly beyond) science. The Chinese government might have accepted this claim if it were not for the sudden protests that materialized in Beijing on 26 April 1999. On that day, 10 000 Falun Gong practitioners amassed in front of Zhongnan Hai (the residential complex for China's highest leaders) to protest the reaction of Chinese officials to a petition against a magazine article that had criticized Falun Gong. After a month-long investigation, the Chinese state began a major propaganda campaign denouncing Falun Gong as a "superstition", an illegal organization, and a "heretical" form of religious teaching.

[12] Goossaert & Palmer 2011, p. 364
[13] Palmer 2007.

The state claimed that Falun Gong had a highly structured organization with a central office in Beijing, 39 instruction centers in major cities, 1900 instruction stations and 28 000 practice locations scattered around the country. The Public Security Bureau (PSB) rounded up thousands of practitioners and they were sent to labor camps or mental asylums, while many others were let off if they agreed to denounce Falun Gong publicly. The state's fear of Falun Gong went beyond its usual dislike of organizations that it did not control, because many CCP members themselves, including high-ranking people in the government and the army, were said to have practiced Falun Gong. Older, retired Party members were drawn to *qigong* practice, in the same way as the general population were, both because it involved social activity and because they believed it promoted good health. As retired Party members can retain influence, Jiang Zemin, the then CCP leader, was said to have feared the formation of a secret organization within the Party itself.[14]

During the first decade of the 21st century, despite continuing defiance by Falun Gong members at first, the crackdown eventually succeeded in silencing Falun Gong within China. The public practice of many other forms of *qigong* has also declined as a result of the protracted campaign. Outside China, however, the popularity of Falun Gong has continued to grow. There are branches of the organization in the North America, South America, Australia, Europe and Hong Kong. Falun Gong members often protest in front of Chinese embassies and consulates, and have started newspapers in both Chinese and English that are extremely critical of the CCP and its record of human-rights violations.

THE FALUN GONG AND THE CHINESE STATE

The war of words between Falun Gong and the Chinese state has been extreme. At the start of its campaign against Falun Gong, the state published a series of newspaper articles and pamphlets that depicted Falun Gong practitioners being driven insane and committing suicide and murder, literally trying to rip a "wheel of law" from their stomachs, dying because they refused medical care after being told by their instructors that Falun Gong alone could cure them, and being manipulated by their instructors to commit all manner of crimes, including cannibalism. Falun Gong, through its newspapers and websites, has responded with numerous writings about human-rights violations in China and the torture and abuse that Falun Gong practitioners have endured while in captivity in China. Such writings depict Chinese

14 Kipnis 2001.

prisoners being burned with irons, shocked with electric batons, having saline solution forced into their noses, having fingernails pried off with bamboo slits, as well as being subjected to rape and sexual torture. While state writings about Falun Gong emerged mostly around the turn of the 21st century, Falun Gong writings continue to be published online.[15]

Wenzhou Christianity

The number of Christians in China is thought to be between 20 and 200 million people, with most estimates falling between 60 and 130 million. Approximately three-quarters of Chinese Christians are Protestant. Survey research on this topic is difficult due to the fact that some Christian churches are illegal and that Party members could lose power if they admitted publicly to being Christians. Nevertheless, even by most of the more conservative estimates, China is one of the largest Christian countries in the world.

Many ethnographic accounts of Christianity in China have focused on rural China and, in the congregations investigated, most members were women, the elderly or sick, or the relatively impoverished. Not all Christian congregations are rural, however. Cao Nanlai researched Protestant Christianity in the Zhejiang province city of Wenzhou, known as "the Jerusalem of China" because of the number of churches there. Cao argues that Wenzhou Christianity is dominated by a group of middle-aged male entrepreneurs known as the "boss Christians" (laoban jidutu). Cao's study focuses attention on the relationship between Wenzhou Christianity and the everyday politics of class, gender and status rather than the official politics of the state regulation of religion that we highlighted in the cases of Tibetan Buddhism and Falun Gong. While there are both official (RAB-certified) and unofficial (illegal) churches in Wenzhou, Cao argues that differences between them are not significant.[16]

Cao identifies several parallels between the ways in which the boss Christians arrange their lives and seek status as businessmen and how they do so in their churches. To begin with, just as some businessmen in real estate hope to display their success by owning large and ostentatious buildings, so some boss Christians dream of building and financing the largest and most ornate church buildings possible. Cao describes a boss Christian who always carries with him a business proposal for constructing a church with a capacity for seating 10 000 people in

[15] For example, see the website <http://www.faluninfo.net>.
[16] Cao 2011.

Shanghai (the Chinese city where real estate is most expensive). In addition, these businessmen take great pride in their Wenzhou identities. Wenzhou natives are famous for starting businesses in other parts of the country and the world, and they often build churches in the places where they start their businesses. When they do so, they prefer to rely entirely on their own finance rather than seeking local partners. In this manner, they can establish the "brand" of Wenzhou churches outside of Wenzhou and demonstrate to the locals how powerful and impressive Wenzhou people are. Boss Christians run their churches in the same way as their businesses. Just as they increase labor specialization by outsourcing aspects of their manufacturing, for example, so do they "outsource" the labor of delivering sermons – that is, instead of each church hiring its own preacher, the bosses organize rotating groups of preachers (including themselves) to circulate among many churches. In this manner, each preacher need only develop a small number of sermons. Finally, some bosses are insecure about their own low level of education. To build up their status as literate and literary men, such boss Christians give sermons and lead discussions on biblical verses.

Boss Christians are evangelical and their church congregations are often very mixed, including people from a range of class backgrounds. Many migrant-worker Christians converted to Christianity after their arrival in Wenzhou. While they had heard of Christianity in their rural homes, they associated the religion with relatively uneducated, elderly women. When they arrived in Wenzhou and became aware of boss Christians, they realized that Christianity can also be linked to upper-class, male modernity, and they become more receptive. Some male migrant workers take a great interest in the Bible and choose to become preachers themselves. In Wenzhou, migrant-worker preachers are sometimes more educated and articulate than the boss Christians, and they deliver eloquent sermons. But no matter how well a particular migrant worker may preach, he is never allowed to do so to boss Christians, because preaching is taken as indicating a potentially hierarchical relationship. So, boss Christians often preach to congregations of migrant workers, migrant workers preach to other migrant workers and boss Christians to other boss Christians. But migrant workers are never allowed to preach in settings where many in the audience are likely to be bosses. Boss Christians also hold many religious events that are organized in expensive settings, reserved exclusively for the bosses and attended by invitation only.

In the Wenzhou church, women also preach only rarely. In the relatively exclusive meetings of boss Christians, Christian women are restricted to the role of greeting men at the entrance and ushering them to their seats. Boss Christians evaluate their Christian sisters on the way in which they handle their familial relationships rather than on their knowledge of the

Image 6.2   A Protestant Christian church in downtown Wenzhou.
Source: Cao Nanlai 2009.

Bible. At all-female spiritual cultivation meetings, Wenzhou sisters sing hymns, make intensely emotional personal disclosures about their family problems, reveal how God has led them to overcome certain problems, and pray together to alleviate illnesses and difficult family relationships. At such meetings, the women often weep. In short, women are expected and encouraged to engage Christianity through familial emotion, not reasoned discussion supported by the Bible.

Confucian "philosophy" as "religion"

The Confucian tradition of philosophical reasoning traces itself back to the *Lunyu* (*Analects of Confucius*), a book written by Confucius' students shortly after his death almost 2500 years ago. The tradition includes many other famous contributors, most notably Mencius (372–289 BCE; disputed by some) and Zhu Xi (1130–1200), the latter of whom is credited with establishing the "neo-Confucian" canon. While many contemporary Chinese scholars engage philosophically with the tradition, the wider public often interacts with Confucianism in a religious manner.

Although the Chinese state classifies Buddhism as a religion and Confucianism as a form of secular philosophy, today both forms of "teaching" might be thought of as blurring the lines between religion and philosophy.

The most important religious aspect of contemporary Confucianism is the many temples devoted to both Confucius himself and later Confucian philosophers. Perhaps the largest Confucian temple (Kong Miao) is in Confucius' hometown of Qufu, in Shandong province. That temple is now a massive tourist complex. It was originally built just two years after Confucius' death and has been rebuilt many times since. During the late imperial period, it had obvious relevance to state politics. In the 18th century, before distinctions between religion, statecraft and philosophy had been as carefully drawn as they would later become, the Qianlong emperor came to the temple eight times to offer major sacrifices. The temple still has buildings for making sacrifices to Confucius, his parents and family members, and other scholar officials in the Confucian tradition. Because familial ethics and sacrifice was a central concern of Confucianism, Confucius' descendants (who took the surname Kong), have reconstructed a vast genealogy that traces Confucius' family down to the current day. Their performance of ancestral and funerary rites is considered an important aspect of the Confucianism on display in Qufu. The family cemetery (Kong Lin) is the second largest tourist attraction in Qufu.

Around the country, many other temples are devoted to Confucius or Confucian scholars. These temples illustrate an important aspect of popular religion in China. Historical personages, including scholar officials, military heroes and exemplary women, were often (and sometimes still are) deified after they died. Temples were built for them, and people come to burn incense for them and make requests to the image and spirit of the "god" contained in those temples. Just as Confucianism and Buddhism may be said to blur the lines between religion and philosophy, so these forms of worship blur the lines between historical personages and gods. Ancestor-worship can be said to do the same thing.

A second religious aspect of Confucianism is the attitude many readers take toward the texts in this tradition. Some who study them treat them in a manner similar to sacred religious texts such as the Bible or the Koran – that is, as texts that might be interpreted in one way or another but which can never be criticized or doubted. Primary school children around the country are encouraged to memorize (without necessarily understanding) some of the basic texts of the Confucian tradition. In Shandong province, since 2005, primary-school children have memorized the whole of the *Analects* by repeatedly chanting verses from it aloud. On 28 September 2009, the 2560th birthday of Confucius, schoolchildren throughout Shandong performed recitations from the *Analects*. In a small Shandong town, Andrew Kipnis witnessed an entire primary school reciting sections of the *Analects* while a small group of girls performed a dance with oversized book covers (representing the *Analects*) as props.[17]

The state as sacred

In China, as in most other countries, the state can be said to adopt a religious attitude toward itself, in its attempts to shore up its legitimacy. State religiosity is apparent in the attitude state officials take toward certain documents, in the manner in which they conduct state rituals, and in the way officials treat as sacred the symbols of the state, such as flags, anthems and images of past leaders. In China, the religious aspects of the state are reinforced by the facts of authoritarianism and one-party rule, which reduce the space for profane attitudes toward the sacred symbols of statehood.

Many parallels have been drawn between Maoism and religion. During the Cultural Revolution, Mao's writings were condensed into a work known as "the little red book" (see Introduction, Image 0.1). All literate Chinese of the time studied the book, passages from it were read aloud over broadcast systems so the illiterate could benefit, and quotations from the book were used by everyone to justify all manner of arguments. The book itself was treated as a sacred object and destroying it was considered a crime. During the Maoist era, communism was treated as a form of heaven that China aspired to reach or become. Political rituals of condemning "state enemies" were carried out in all villages and state *danwei* (work units), allowing for, and requiring, a high degree of mass participation. Though Mao is dead, the religious aspects of the cult of Mao have not disappeared. His writings, if not as widely read as before, are still taught in Chinese schools and still considered above criticism. His image hovers above Tian'anmen Square and his body has been embalmed and displayed in the Mao Zedong Mausoleum in the center of Tian'anmen Square. Many people use amulets with his image as a good-luck charm. Temples have also been built to him, and people burn incense to his image.[18]

In the post-Mao era, religious aspects of state rule have lost some of their lustre, but still continue. The writings of all China's past and current leaders are treated as sacred documents, studied but not criticized. While many people ignore these texts, the more than 70 million members of the

[17] For more on the way educational institutions approach classic Chinese texts in a sacred manner, see Billioud & Thoraval 2007.

[18] For more on the Mao Cult, see Barmé 1996.

CCP are required to study them at special schools for Party members. The canon now consists of works by Mao Zedong, Deng Xiaoping, Jiang Zemin, and Hu Jintao. New leaders aspire to secure their legacy by adding their own writings to this canon. At Monday morning flag-raising ceremonies, schoolchildren learn to adopt a sacred and solemn attitude in front of the national flag and when the national anthem is playing. The words of national leaders are often invoked at these ceremonies.

The state also runs large rituals on holidays and special events, through which it renders love for the nation sacred and attempts to portray itself as the ultimate promoter of the nation's interests. One of the most spectacular state rituals of recent years occurred at the opening ceremony of the 2008 Olympic Games in Beijing. Eight is considered a lucky number in China, and so the ceremony began on 8 August at eight in the evening (that is, 08/08/08 at 8 p.m.). The ceremony itself featured many religious and cultural symbols from China's past: children dressed in the traditional outfits of each of China's 56 officially recognized ethnic minorities, representatives of China's military, military-style marching, famous and popular Chinese gold medal–winning athletes of previous Olympics, and the ample use of fireworks, which were trumpeted as a Chinese cultural invention. The official Chinese press declared that more than 800 million Chinese citizens (between 63 and 69 percent of the Chinese population) watched the ceremony on television, making it the most viewed ceremony ever. Hu Jintao, then President of the PRC and General Secretary of the CCP, officially declared the 2008 Olympics open.

Summary

Religious behavior shares much in common with politics, moral reasoning and philosophy. In all of these fields, broad arguments about the way the world is, and the way it should be, are used as focal points for the formation of social identities. A categorical separation of religion from politics, science, philosophy and superstition began in China in the 19th century and continues today. The arbitrary aspects of this separation allow many concrete activities to be seen simultaneously as religious and as something else. To get away from categorical difficulties, many scholars use the term "religiosity" instead of religion.

Most religious activity in China was suppressed during the Cultural Revolution. The post-Mao era, however, has seen a revival of all kinds of Chinese religiosity, including *qigong* practice, participation in the five official religions (Protestant Christianity, Catholicism, Islam, Buddhism and Daoism), the rebuilding of local temples, Confucianism, fortune-telling, geomancy and continued Mao-worship. The CCP tolerates many aspects of this revival and tries to co-opt aspects of it to bolster its own legitimacy, but also cracks down hard when it feels threatened by the potentially political identities that religious practice can consolidate. Religious practice further interacts with other aspects of social identity, including those of class, gender, region and ethnicity. Finally, as most forms of religious practice are able to cross national boundaries, Chinese religiosity is apt to become caught up in various kinds of international politics.

Discussion questions

1. What forms of politics (international, national, local and familial) are evident in the examples of Chinese religiosity presented in this chapter?
2. What might a study of China tell us about the relationship between modernity and religiosity?
3. What is distinctive about religiosity in contemporary China and how are these distinctive features categorized by the government and enacted by the public?
4. What is international about Chinese religion?

Recommended reading

Ahern, Emily Martin 1981, *Chinese Ritual and Politics*. Cambridge, UK: Cambridge University Press.

Cao, Nanlai 2011, *Constructing China's Jerusalem*. Stanford, CA: Stanford University Press.

Chau, Adam Yuet 2006, *Miraculous Response: Doing Popular Religion in Contemporary China*. Stanford, CA: Stanford University Press.

Feuchtwang, Stephan 2001, *Popular Religion in China: The Imperial Metaphor*. Richmond, UK: Curzon.

Goossaert, Vincent & Palmer, David A 2011, *The Religious Question in Modern China*. Chicago: University of Chicago Press.

Palmer, David A 2007, Qigong *Fever: Body, Science, and Utopia in China*. New York: Columbia University Press.

Weller, Robert P 1987, *Unities and Diversities in Chinese Religion*. Seattle: University of Washington Press.

Wolf, Arthur P (ed.) 1974a, *Religion and Ritual in Chinese Society*. Stanford: Stanford University Press.

7   Ethnicity

The relationship between ethnic and regional identities in China is complex. Some regions of the country, even entire provinces, are politically labeled as "minority regions", such as the "Xinjiang [provincial-level] Uyghur Autonomous Region", or the "Diqing Autonomous Tibetan Prefecture" in Yunnan province. More important than this simple geographical overlap is a broader political question: why are some differences in language, religion, food and dress considered "regional" in China, while others are considered to be "ethnic"? The answers to this question are historical and political rather than intrinsic to particular groups of people.

This chapter focuses on the issue of ethnic difference in China. It traces the relationship of ethnic and regional categories, the historical origins of various ethnic categories, the manner in which these differences map onto present-day identities, and the way that they structure current patterns of ethnic inequality and conflict.

Regional difference and identity in China

As noted in the introduction, China has historically been constituted by wide regional differences. Different parts of the country grow different grains and consequently eat different staple foods. Regional "dialects" are as different as the languages of the countries of Europe. Strong patrilines and lineage halls are more likely to found in southern than northern China. The main styles of (non-staple) cooking in China – Sichuan food, Cantonese food, Hunanese food, Shandong food and so on – are named after provinces. Forms of traditional opera are named after the places (usually provinces) from which they originated, as are varieties of music associated with that opera. Many forms of family rituals – weddings, funerals and so on – vary depending on the place, and many villages, towns and cities have temples devoted to gods that are said to reside in that particular place and at which only local people worship. These differences have informed patterns of regional, local and provincial identities for centuries.

Over the past few decades, processes of urbanization, industrialization and nation-building have vastly increased cultural commonalities across the country. As education has become universally accessible and standardized, almost all young people have learned to speak Mandarin, as well as becoming literate in Chinese characters and learning standardized approaches to mathematics, science, history and other subjects. Television has likewise increased the ability of people from across the country to understand Mandarin. The internet has facilitated interaction among people from different parts of the country, and improved roads, airports and rail lines mean it is now easier to travel around the nation for work, study or tourism. As China has industrialized and become wealthier, fewer people simply eat what they grow. New supermarket chains enable people to purchase almost any type of staple food, anywhere in the country. Newly popular musical pastimes, such as karaoke, encourage people to learn songs that are popular across the country rather than those associated with their home district.

But these processes of constructing cultural commonality across the country have not by any means led to the end of provincial and local identities. Paradoxically, it could be argued that, in many contexts, the existence of greater commonality leads to the re-assertion of local and provincial identities. For example, as hundreds of millions of migrant workers move around the country in search of jobs, they tend (to the best of their ability) to speak Mandarin to employers and locals in the places to which they move. Some locals then insist on using local dialect to speak to one another, to distinguish themselves from migrant workers. Since the wealthier areas on China's eastern seaboard tend to attract the most migrant workers, it is, paradoxically, in the wealthiest and most educated parts of China where local dialects have gained the most importance. Shanghai dialect in Shanghai, Wenzhou dialect in Wenzhou, and Cantonese in Guangzhou may be seen as elite languages.[1]

Another example of the re-assertion of local identity is the manner in which various localities promote themselves on the rapidly expanding market for domestic tourism in China. To attract tourists, almost every locality claims to have some special local products, known by the colorful term *tuchan* ("products from the earth"), which somehow distinguish their area from those around them. Local temples – many of which were destroyed during the Cultural Revolution or various 20th-century wars – are much more likely to be rebuilt in order to promote tourism than for any religious purpose.

---

[1] For more on constructing commonality and nation-building in China see Kipnis 2011a; Kipnis 2012.

Ethnic categorization in China: the 56 "nationalities"

The Chinese nation officially comprises 56 ethnic groups, a number that was first approximated after the newly founded PRC's Ethnic Classification Project in 1954, and that has been more rigidly upheld since 1982, with more minor adjustments in between. These groups are sometimes termed "nationalities", using the slightly ambiguous Chinese term *minzu*. They include the majority Han, who account for more than 90 percent of the country's population, and 55 other minority groups.

Although these ethnic categories have now been in place long enough to be accepted as natural by the vast majority of both Han and non-Han Chinese people, there is nothing natural about this categorization. Many more or many fewer ethnic groupings might have been possible. Because of the importance of these 56 categories to contemporary Chinese society, a closer look at the historical process of their emergence is necessary.

Ethnic group	Population (millions)	Major provincial locations
Zhuang	16.9	Guangxi, Yunnan
Hui	10.6	Ningxia, Gansu, Henan, Yunnan
Manchu	10.4	Liaoning, Hebei
Uyghur	10.1	Xinjiang
Miao	9.4	Guizhou, Hunan, Yunnan
Yi	8.7	Sichuan, Yunnan
Tujia	8.4	Hunan, Hubei
Tibetan	6.3	Tibet, Sichuan, Qinghai, Yunnan
Mongol	6.0	Inner Mongolia
Dong	2.9	Guizhou
Buyi (Buyei)	2.9	Guizhou
Yao	2.8	Guangxi
Bai	1.9	Yunnan
Korean	1.8	Jilin
Hani	1.7	Yunnan
Li	1.5	Hainan
Kazak	1.5	Xinjiang
Dai	1.3	Yunnan

Table 7.1 Approximate population and major provincial locations of the 18 largest minority ethnic groups

Source: Population Census Office 2012, pp. 35–55.[2]

---

[2] This table includes all minority ethnic groups with a national population of more than 1 million at the time of the 2010 population census. Because of migration, there are members of most ethnic groups living in every province. The locations refer to the largest population concentrations. See also Introduction, Map 0.2.

Dru Gladney has pointed out that the creation of a numerically predominate majority ethnic group (the Han) was a deliberate political choice.[3] The Han could easily have been divided into many separate groups with the "regional identities" of the Cantonese, Hakka or Fujianese all being reasonable candidates for a separate "ethnic identity". Indeed, in Taiwan, people who, in mainland China, would be classified as Han make up 98 percent of the population, but the four main "ethnic" categories are Hakka speakers, people of Fujianese origin, "mainlanders" (almost entirely Han people who came from other parts of mainland China with the Nationalist army during the late 1940s) and aboriginals. The PRC's decision to place the vast majority of Chinese people into one category – the Han – reflected a political desire to avoid the ethnic conflict that might have emerged if there were several sizeable groups, none of which constituted an absolute majority of the population.

From an outside perspective, many of the choices the 56 categories represent seem arbitrary. For example, the ethnic group known as the Hui is defined primarily by their Islamic religious affiliation but otherwise seemingly Han-like ethnicity. The Hui are Muslim Chinese who speak a Chinese dialect and are not identified with Muslim groups living outside of or in the border regions of China (as is the case with other Islamic minorities such as the Uyghurs or the Tajiks). But if mainstream Chinese who adhere to Islam can be said to constitute an ethnic group, why are mainstream Chinese who adhere to Christianity not also considered a separate ethnic group? The answers to such questions partly reflect the historical legacies that the CCP inherited from previous regimes and partly the choices made during the Ethnic Classification Project itself.

The ruling regime of the Qing dynasty issued official documents in up to five languages (Chinese, Manchurian, Mongolian, Tibetan and Uyghur) to reach out to significant populations who dominated the border regions of the empire.[4] The Manchus led the dynasty and enacted many laws and policies directed at creating and maintaining the ethnic distinctiveness and privilege of their own group. In addition to these five groups, Qing dynasty government gazetteers reported hundreds of varieties of "barbarians" living in the frontier regions of the country, with the southwestern provinces of Yunnan and Guizhou becoming known as sites of a particularly diverse population. The Nationalist Party regime later reached out to peoples living in the border region by describing China as a "Republic of Five Peoples", namely the Han, Tibetans, Mongolians, Manchu and Hui.

In short, the CCP did not start with a blank slate, from which it could imagine the ethnic groups of China into existence. At the same time,

[3] Gladney 1998.
[4] For more on language usage during the Qing, see Yoshida 1990.

Image 7.1 Hui Chinese at a Sufi shrine in Lanzhou.
Source: Andrew Kipnis 2012.

however, the notion that there were *exactly* 56 distinct groups did not exist before CCP rule.

When the CCP came to power, it took seriously the task of granting autonomy and representation to Chinese minority groups. It owed some of these groups consideration because of the way they had protected the Party when its army and members were in desperate situations during the Long March (1934–35). The CCP also wished to differentiate its policies toward minorities from the more assimilationist policies of the Nationalists. Toward this end, the new CCP-led state borrowed policies from the Soviet Union including the creation of Special Autonomous Regions for minority groups, where officials of particular ethnic backgrounds would be assured positions of local leadership,[5] representation for minority groups in the NPC and various cultural and legal benefits.

---

[5] The extent of this "autonomy" is debated. On the one hand, local leaders in autonomous regions can do nothing to promote independence from the rest of the country. In places such as Xinjiang and Tibet, where there are significant independence movements, such leaders must also crack down on any religious or social actions that the CCP leadership sees as related to independence movements. On the other hand, especially outside of Xinjiang and Tibet, local leaders of autonomous regions can take actions that disproportionately benefit members of their minority group within their regions.

However, just as the generous citizenship entitlements afforded people with urban *hukou* (household registration) were accompanied by measures to limit the population with such registration (see Chapter 3), the generous policies toward minority groups created political pressure to limit the number of minority groups recognized.

The contradictions reached a peak in the southwestern province of Yunnan. During the 1953 census there, in which people were given the option of naming their ethnicity without any limitation on the choice of ethnonym, almost 200 different ethnonyms emerged. It was not even clear how people interpreted the term "ethnicity" when asked the census question. As a consequence, in 1954 an ethnic classification team was given six months to come up with an authoritative list of ethnic groups in Yunnan. While the story of how they did this is complex, in the end they based their classification primarily on scholarship that descended from the research of an early 20th-century British military officer, Henry Davies, who had used the work of various amateur linguists to create a taxonomy of linguistic varieties in Yunnan. Working hard to convince various smaller groups that they could merge with each other or the larger groups because of affinities of language (or culture), the team ended up with roughly 25 different groups in Yunnan (which, when combined with the relatively easier work done by other teams in other parts of the country, eventually led to 56 groups nationwide).[6]

Once the 56 groups were set, regardless of the extent to which they represented social reality before the classification, they were made into social reality. Officials and political representatives were selected because they belonged to one of these 56 groups; affirmative action in university admittance was based on this membership; forms of dance, dress and artistic expression received state sponsorship because they were deemed to represent one of these groups; museums set up displays about the 56 groups; and knowledge about the 56 ethnic groups of China was spread through the school curriculum and state propaganda apparatus. Today, state-issued identity cards and *hukou* booklets list the holder's ethnicity. When children whose parents belong to two different ethnicities reach the age of 18, they may choose to belong to either one, but may not officially assume a hybrid or hyphenated identity. In this manner, each and every Chinese citizen belongs to only one ethnic group. As the system has now been in place for more than 50 years, the majority of today's Chinese were born into one of these 56 groups. While there are still a few cases of groups of people who claim to belong to an ethnic group other than the 56 official ones and petition the state for recognition of their ethnic identity, the vast majority of ethnic minorities accept their

[6] Mullaney 2011.

ethnic classifications as natural. The state has refused to recognize any new ethnicities since the classification system of 56 was settled in 1982.

THE ETHNOGENESIS OF UYGHUR IDENTITY

Anthropologists use the term "ethnogenesis" to describe the process by which a particular ethnic group comes into social existence. In 1990, the anthropologist Dru Gladney argued that the Uyghurs, now one of the largest minority groups in China, owe much of their sense of identity as a particular people to events after 1940. Before then, identities in the region now called Xinjiang were quite fluid. The people who are today called Uyghurs more often defined themselves in terms of the particular oasis (Xinjiang is mostly desert and the towns all grew around oases) where they lived, which often marked the dialect they spoke, or in terms of local religious and political factions. But as Xinjiang has experienced extensive and continual in-migration of Han and Hui populations from China since the 1940s, as communication and transportation advances within Xinjiang have made travel and communication between oases more common and convenient, and as Xinjiang has been incorporated into the PRC, Uyghurs are increasingly seen as, and themselves identify as, a distinctive ethnic group. On the one hand, the PRC's ethnic policy reifies Uyghur identity in particular ways – a standardized version of Uyghur language is taught in bilingual schools; there are opportunities in the government for educated individuals who are labeled as Uyghurs; and admission to university and the birth-control policy are applied differently to Uyghurs than to the Han. On the other hand, in-migration by Han and Hui, ethnic discrimination against Uyghurs, and the ability to travel around Xinjiang and be treated as a Uyghur by both other Uyghurs and by the Han all create experiences that reinforce a sense of ethnic identity. Today, Uyghurness is defined primarily in opposition to the Han, Hui and a few smaller ethnic groups. That is to say, the contemporary meaning of Uyghur ethnicity – a Turkic-speaking Muslim group of people in Xinjiang, descended from those who lived in the oasis towns – distinguishes the Uyghurs from the Han (who are not Muslims), the Hui (who originated from outside Xinjiang and do not speak a Turkic language), and other small, formerly nomadic Islamic groups (who do not descend from ancestors who lived sedentary lives in a particular oasis).[7]

---

[7] For more detail on this process see Gladney 1990; Rudelson 1997.

Image 7.2 Propaganda poster, 1957.
  The title reads "Long live the great unity of all the peoples of the whole nation". Note the use of women in traditional ethnic dress to represent diversity.
Source: Stephan Landsberger Collection, International Institute of Social History (Amsterdam).

Because much of the official discourse on the 56 ethnic groups emphasises their harmonious coexistence and their shared Chineseness, the public presentation of ethnicity in China often emphasizes colorful ethnic clothing, as well as dance, music, marriage customs, and other easy-to-appreciate aspects of ethnic distinctiveness. With the rise of domestic tourism in China, such attributes are often standardized by minority leaders and commoditized for the purpose of tourist consumption. Louisa Schein has written at length about how the combination of government presentations of ethnic harmony and competition for the tourist dollar leads to the feminization of ethnicity. Cultural performances and images of minorities feature pictures of women (dancing or wearing the traditional clothing of their ethnic group) much more often than men. Just as some airlines might sell airline tickets with images of female flight attendants serving male customers, so ethnic representations of minorities in China emphasize the feminine to make ethnicity less threatening and more palatable to visitors. In this manner, the relationship between the majority Han and the various ethnic groups is likened to the relationship between men and women.[8]

[8] Schein 2000.

Because enormous political effort has gone into defining the 56 ethnic groups of China, promoting their harmonious integration and minimizing their cost, the Chinese state has been extremely reluctant to make any changes to the classification system. This intransigence prevents the state from understanding, let alone developing policy for, its diversifying population. As China prospers economically, it increasingly attracts a variety of immigrants: brides from Southeast Asian countries; Filipino maids; refugees from North Korea; traders and skilled workers from Africa and the Middle East; managerial workers and English teachers from wealthier nations; and students from all over the world. Some of these immigrants have spent most of their lives in China, have raised children in China and have no plans of leaving. As we discussed in Chapter 4, in Guangzhou there are established communities of African traders, in Shandong there are "Korea-towns", and in Shanghai there are entire housing subdivisions filled with expatriate businessmen from Taiwan, Singapore and other developed economies. But there is no place in China's ethnic imagination for new immigrants, so these communities are conceptualized as foreigners.[9]

Ethnic inequalities and conflict

As in most countries, various forms of ethnic conflict occur in China. These conflicts range from large-scale riots linked to long-term grievances and secessionist movements, as in the case of Tibetans and Uyghurs, to unstated grudges and prejudicial assumptions. While many forms of conflict are between the majority Han and various minority ethnicities, there are also conflicts among minority groups. In autonomous regions designated for one particular ethnic group, for example, policy guarantees affirmative action in favour of members of the designated group who apply for jobs in the state sector. Members of other minority ethnic groups who live in that region, lacking the benefit of affirmative action, may encounter less favorable socioeconomic conditions, and this creates resentment of the favored group.

Affirmative action and other advantageous policies toward minority groups have varied with the specific ethnic group, the specific locality and the period in question. Several types of benefit have been relatively common. In addition to reserving positions for officials of designated ethnic backgrounds in autonomous regions, in many parts of the country ethnic minority women who live in rural areas are permitted in law to give birth to up to three children instead of the usual two. In many provinces, members of ethnic minority groups enjoy advantages in the

---

[9] Pieke 2012.

competition for university admission, either in the form of bonus points on the university entrance exam (UEE) or in the form of reserved places in certain subjects at certain universities. But such policies do not end ethnic conflict. They can reinforce prejudice among some segments of the Han public, who argue, for example, that members of minority groups are "lazy and stupid" and unable to succeed academically on their own, and they can become bandages that merely cover up differences in educational opportunities that exist among different parts of the country.

One of the most intractable aspects of ethnic inequality relates to language. As standardized Mandarin has become the primary language of an increasing percentage of the population of China, as literacy in Chinese characters spreads and education levels rise, and as the Chinese economy grows, the economic value of literacy and fluency in Mandarin grows in relation to the economic value of literacy and fluency in Tibetan, Uyghur, Mongolian, Thai or a host of other minority languages. A person who is literate in one of these minority languages without being equally literate in Mandarin has a severely limited choice of jobs. Because of the intensity of competition in the education system, it is virtually impossible to succeed on the UEE if any significant portion of one's education takes place in a language other than Mandarin. This linguistic situation makes bilingual education in minority areas economically viable if, and only if, the government reserves university places and jobs specifically for the graduates of those programs. One policy response to this predicament has been to increase monolingual Mandarin educational opportunities for certain minority children. The most famous of these opportunities are the boarding junior and senior secondary schools for Tibetan and Uyghur students, established in large Chinese cities on the eastern seaboard. Tibetan and Uyghur children must leave their homes, families and communities to attend these schools, yet demand for places is high and competition for entrance keen. At these schools, the entire curriculum is taught in Mandarin and a political emphasis is placed on teaching students to be "patriotic" and supportive of "ethnic unity". While these schools are popular among some parents because of the economic opportunity they offer, and while the schools have been successful in raising the number of ethnic Tibetan and Uyghur young people who later graduate from university, they are also criticized as attempts to erase Tibetan and Uyghur language and culture.[10]

Uradyn Bulag, an ethnic Mongolian from China, has written about the tensions between Mongolian language and Mandarin in his own life and those of his friends, classmates and family members. He describes how his elder sister went to a Mongolian-language primary school, while he

[10] Grose 2010.

had to go to a Chinese-language one because there was no room for him in the Mongolian language school. His family then moved from a rural to an urban area and both he and his sister had to attend a Chinese-language primary school. The Han Chinese students there often teased him as a "stinking Mongol Tartar" and, internalizing this prejudice, he began to be embarrassed that his sister's Mandarin skills were poor in comparison to those of the Han students and his own. Bulag himself was successful enough in the Chinese education system to enter a university in Inner Mongolia in the early 1980s, but once there he was embarrassed by a revival of Mongolian culture and found that his many Mongolian class-mates (admitted as minority-language students) had better Mongolian than his own. He forced himself to become literate in Mongolian as well as Chinese, an effort that was aided by his memory of speaking Mongolian as a child and the fact that written Mongolian uses an alphabetic script. He eventually used his excellent linguistic skills (being trilingual in Chinese, Mongolian and English) to win a scholarship to study for his doctorate in anthropology at the University of Cambridge, with a research focus on Mongolian culture. Meanwhile, his sister and his Mongolian-educated friends had a difficult time back home on the job market. Because of this experience, his sister wanted to send her own child to a Chinese-medium school, but Bulag, convinced of the importance of language maintenance by his own experience and his study of anthropology, wrote angry letters home, which convinced her and his brother-in-law to send their child to Mongolian-medium schools. When Dr Bulag returned home from Cambridge with his PhD in 1993, however, he painfully learned that his sister and their family had come to blame him for their son's poor career prospects and supposedly "diminished" intellectual capacity.[11] As Bulag's experience shows, the current linguistic, education and employment situation in China places minority-language speakers in a double bind that causes pain whatever choices they make about their education and career.

Another source of grievance for some ethnic minorities in China has been the experience and memory of religious repression. As we described in Chapter 6, for many Tibetans, religious repression remains an irritant and a source of suffering. Though for most Chinese citizens, both Han and minority, opportunities for religious experience have greatly expanded since the end of the Cultural Revolution, for those minorities whose religious identities relate to secessionist movements, including both Tibetans and Uyghurs, state attempts to control religious practice feel very much like Han ethnic repression. Moreover, both in

---

[11] Bulag 2003.

religion and more generally, the Cultural Revolution hit minority communities especially hard. Marauding groups of Red Guards were often Han, and their attacks often targeted religious institutions and people who were suspected of being "spies" because of relationships to people outside of China or simply because they seemed different. During one infamous Cultural Revolution incident, as many as 100 000 ethnic Mongols were killed.[12] In short, for one reason or another, during the Cultural Revolution minority communities often found themselves attacked by members of the Han majority. In many places, especially during the 1980s and 1990s, popular understandings of the justification for affirmative action policies for minority groups related to the persecution they suffered during the Cultural Revolution.

Han perspectives on ethnic relationships in China are complex, but James Leibold identifies three main discursive strands. The first is Soviet-style multiculturalism, which is reflected in the policies we have already described, namely, the identification of official ethnic groups, the formation of autonomous regions for those groups, the establishment of various forms of affirmative action and beneficial policies for minorities and the presentation of the nation as a harmoniously unified community of 56 distinct ethnic groups. The second is Han ethnocentricism, a prejudiced view of the Han as the most "advanced" ethnic group in China, which naturally should lead the more "backward" minority groups into modernity. More moderate forms of Han ethnocentrism romanticize the primitivism of minority peoples, while more aggressive forms can insist that the Han are the backbone of the Chinese nation and that steps should be taken to preserve the purity of the Han race and prevent minorities from becoming too demanding or slowing the progress of the Chinese nation. Leibold labels the third discursive strand "Confucian Ecumenism", a perspective that denies the existence of separate ethnic groups and thinks that all people should improve themselves by internalizing the universal values of Chinese Confucian civilization. Individuals adopting this perspective believe that Soviet-style multiculturalism gives rise to ethnic conflict and that affirmative action policies are counterproductive. They also believe that only Mandarin should be taught within the Chinese education system as this is the only language of true civilization.[13]

The extent of economic inequalities among ethnic groups varies considerably but they can sometimes be extreme. Xiaowei Zang has measured the extent and origins of income inequality between Hans and Uyghurs in Urumqi (Urumchi), the capital of the Autonomous Region

[12] For, more detail on the "Nei ren" incident, see Jankowiak 1988.
[13] Leibold 2010.

of Xinjiang. He found that, between 2005 and 2008, the average monthly income for Han workers was 1141 *yuan* per month, while for Uyghurs it was 892 *yuan* per month. While some of this difference was attributable to education levels, some of it related to the prejudice of private-sector Han employers. While affirmative action policies have ensured that Uyghurs working in the state sector earn as much as their Han counterparts, in the private sector such policies do not apply and Uyghurs earn considerably less. Zang's interviews showed that many private-sector employers who were Han believed that Uyghur workers are lazier and more troublesome than Han workers and, therefore, refused to hire them.[14]

The state has tried to improve ethnic relations, particularly in Tibet, by increasing the incomes of Tibetans. It has devised programs to help rural Tibetans build new houses, bring infrastructure improvements such as running water and electricity to rural villages and give start-up capital to rural businesses. Some of these programs have been more successful than others. The housing program has given substantial numbers of rural Tibetans new homes, with the added benefit of providing employment for rural Tibetans in house construction. However, the income of rural Tibetans still lags behind that of rural Han.

As more and more rural Tibetans become migrant workers, it is likely that vigorous vocational education and affirmative action programs will be needed to enable rural Tibetans to catch up with the income levels of the rural Han.[15] In addition to the difficulty of running an economic development program in a rural area – as in other countries, there is a high risk that a program will fail to meet expectations – there is a larger question of whether it is possible to ameliorate ethnic tension in Tibet (or indeed in Xinjiang – see the text box below) through economic policy alone, as the state hopes, or whether the causes of conflict are cultural, religious and linguistic as much as economic.

ETHNIC RIOTS IN XINJIANG

Since 2006, the Chinese state has sponsored a program by which Uyghur workers from rural areas are brought in as migrant workers to factories in Guangdong province. Many tensions surround the program as migrant worker life is tough. Workers of all ethnicities live in dormitories and have little time off. For Uyghur workers, language, diet and cultural factors increase the sense of isolation. Some Han workers resent having to compete with workers from so far away and

---

[14] Zang 2011b.
[15] Goldstein, Childs & Wangdui 2011.

blame the Uyghurs for keeping wages down. Many of the Uyghur workers are young women and some Uyghurs say the purpose of the policy is to prevent Uyghur women from marrying Uyghur men and thereby reduce the population of Uyghurs. Other Uyghurs find it suspicious that Uyghurs are brought to Guangdong to work at the same time as so many Han migrate to Xinjiang for work. Demographic figures are widely disputed, but some contend that Uyghurs have gone from being the vast majority of the population of Xinjiang in 1949 to a numerical minority in their own home province.[16]

On 26 June 2009, at the Xuri toy factory in Shaoguang, Guangdong province, Han workers stormed Uyghur dormitories with clubs and machetes after a rumor had spread that Uyghur workers had raped a Han woman. Newspaper accounts suggested that 118 people of unspecified ethnicity were injured and that at least two were killed. Internet videos of the melee spread across the country and rumors as well as angry and racist postings filled internet blogs. On 5 July, Uyghurs in Urumqi, who suspected a cover-up of the incident, organized a protest march, to which Uyghurs from all over Xinjiang came. The demonstration was dispersed in a violent police crackdown, after which some Uyghur protestors began to riot, killing people who they identified as Han, looting Han businesses and destroying motor vehicles. Although the Chinese government has never released figures of how many Uyghurs were killed by the police, it has reported that 197 people were killed and 1700 more injured, and 331 shops and 1325 motor vehicles burned or destroyed during the riots. To slow the circulation of rumors, the Party secretary of Xinjiang, Wang Lequan, shut down the internet in the province on the morning of 6 July 2009.

The next day, Han demonstrators or mobs launched counter protests and riots throughout Xinjiang. No police were deployed to curb these protests, though some Uyghur neighborhoods organized defence groups armed with clubs and other weapons. It is not known how many people were killed and injured on this day. The violence of 5 and 7 July was captured on video and posted on the internet (and viewed widely outside of Xinjiang). In August, rumors circulated that Uyghurs were attacking Han in the streets with hypodermic needles. Hundreds of cases of such attacks were claimed though not one was

---

[16] According to 2010 Population Census data, Uyghur, Han and Hui people make up respectively 45.8 percent, 40.5 percent and 4.5 percent of Xinjiang's total population. Kazaks comprise a further 6.5 percent (Population Census Office 2012, pp. 35–41).

ever confirmed. On 3 September, thousands of Han protestors again marched in Urumqi (Urumchi), claiming that Wang had been too soft on the Uyghurs and demanding that he step down. The Xinjiang Han felt that because they had moved to Xinjiang to help the government colonize and develop the region, the government owed them (rather than Uyghurs) protection from ethnic violence and preferential treatment. Wang was forced to step down and money was allocated for increasing the income of people in Xinjiang who worked in state *danwei*. The riots demonstrate the demographic and gendered tensions that frame ethnic relations in Xinjiang, as well as the place of rumor and new communication technologies in contemporary ethnic relations.[17]

Not all ethnic relations in China are as contentious as those between the Han and the Tibetan, Uyghur and Mongolian ethnic groups. These sizeable groups are identified with large provincial-level territories in China and are threatened by Han in-migration, linguistic extinction and religious suppression. There are many ethnic groups in China that identify more closely with the regime. In southwestern Yunnan, for example, members of the Dai ethnic group are closely related to Thai-speaking peoples who traverse the Laos, China, Burma and northern Thailand region, and have historically had many options of ethnic identification, depending on the national context. As China has developed rapidly over the past few decades, many young Dai find it most comfortable to accept the ethnic label that the Chinese state ascribes to them, speak Mandarin, and present themselves as Dai-Chinese, which is precisely the result that ethnic policy in China aims for.[18]

Summary

For many years, China has had 56 official ethnic groups, comprising the majority Han and 55 ethnic minorities. These categories are not natural, but the result of political relations and historical processes, the most important of which was the Ethnic Classification Project of the early 1950s. The fact that the Han are considered a single, unified group, rather than different groups based on regional differences, means that there is an official distinction between people's regional and ethnic identities. Today, the vast majority of Chinese accept the official ethnic categories,

[17] Cliff 2012; Millward 2009.
[18] Diana 2009.

and yet this acceptance does not mean that there are no ethnic tensions. Sizeable ethnic groups concentrated in China's peripheral regions – Tibetans, Uyghurs and Mongols – see Han in-migration as a form of colonization. Linguistic extinction and religious repression threaten these groups and a few others, causing resentment. In turn, many Han resent the affirmative-action policies that favor minority groups in certain regions. Modernization processes that have shaped regional and ethnic identities include the improvement of transportation and communications infrastructure; the standardization of Mandarin and the expansion of a Mandarin-based education system; industrialization, urbanization and increased population mobility; and the rise of a significant tourist industry.

Discussion questions

1. How have ethnic relations in China developed over recent decades? What has changed and what remains the same?
2. Describe the ethnogenesis of a particular ethnic group in China.
3. What are the key factors shaping different ethnic groups' experiences of, and relationship to, state ideology and policy on ethnicity?

Recommended reading

Gillette, Maris B 2000, *Between Mecca and Beijing: Modernization and Consumption among Urban Chinese Muslims*. Stanford, CA: Stanford University Press.

Gladney, Dru 2004b, *Dislocating China: Reflections on Muslims, Minorities, and Other Subaltern Subjects*. Chicago: University of Chicago Press.

Harrell, Stevan (ed.) 1995, *Cultural Encounters on China's Ethnic Frontiers*. Seattle: University of Washington Press.

Litzinger, Ralph A 2000, *Other Chinas: The Yao and the Politics of National Belonging*. Durham, NC: Duke University Press.

Mackerras, Colin 1994, *China's Minorities: Integration and Modernization in the 20th Century*. Hong Kong: Oxford University Press.

Meriam, Beth 2012, *China's "Tibetan" Frontiers: Sharing the Contested Ground*. Leiden, Netherlands: Global Oriental.

Mueggler, Erik 2001, *The Age of Wild Ghosts: Memory, Violence, and Place in Southwest China*. Berkeley: University of California Press.

Mullaney, Thomas S 2011, *Coming to Terms with the Nation: Ethnic Classification in Modern China*. Berkeley: University of California Press.

Schein, Louisa 2000, *Minority Rules: The Miao and the Feminine in China's Cultural Politics*. Durham, NC: Duke University Press.

8   Education and the Cultivation of Citizens

Competition in China's education system is intense. The causes and consequences of this competition are complex and involve social stratification, gender and ethnic relations, economic inequality, political legitimacy, international migration and ideologies of development. In this chapter, we introduce the education system in China and assess the factors that contribute to its intensity and the consequences of intense educational competition for Chinese society. We also discuss state and popular discourses that promise the salvation of the Chinese nation through the cultivation of citizens. These discourses feed on, and contribute to, popular desires for educational success.

Educational structures in China

In China, it is compulsory to complete nine years of education (usually six years of primary school and three years of junior secondary school). Across most of the country, these nine years of education are now available for free to all citizens. This level of educational provision is an accomplishment that was gradually achieved over the course of most of the 20th century. It has only recently been attained in many rural areas. Because local governments have provided a good percentage of the funds for education, impoverished localities have been the last to be able to provide nine years of education for everybody. Recent efforts to increase the level of central and provincial funding for education in impoverished areas have been important to this success, as has the central state's requirement, as of 2006, that rural primary and junior secondary schools remove all tuition fees.[1]

---

[1] In earlier periods, limitations on tuition fees resulted in schools devising other sorts of fees ("heating" fees, "miscellaneous" fees, and so on) to supplement school funding. The abolition of tuition fees in 2006 has been much more successful both because it was accompanied by higher levels of central funding and because previous tax and fee reforms across a wide variety of sectors have made it more difficult for local government institutions to levy new types of fees.

Despite the general availability of nine years of education, some children fall between the cracks. Migrant workers sometimes have difficulty enrolling their children in schools because they do not hold a local *hukou* (household registration), because some urban public schools discriminate against migrant children, either charging them high fees or denying them entry, or because there are no affordable migrant-run schools nearby. Children whose birth was illegal according to the birth-control policy and who therefore lack a *hukou* may likewise fail to attend school. Children who have a disability, who live in extremely remote areas, or whose parents abuse or neglect them may also have difficulty attending school. Finally, some children choose to drop out of junior secondary school because they cannot stand the intensity of the education system, or for some other reason. Of course, there are young dropouts and abused children in most societies. At least according to official statistics, roughly 90 percent of children born in China today complete nine or more years of education.

In most parts of the country, children attend school for far longer than the compulsory nine years. In all urban areas and in moderate to wealthy rural areas, the vast majority of children attend three or more years of preschool before they attend primary school. Then, after completing junior secondary school, about 80 percent of the children in these areas attend some form of senior secondary school.[2] There are both academic and vocational senior secondary schools and sometimes different grades of academic senior secondary schools. The senior secondary school entrance exam, administered on a city or countywide basis, determines which senior secondary school a student is eligible to attend. The academic senior secondary schools prepare students for the university entrance exam (UEE), while vocational senior secondary schools prepare students to enter the workforce straight after they complete their schooling.

Almost all students who graduate from an academic senior secondary school sit the UEE. A student's score on this exam determines which, if any, university programs they will be admitted to attend. Each Chinese province or provincial-level city administers the UEE, in a process closely overseen by the national educational bureaucracy. Each province holds its UEE over the same three-day period in June. All UEE students may take the sciences or the humanities version of the exam or choose to sit more specialized and less prestigious exams in subjects such as Art,

---

[2] According to the 2009 *Zhongguo Jiaoyu Tongji Nianjian 2009* [*China Education Statistical Yearbook*] 2009, p. 15), 79.2 percent of senior secondary school aged children were enrolled in a senior secondary school in that year. This number seems on the high side given the experiences of the authors in poorer parts of the country, but it does accurately reflect our experiences in moderately well-off areas.

Music and Physical Education. The content of each province's exams is roughly comparable and the final results are calculated on a scale that is calibrated by the percentile of a student's raw score in relation to the average score for all students in that province. In this manner, a student who receives a result of 600 in one province will be directly comparable with a student who receives a 600 in another province (given the large number of students who take the exam in each province, this comparison is usually quite equitable). Provincial governments control most universities, and universities admit students from their home provinces with scores lower than students from other provinces. Consequently, it is easier for students from provinces with a high number of universities (especially prestigious universities) per capita to get into a good university than those from other provinces. Most notoriously, many of the best universities in the country, including Peking University and Qinghua University, are located in Beijing, and a student who holds a Beijing *hukou* can get into a Beijing university with a much lower UEE score than students from other parts of the country. Shanghai also has more than its fair share of excellent universities. In addition, in some provinces, some urban universities offer easier admission to students from the same urban area. Overall, this system of distributing university places creates considerable inequality in educational opportunity for students from rural areas in poorer provinces. Students from families who live and work in places other than their *hukou* (including most migrant-worker families) must return to the district in which they are registered to take the UEE, even if they attended senior secondary school somewhere else. This requirement is a source of great disadvantage and resentment among migrant-worker families in Beijing and Shanghai.

In 2012, some 9.15 million students, or 44 percent of students born in 1994, sat the UEE. As a result of the recent rapid expansion in university places, across the country there are university places for about 6.86 million of these students, or nearly 33 percent of the age cohort. So, there are places for about three-quarters of UEE students,[3] though these are unevenly distributed, with some provinces having many more places per capita than others. Many students who do not do well enough on the UEE to gain admission to the university course of their choice retake the final year of senior secondary school and re-sit the UEE at considerable expense. Others attempt to attend universities outside China. The intensity of preparation for the UEE and the fact that such a high proportion of Chinese youth choose to sit the exam makes it a rite of passage for many of them. Students discuss the "bitterness" they have "eaten" in

[3] See Wong 2012. Data on the age cohort size (21 million) comes from *Zhongguo Renkou Nianjian 2007* [*China Population Yearbook 2009*] 2007, p. 365.

Image 8.1   The midday break in a class for students preparing to re-sit the UEE.
Source: Tamara Jacka, Yunnan 2012.

order to prepare for the UEE as a form of sacrifice that makes them both filial family members and worthy citizens of the nation.

After a student completes four years of undergraduate education, they may choose to pursue a masters or doctoral degree; these are available in almost every conceivable field. Most postgraduate degrees in China are three-year programs, and admittance to these programs usually involves an exam administered by the university where the degree program is hosted. There are also special schools for Party members to further their education and knowledge of Party policy, history and ideology, and adult schools for those who wish to further their knowledge of a particular topic or their qualifications in a particular area.

Discourses of cultivating citizens

Since the late 19th century, discourses of saving the nation by cultivating strong, intelligent, morally upright and patriotic citizens have circulated in China. Often, these discourses are opposed to those that advocate strengthening China by reforming political, economic and social institutions. As such, discourses of cultivating citizens may be politically conservative. The argument goes that, if the key to saving the country is the cultivation of citizens, then political reform is not necessary.[4] In addition, these discourses have often valued "science" as the ultimate form of knowledge. This preference helps to explain the fact that a large number of university places in China is reserved for students in the natural sciences.

During the post-Mao period, two keywords of such discourses have been *wenming* (civilization) and *suzhi* (quality). The word *wenming* is usually invoked during campaigns to encourage the population at large to behave in a more "civilized" manner – that is, not to litter, spit, swear, or speak loudly in public, to be neat in appearance, to obey political edicts, and so on. *Suzhi* discourse developed alongside the birth-control policy. Birth-control advocates argued that by reducing the "quantity" of the population they could improve its "quality". During the 1980s, when initially designing and promoting the policy, these advocates felt that, by requiring parents to have fewer children, they could increase the amount of economic and emotional investment parents would make in each of their children. For the large part, this expectation has been proven correct. Parents and teachers often argue that the birth-control policy has led parents to a "psychology of hoping one's child becomes a dragon" (*wang zi cheng long de xinli*), in which every parent holds very high educational ambitions for their only child or two children. Government officials most commonly invoke the word *suzhi* when discussing means of improving the quality of the population.

In the 1990s and 2000s, *suzhi* discourse became tightly enmeshed in debates about education reform. Since then, any sort of education reform has been described as "education for quality" (*suzhi jiaoyu*). Regardless of whether a particular reform advocates more military training and political indoctrination in secondary schools or recommends a more relaxed, creativity-enhancing, child-centered form of education, it has to conclude its arguments with the claim that it will lead to improvements in the quality of school children. As a consequence, the meanings of the phrase "education for quality" have become quite contradictory.

The tensions around "education for quality" are particularly evident in classes in the social sciences, such as Political Education and History. On the one hand, these subjects seem ideal areas to promote the "creative quality" of students by using teaching techniques that emphasize open-ended discussion. On the other hand, these subjects are also places where the "political quality" of students can be enhanced by requiring them to memorize the Party line on political and historical events and practicing the habit of never questioning Party edicts. The result of this

---

[4] See Kipnis 2006.

contradiction is often that political education is short-changed and that students develop cynical attitudes toward politics.

The term *suzhi* is also commonly used to justify social hierarchies. People of "higher" *suzhi* are seen as naturally deserving leadership positions in all aspects of life. In such justifications, *suzhi* becomes an all-encompassing attribute. People of high *suzhi* are assumed to be simultaneously more intelligent, physically stronger, and less morally corruptible than those of low *suzhi*. As a consequence, disparaging someone as "lacking" *suzhi* or being of "low" *suzhi* is a serious insult. In their attempts to improve the *suzhi* of themselves and their children, people read a wide variety of books, consume nutritional supplements, obtain clothes, exercise equipment and medicines, and join educational programs.

Suzhi discourse is also important to Party self-governance. Aware of the problems it has with corruption, and distrustful of what it sees as "western" democratic institutions, such as a free press, independent judiciary and elections, the CCP vows to fight corruption by improving the *suzhi* of its members. This process involves educational institutions in two ways. First, the CCP now selects its members primarily from among graduates of the senior secondary school and university systems, and requires those already working within its ranks to have a university degree before seeking promotion. The importance of degrees for opportunities to enter and climb the ranks of the Party hierarchy have made UEE success even more central to parents who hope that their children become "dragons". Second, the CCP requires members who wish to advance in the Party hierarchy to attend classes in policy, history and ideology at the special Party schools we have described.

As indicated in the relationship of Party hierarchies to the UEE, *suzhi* discourse involves ideals of meritocracy. These ideals reinforce the importance of examinations throughout all aspects of Chinese society, especially the education system. The all-encompassing aspects of the Chinese notion of *suzhi* imply that those who have succeeded on the UEE are not just better at taking tests than those who have not, but that they are intellectually superior in every way, more morally upright and perhaps even physically fitter. Efforts to place officials above criticism also employ the all-encompassing nature of *suzhi* to reinforce the authoritarian aspects of China's political system. An official who has received a high degree must naturally be morally incorrupt, the logic suggests. Nevertheless, the meritocratic aspects of the UEE seem preferable to the alternatives for both Party leaders and average citizens. For average citizens, reliance on the UEE suggests that even people without social connections to Party members have a chance of advancing in society. Without reliance on the UEE, political and economic leaders would be more likely to appoint their own friends and relatives to important posts, without giving anyone else a chance. For Party leaders, reliance on the UEE inhibits corruption of those lower down the Party hierarchy and is preferable to the democratic methods of curbing corruption used in the west.

Educational intensity

In China today, the intensity of competition for UEE success is extreme, thanks to the combined effects of the psychology of hoping one's child becomes a "dragon", the meritocratic polices and discourses of the state, and the growing employment competition that has followed market reforms since the 1980s. For students, this intensity peaks during senior secondary school but, in many places, the competition during junior secondary school is nearly as strong. In some places, even primary school involves large amounts of homework. Especially in rural areas, secondary schools tend to be boarding schools. At these schools, it is typical for eight students to sleep in each dormitory room, and they lead a very structured life. Their time is organized around studying, from wake-up bells at six in the morning to lights out at 11 in the evening, seven days a week.[5] At most of these schools, students are allowed one Sunday off, once or twice a month, but sometimes not even that during the lead-up to the senior secondary school entrance exam and the UEE. Even some rural primary schools have spaces for boarders, especially during years four, five and six (ages 10–12).

In urban areas, there are few boarding schools and secondary school students can lead less structured lives, but homework loads are still quite high and most serious students receive private tutoring or attend private "cram schools" (*buxi ban*) in addition to their regular secondary school classes. As in Japan, the after-school tutoring and cram-school business sector is highly developed and profitable. Some students and parents even accuse teachers of colluding with the entrepreneurs who run these schools, leaving crucial information out of their lectures so that students must pay fees to attend an after-school class if they wish to learn everything necessary to do well on the exams.

Of course, not all students are very studious; some spend many more hours playing internet games than doing homework, daydream during class, jump the walls at their boarding school to go out at night, or skip classes during the day. Such students, however, are in a minority and do not tend to do well on the secondary school entrance exams or the UEE. They generally either drop out of school or end up in the vocational schooling sector.

---

[5] For more on school schedules see Kipnis 2011b.

UEE success can bring considerable glory. Students who win scholarships or admission to top university programs may be interviewed on television or photographed for newspaper stories, or depictions of their accomplishments may be displayed on posters in prominent public places. Senior secondary schools also discuss their students' accomplishments in their own publicity materials. Andrew Kipnis has interviewed many parents in Shandong villages who could tell him which children in their village had been admitted to which university, demonstrating that the academic accomplishments of children are a common topic for gossip even among relatively uneducated people.

The glory of academic success extends to student social groups as well. The notion of a nerd or a geek – someone who is socially unpopular because of his or her success in academic endeavours and the amount of time he or she devotes to study – does not translate well into Chinese academic spaces. Secondary-school students told Kipnis that academically successful students were the least likely to be bullied. Relatedly, China has a strong tradition of "literary masculinity". That is to say, rather than stereotyping studious men as those least likely to attract girlfriends, as do English-language television shows such as *The Beauty and the Geek*, Chinese stories and dramas tend to depict academically successful men as the objects of considerable female attention. Literary masculinity and meritocratic examination systems are common across contemporary East Asia (examples can be found not only in China but in Japan, Korea, Taiwan, Hong Kong and Singapore) and relate historically to the Confucian traditions of government in those countries.

Finally, the intensity of education in China can be seen in the amount of money that both local governments and individual families spend on it. When the Chinese government began expanding university enrollments during the late 1990s, its primary role was to stimulate the economy. The government reasoned that rural Chinese parents would be eager to spend their money on university tuition if their children had the chance to attend university. By building new universities, expanding existing ones, and raising tuition to cover this building spree, the government successfully stimulated internal demand in the wake of the Asian financial crisis. Despite the fact that room, board and tuition at university cost the equivalent of between one and two years' average annual income, the Chinese parents whom Kipnis interviewed between 2005 and 2011 were willing to spend all their savings and to borrow heavily to give their child or children the chance to go to university. In urban areas, spending on cram schools, private tutoring and extra fees for attending senior secondary schools (when one's score on the senior secondary school entrance exam was slightly too low for regular admission) is likewise quite high. China's extreme economic inequalities, and the fact that,

Image 8.2   Primary-school facilities in Shandong.
Source: Andrew Kipnis 2008–09.

for rural and working-class families, educational success seems the only path toward social mobility, cause many parents to spend heavily on their children's educational success.

Local governments are also willing to spend their money on good schools when possible. The ability to provide schools with excellent facilities that give local students a chance at UEE success is a source of legitimacy. Many local governments have fallen into financial trouble by borrowing money to raise the standard of their schools, and many schools in China have facilities that are of exceptional quality. In 2010, Kipnis judged that the quality of public-school facilities in Shandong was roughly the equivalent of the quality of public schools in Australia, though Australia's per-capita gross domestic product (GDP) is many times higher than that of Shandong.

Education and inequality

There are multiple relationships between education and inequality, but they are sometimes illusory. Although university degrees often lead to better, higher paying jobs for graduates than do vocational schools – which

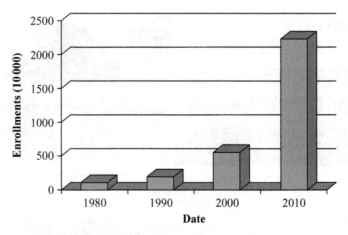

Figure 8.1   University enrollments, 1980–2010.
Source: Data from NBS 2011.

was almost always the case during the PRC's first 50 years – the rapid expansion of university places during the late 1990s and early 2000s has meant that there are many university graduates who cannot find work at all, let alone work that can allow them to repay their family members for debts they incurred while at university. In big cities with many universities, such as Beijing, recent graduates often live in poor conditions, packed into rental rooms in low-rent outer suburbs, where they are known as the "ant tribe" (*yizu*). In contrast, graduates of vocational schools system, who have skills in fields such as automobile repair, welding, and electronics, often quickly find relatively high-paying jobs, though never prestigious ones. Some university and academic senior secondary school students attend vocational school after they graduate because, despite their degree, it is the only path toward work. In China today, to secure a good white-collar job a person needs a degree from a top-rated university – not just any university – and, most often, good luck or social connections as well.

The relatively clear hierarchy of universities in China today is another aspect of educational inequality. There are many rankings and groupings of elite universities. The most powerful universities band together to lobby the government for more research funds, resulting in organizations such as the "C9" (a consortium of nine research universities) and the "211" (the top tier of universities in China). For students, the clear rankings of universities, the fact that many of the wealthier provinces and provincial-level cities give preferential admission to their own students, and the clear differences in required admission scores between different universities illuminate the inequalities in Chinese society.

Students who have little chance of getting into any university find that other forms of inequality loom large. In the most impoverished of rural areas, the schools are not good enough to give students a chance of competing with those from wealthier districts in the race to secure academic senior secondary school places. Because they do not have access to preschool, students from such areas start primary school later than students from wealthier areas do. The quality of instruction in such schools often suffers because teachers dislike teaching there, and, especially in the past, because they offer lower salaries than schools in wealthier districts. Students from these areas often make the calculation that since they will never make it to an academic secondary school, let alone university, they are better off dropping out of junior secondary school and becoming a migrant worker sooner rather than later. While such a strategy might allow a young person to start earning money at an early age, it also brings the stigma of becoming a school dropout, and increases their chances of being disparaged as low *suzhi*.

Educational inequality can also take on ethnic dimensions. Some of China's minority ethnic groups, including Mongolians, Tibetans and Uyghurs, have traditionally used forms of writing other than Chinese characters. Within these communities, many people would prefer to be educated in their own language rather than Mandarin. Even where programs for bilingual education exist, however, the types of economic opportunities available for graduates of such schools are a distant second to those available for graduates of Chinese-language schools. Just as the hegemony of English in the world economy has reduced the value of education in other languages around the globe, so has the economic hegemony of Mandarin reduced the value of education in other languages in China.

There are far fewer graduates of Chinese universities among ethnic Mongolians, Tibetans and Uyghurs than among the majority Han. As we noted in Chapter 7, to encourage students from Tibet and Xinjiang (where most Uyghurs live) to study Mandarin, the government has set up special boarding schools in Shanghai, Beijing and other eastern provinces, where minority secondary-school students from these provinces can enroll. They receive extra language training during the first years of tuition, and are given bonus points on the UEE to enable many of them to reach university. However, and not surprisingly, most students who attend such boarding schools report a decline in their linguistic ability in Tibetan or Uyghur.

Until the mid-2000s, rural girls sometimes faced significant difficulties in receiving an education. Rural parents preferred to devote their limited resources to the education of their sons, as they knew their daughters would marry into other families. As a result of the birth-control policy, which reduced family size, and policies reducing the costs of education for villagers, as well as urbanization and the consequent shift away from virilocal marriage, almost all families today invest equally in the education of daughters and sons. On average, women today are just as likely to succeed in the UEE as men, although among older generations in rural areas, women are more likely to be illiterate than men. At the other end of the scale, employers in some areas of work explicitly discriminate against female applicants, and some universities discriminate against women applying for majors related to those areas of work, requiring higher UEE scores from them than from male applicants.[6]

Because of their general lack of prestige, vocational schools in some parts of China are drastically underfunded. The anthropologist Terry Woronov examined private vocational schools in the city of Nanjing and found that the facilities were atrocious and the teaching poor. Because of the prestige associated with traditional forms of education, as well as a lack of proper equipment, the teachers emphasized abstract knowledge rather than hands-on learning. The students could not follow their teachers' lectures and the whole exercise seemed a farce, with no real "vocational" training occurring at all. The school survived only because its students wanted to spend their teenage years in a school environment to avoid the stigma of dropping out and because its teachers needed a job.[7] Some provinces are now putting more emphasis on vocational schools, but the field remains quite underdeveloped and the quality of vocational schools varies widely.

EDUCATION IN TWO ETHNIC COMMUNITIES IN YUNNAN

During the mid-1990s, Mette Halskov Hansen conducted comparative research in schools in two ethnic communities in Yunnan province. The first community consisted of members of the Naxi ethnic group in the northern part of the province. The second consisted of members of the Tai ethnic group in the southern part of the province. In some ways the groups were very different. The Tai had their own distinctive form of written language that was taught in Theravada Buddhist monasteries and was historically derived from the former Sipsongpanna kingdom. Many Tai families preferred their sons to study in the monasteries rather than state schools. In contrast, the Naxi had long ago embraced education in Chinese characters as a means for social advancement and participated enthusiastically in the state education

---

[6] Tatlow 2012.
[7] Woronov 2011.

system. Ironically, in both cases the presence of the state education system served to reinforce non-mainstream ethnic identities. For the Tai, the state's pressure on them to educate their children in a different language highlighted the fact that their language made them ethnically distinct from the majority of the Chinese. For the Naxi, success in the education system enabled some of their members to gain a foothold in the Chinese bureaucracy as officials hired as representatives of the Naxi. Because their careers as state officials marked them with the label of being an ethnic minority, they were constantly reminded of their ethnic difference and often required to work for the benefit of their ethnic communities. Although the education system itself, and the educational choices of these two communities, have most likely evolved considerably since Hansen's study, the lessons she derived about how state education reinforces ethnic identity remain valid.[8]

Social consequences of Chinese education and discourses of cultivation

The Chinese education system influences patterns of government, demographic trends and class, and ethnic and gender relations. Images of ideal partners for men and women often draw from ideals of academic success; one stereotypical ideal is denoted by the phrase "the scholar and the beauty" (*caizi jiaren*). While this phrase seems to emphasize academic success for men and beauty for women, we should remember that the specific qualities the phrase mentions imply broader notions of "quality". Men who are "scholars" are thought of as being more successful than mere cloistered academics, because in the Chinese tradition a person's scholarly success links directly to their prospects of promotion in the state bureaucracy. Arguably, another legacy of Confucian tradition is that even academics feel attracted to positions where they might offer advice to the government, while government officials often portray themselves as knowledgeable in a scholarly fashion. In short, the scholar/official ideal influences both academics and officials. In addition, "beauties" are understood to be highly intelligent, educated and moral (especially in terms of familial morality), an image that comes across better in the Chinese word *jiaren* than in the English word "beauty". The *caizi jiaren* stereotype does, however, imply that husbands should be at least as educated as their wives and, on average, a Chinese groom will have at least as much education as his bride. Less educated men, and very highly educated women, may struggle to find a partner.

---

[8] Hansen 1999.

One of the practical reasons that a man may desire an educated wife is that child-raising is stereotypically a female responsibility, and one of the most important aspects of child-raising is enabling the child to do well at school. The intensity of competition in the Chinese education system means that this responsibility is not an easy one. In urban areas where there are no boarding schools, Chinese mothers discipline and closely supervise their child or children to ensure that they do their homework; give help when the child cannot do his or her own homework; and select tutors or cram schools for their child. Many mothers report feeling strongly ambivalent about their roles as "education moms". On the one hand, they long for a relatively easygoing relationship with their child, and want to help them to be happy and well rounded rather than just a "studying machine". On the other hand, they strongly feel the responsibility for helping their child to become a "dragon" and that success in educational endeavours is the only way to ensure this outcome.[9] The incredible effort and expense required to raise a child who can succeed in the education system is a common reason parents give for not wanting more children in Chinese cities, and thus is a factor in declining birth rates.[10] In the largest Chinese cities, surveys show that the birth rate would be extremely low even without the birth-control policy, in the same way as in all other highly urbanized East Asian societies where there is intense educational competition, including Japan, South Korea, Taiwan, Hong Kong and Singapore.

The intensity of the education system also influences ethnic relations. As we discussed earlier, China enacts affirmative action for minority students by giving them bonus points on their UEE scores. While these policies enable higher numbers of minority students to reach university, they also stigmatize minority students as unable to compete with members of the Han majority. In parts of China where, for whatever reason, minority students are less committed to educational advancement than their Han classmates, even teachers will make comments about minority students being stupid and lazy. In such settings, ethnic relations tend to revolve around stereotypes that derive from the cultural association between Han ethnicity and school success.

The intensity of the education system limits the type of education that can be delivered; many Chinese education reformers bemoan the fact that students must spend most of their time preparing for tests. Such education, they claim, reduces students' creativity, increases the chances of certain types of mental illness, and prevents the education of better rounded young people. These sentiments are echoed in discussions

[9] Kuan 2011.
[10] Ibid.; see also Greenhalgh & Winckler 2005, p. 232; Kipnis 2011b.

about education for quality among secondary school teachers and students themselves, who claim that no matter how much emphasis is placed on education for quality, all that is possible in secondary school is the memorization of useless facts for the UEE. The only realistic way of improving your "quality" (*suzhi*) is to first prepare well for the UEE and then, only after arriving at university, focus on activities that might raise your *suzhi*. Whether such claims are accurate or not, it is clear that the reality of the system does influence student psychology, sometimes with important social effects. The ubiquity of students' desire to attend university and the problems with vocational education, for example, starve many sectors of the economy of skilled workers.

Educational practice in Chinese society has more subtle effects in the area of governance. In many ways, ideologies of meritocracy affect how China is governed. The experience of the UEE and the debates about exams as a means of curbing corruption mean that exams are the expected way to select people for desirable positions. Exam results, and not undergraduate transcripts, writing samples or application essays, are the primary criteria for selecting students for MA and PhD programs. They are also used in the selection of applicants for government posts, for promotions in the state sector, and for employment in a wide variety of positions outside government.

Exams in China are often scored on an extremely detailed point scale. The UEE scale has roughly 700 points and the difference of a single point can have significant consequences. Similarly, point schemes for measuring the performance of employees in a variety of workplaces, including the government itself, use extremely detailed point schemes. Just as UEE scores depend on tallying responses to a wide variety of questions, so do performance scores reflect the totalling of performance measures from a wide range of perspectives. Furthermore, just as UEE score differentials of just one point can drastically influence a student's future, so small differences in a performance score can have a large impact on how employees are treated. While tests and performance audits exist in workplaces around the world, in contemporary China these bureaucratic methods are taken to extremes. Arguably, such forms of evaluation have become dominant because of students' experience of being examined under high pressure and the fact that those who succeed in the UEE become the country's leaders.

Summary

The intensity of educational competition in China affects many aspects of Chinese society. On the one hand, China's rapid economic development and extreme economic inequality cause young people to fear being left behind, and bring parents to drive their child or children to get ahead through the education system. On the other hand, *suzhi* discourse is used to imply that extremes of social hierarchy and inequality are justified, since leaders are those who have higher *suzhi*, as demonstrated through UEE success. The state looks to meritocratic discourses to legitimate its own leadership and authoritarian attitudes. Such discourse suggests that, if the CCP is selecting high-*suzhi* leaders, the rest of society need not concern itself about corruption or political reform. The intensity of educational competition also affects ethnic relations, both because attitudes toward educational competition often link to ethnic identity and because it tends to exacerbate inequalities in education between the majority Han and other ethnic groups, in turn both feeding off and compounding other kinds of inequality between ethnic groups. Competition in education raises issues in gender relations because of the place of academic success in ideals of masculinity and femininity and the pressure that nurturing successful students places on mothers. It also affects birth rates, labor markets and almost every other aspect of Chinese society.

Discussion questions

1. How do attitudes toward educational competition relate to ethnic identity and ideas of masculinity and femininity in China?
2. How do different groups in society employ *suzhi* discourse, and what are the social and political effects of this discourse?
3. What effects do examinations and discourse about examinations have on the way China is governed?

Recommended reading

Bakken, Børge 2000, *The Exemplary Society: Human Improvement, Social Control, and the Dangers of Modernity in China*. New York: Oxford University Press.

Jacka, Tamara (ed.) 2009, "Quality and Citizenship in China", *positions: east asia cultures critique* vol. 17, no. 3 [special issue].

Kipnis, Andrew 2006, "*Suzhi*: A keyword approach", *The China Quarterly*. vol. 186 (June), pp. 295–313.

Kipnis, Andrew 2011b, *Governing Educational Desire: Culture, Politics, and Schooling in China*. Chicago: University of Chicago Press.

Nie, Hongping Nannie 2008, *The Dilemma of the Moral Curriculum in a Chinese Secondary School*. Latham, MD: University Press of America.

Postiglione, Gerard A (ed.) 2006, *Education in Social Change in China: Inequality in a Market Economy*. Armonk, NY: ME Sharpe.

Stafford, Charles 1995, *The Roads of Chinese Childhood: Learning and Identification in Angang*. Cambridge, UK: Cambridge University Press.

Thøgersen, Stig 2002, *A County of Culture: Twentieth-Century China Seen from the Village Schools of Zouping, Shandong*. Ann Arbor: University of Michigan Press.

Unger, Jonathan 1982, *Education under Mao: Class and Competition in Canton Schools, 1960–1980*. New York: Columbia University Press.

9   Modernity, Youth Identities and
        Popular Culture

How do young adults – people in their teens, twenties and thirties – build a sense of self and identity for themselves? And what impact does modernization have on young peoples' sense of identity, self-expression, values, and desires? These questions dominate the literature on youth in contemporary China, and form the framework for this chapter.

In the social sciences, as we noted in the introduction, modernization and modernity are commonly seen to entail urbanization, industrialization, the spread of mass education, commercialization, and advances in technology that enable the rapid flow of goods, values and people over increasing distances. Together, these are seen to lead to a breaking down of "traditional" social institutions, which previously socialized young people; clearly staked out how they were to move from childhood to adulthood; gave them stable identities; and fixed them in a rigid, hierarchical social order. As Marshall Berman, citing Marx and Engels, put it, "all that is solid melts into air".[1] With rapid change and cultural contact come uncertainties about our place in the world, and the future becomes less predictable. Possible identity schemes multiply, the formation of identities is less rigidly determined by existing local institutions such as the family and religious institutions and becomes more an individual project, and both the anxieties and freedoms associated with shaping an identity increase. Indeed, as the sociologist Anthony Giddens has seen it, self-identity becomes a question and a problem for the first time under modernity, and with "late modernity", a person's life becomes more and more an individualized, reflexive project; a matter of actively choosing an identity, selecting a lifestyle, and identifying and planning life goals and how to actualize them.[2]

The links made here between modernity and identity can be challenged. Richard Jenkins, for example, writes that there is nothing particularly "modern" either about changes and upheaval that challenge social institutions and the formation of identities, or about philosophical,

---

[1] Berman 1982.
[2] Giddens 1991.

religious and popular reflections on personhood and the self.[3] We might also note that experiences of "modernity" vary from one place to another and between differently situated people. Among scholars of China, there has been a great deal of interest in the ways in which the beginnings of modernity in the 19th and early 20th centuries led to an intense questioning of social institutions and personal as well as national identities among young students and scholars in the cosmopolitan urban centers. However, this questioning had little impact on the majority. Instead, desperate poverty, famine, banditry and war acted to undermine the family and other institutions, posing severe challenges to the attempts of millions of Chinese to establish stable, positive social identities.

How are we to understand modernity and identity in the Maoist period and afterward? At the time, Maoist leaders saw themselves as achieving a form of modernity in China superior to that of the capitalist west. Today, though, most scholars in China and elsewhere portray the processes of modernization as stalled by Maoism. Studies of youth and youth cultures in contemporary China sometimes liken recent trends to those of the early 20th century in Shanghai and other metropolises, but generally assume a radical disjuncture between the present and the more recent Maoist past. In most studies, the Maoist period represents a baseline of stasis; a time when state institutions imposed rigid limits on young people's identities and self-expression. Modernity, with its accompanying proliferation of identity schemes and freedom of self-construction and self-expression, is seen to begin with the "open-door policy" and the beginnings of China's market economy in the 1980s.

In some ways, this periodization is highly ironic, given the extent to which the Maoist state reorganized society and challenged "traditional" institutions and values pertaining, for example, to kinship and gender, not to mention the social upheaval caused by the Great Leap Forward and the Cultural Revolution. All the same, from the vantage point of the present, the Maoist period as a whole is perhaps most noteworthy for, on the one hand, overcoming the threats to institutions and stable identities posed by war and desperate poverty in the past, rather than demolishing them. On the other hand, the state assigned and maintained rigid individual and group identities, restricted intra-national and international cultural contact between people, and curtailed Chinese people's opportunities and freedoms to choose different identities, lifestyles and forms of self-expression. In comparison, the variety of identities and forms of self-expression, and the reflexive and active choices of identity and lifestyle that Giddens and others associate with modernity and late modernity are much more apparent in China today.

[3] Jenkins 1996, pp. 7–10.

Aside from this, modernization has contributed to particular social trends in contemporary China that, while unique in their details, are nevertheless broadly similar to some of the trends noted in the literature on modernity, late modernity and postmodernity more generally. In previous chapters, we touched on the impact of modernization on social institutions, relationships and communities. In this chapter, we look at the impact of modernization on identities and values, specifically among young people. We focus on two aspects of modernization that have been particularly important in shaping youth identities in the post-Mao period: first, a growth in consumption and consumerism, and second, a boom in the use of communications technologies, especially television and the internet.

Consumption and consumerism

In the post-Mao period, global capitalism, unprecedented economic growth and improvements in personal incomes have contributed to huge increases in the quantity and variety of material goods and services Chinese citizens purchase. In addition, advertising and marketing, non-existent in the Maoist period, have become powerful forces in the shaping of cultures and identities.

Consumption has brought enormous pleasure to many people, who have experienced it as a liberation from the constraints of poverty and the limits on self-expression the state previously imposed. Consumer-driven capitalist economies, however, do not just enable people to fulfil material needs and desires: they are fuelled by the cultivation of new desires and aspirations, and the creation of a population able and keen to spend money on fulfilling those desires. In China, both product advertising and state policy aimed at increasing economic growth and cultivating a high-*suzhi* (quality) population have played crucial roles in this process.[4]

Around the world, manufacturers, retailers and advertisers target children and teenagers, recognizing that they are simultaneously a "primary market" spending their own money, an "influence market" putting pressure on their parents to spend big, and a "future market" comprising the adult consumers of the future. Unsurprisingly, then, children were crucial in the making of Chinese consumerism in the 1980s, and remain one of the most important categories of consumers today. In addition, by the early 21st century, young people born in the early years of market reform had indeed become China's big spenders and consumers. One

---

[4] The state's efforts at cultivating a high-*suzhi* or "quality" population are discussed in Chapter 8.

study reported that, in 2011, there were more than 300 million Chinese people between the ages of 16 and 30, whose consumption amounted to US$136 billion, or about 50 percent of all households' spending across the country.[5] Parents often cite the younger generation's excessive expenditure as justification for household division. Market advisors have noted the significance of the "one-child" birth-control policy in creating "little emperors". Such children, they observe, grow into young people who have high expectations for personal, material consumption, but who also tend to be lonely. This, they suggest, may be a factor driving Chinese youth in particular to buy and use so many communications' technologies, such as mobile phones and internet services. Some market advisors claim that being an only child also means that, for many young Chinese, the wish both to "fit in" and to "stand out" is particularly intense, as is the pressure to be socially "successful". Apart from consumption of communications' technologies, they suggest, these desires and pressures contribute to high levels of spending among young people on forms of consumption that readily serve as publicly visible markers of identity and status, such as cosmetics, clothes and accessories, meals in expensive restaurants, and (among the very wealthiest), imported luxury cars and expensive apartments and villas with luxurious furnishings.

These trends in youth consumption are easily observable, but the causal significance of China-specific characteristics, such as the birth policy, may be exaggerated. After all, the trends are by no means unique to China: they are characteristic of young people in advanced capitalist economies. This raises some questions. Do global marketing advisors themselves create the very trends in consumer desire that they identify? Are the trends simply the result of global capitalism's push to increase profits by creating new consumers and stimulating the desire for new goods and always more rapidly changing fashions? Or does this accord too much weight to impersonal forces and too little to the agency of individual young people?

Regardless of the answer to these questions, youth trends in consumption are clearly also shaped by and contribute to the particular patterns of social differentiation that characterize contemporary Chinese society. Most obviously, young people's incomes and purchasing power and the availability of goods and services tend to be far greater in wealthier urban centers and coastal regions than in the small towns and villages of the interior. And in cities, most migrant workers and poorer or unemployed locally registered residents have less money to spend than do professionals and successful entrepreneurs.

---

[5] Wharton School of the University of Pennsylvania 2011.

This is not to say, though, that less privileged young people do not aspire to consume. In China as elsewhere, trends in consumption are heavily shaped by a "status game" in which young people buy goods in order to improve or maintain social status. Less privileged youth participate in the status game as energetically as others. Some emulate the consumption of the middle class, in order to obtain a middle-class social status, while others seek a superior identity by pouring scorn on the consumer choices of the wealthy or middle class and spending their money differently. Meanwhile, even those with high social status, feeling that status threatened, try to maintain their distinction from others by spending yet more money on new and novel products and pursuits.

As discussed in Chapter 10, the Chinese state has promoted the status game, or at any rate, aspirations for middle-class status, seeing the middle class (or "middle stratum") as a group who will spearhead consumption and serve as a model of high-*suzhi* social behavior. At the same time, manufacturers, retailers and advertisers have fed off and fuelled the status game, creating demand for new forms of cultural capital, that is, culturally valued knowledge, skills, style and looks, and other qualifications and attributes that will enable young people to "get ahead" in a host of different ways. The status game, and the consumerism that accompanies it, have contributed to, and been shaped by, the development of new youth subcultures. Jing Wang illustrates this with a discussion of "bobos", the "neo-neo tribe" and other subcultural "tribes" that have proliferated in urban China in the early years of the 21st century. She writes that

marketers only need to take a tiny step to turn a popular discourse about a tribe into a new marketing phenomenon. And one can certainly argue the reverse. Indeed, it is difficult to tell which comes first – a real-life tribe or its incarnation as a market segment. Either way, when marketing meets culture, can a new pop culture movement be far away?[6]

"BOBOS" AND THE "NEO-NEO TRIBE"[7]

In 2002, the translation of David Brooks' book, *Bobos in Paradise: The New Upper Class and How they Got There* became an instant best seller in urban China. Brooks' book was a satirical examination of the rise of a new information-age elite – people he referred to as "bourgeois bohemians" or "bobos", because they had "one foot in the bohemian world of creativity and another foot in the bourgeois realm of ambition and worldly success". In China, though, the bobo quickly became a

---

[6] Wang, Jing 2005, p. 548.
[7] This discussion draws on Wang, Jing 2005, pp. 534–6; 546–7.

"poster child without a hint of irony",[8] as Jing Wang puts it, with marketers soon cashing in on wealthy young urbanites' desire for the bobo lifestyle and image. A promotion for a cell phone, for example, went as follows:

> Have you ever heard of "bobos"?... a social group in search of freedom, challenges and spiritual fulfilment. They are keen on creating the genuine meaning of life for themselves. A bobo demands the best from life. They are seeking products of exquisite taste and quality, but more importantly, products that display character and an essence of free spirit. Bobos have been looking everywhere for an ideal cell phone. Not until now did they spot the new...[9]

But the bobo was only one of several images and subcultures, and within a few years others had taken over its "coolness". Among those in their teens and early twenties, the mid-2000s saw the rise of the *xin xin renlei or* "neo-neo tribe" (*Xin xin renlei* is a transliteration of the Japanese term *shin shin jinrei*, introduced to mainland China via Hong Kong and Taiwan). The neo-neo tribe is an East Asian phenomenon: technologically savvy and irreverent teenagers who have grown up glued to cell phones and hunched over computers in internet cafés. Nurtured on Japanese manga and fast food, they have little knowledge or interest in history or tradition, are more independent and self-centered, and have a greater thirst for instant sensory stimulus and gratification than previous generations.

Television and the internet

Together with consumerism, one of the most outstanding features distinguishing Chinese sociocultural life of the last few decades has been an unprecedented increase in the flow of ideas, images and values, as well as goods, both around the country and between China and the rest of the world. Enabled by the state's loosening of restrictions and by technological developments, this communication has been spurred on by the efforts of both private business and the state to increase profits and economic growth by stimulating innovation and consumption. The growth of television and the internet has been particularly important in influencing youth identities and culture.

Television came late to China. The first two TV stations were set up in Beijing and Shanghai in 1958, but into the 1960s and 1970s,

---

[8] Wang, Jing 2005, p. 534.

[9] "*Bubozu' de xin chonger: Aerkate OT715*" ("The new pet toy for bobos: Alcatel OT715"), Alcatel product advertisement, cited in Wang, Jing 2005, p. 535.

further stations were established only slowly and programs produced equally so, with major setbacks along the way. Further, very few people owned or had access to a TV set at that time, and the stations broadcast only for a few hours each day. From the late 1970s onward, however, there was a boom in the manufacture and sale of TV sets, and more stations, channels and programs were set up. In 1978, a mere two percent of Chinese households owned a TV; by 2004, more than 95 percent had one, and a survey estimated the number of viewers to be about 1.2 billion. According to this survey, an average viewer watched about three hours of TV per day. Aside from the national broadcaster, China Central Television (CCTV), there were hundreds of national, provincial and municipal stations with thousands of channels, broadcasting more than 25 600 hours of programming every day. The major local channels were available by satellite across the country, and viewers also had access to cable TV and global satellite services based in Hong Kong.[10]

The state still owns all Chinese TV stations, and TV broadcasts come under state surveillance and control. Caught between "the Party line and the bottom line",[11] most TV programming and production is primarily guided by the desire to generate profits by expanding advertising revenue as well as audiences. However, it continues to be shaped by state efforts to limit political threats and to cultivate a high-*suzhi* citizenry.

Television is dominated by entertainment programs, especially television dramas. In terms of the numbers produced, the size of audiences and advertising revenue, TV dramas are far more important than cinema in China. They are also the "number one myth-making engine in popular culture".[12] Many of the most popular TV dramas among young Chinese are either those produced overseas or in conjunction with overseas companies, or historical dramas. Imported dramas, although there are fewer of them than local productions, have been very popular and influential, and the most successful of these have come from other parts of East Asia, especially Hong Kong, Taiwan and Korea. Japanese dramas were popular in the 1980s, but by 1990 these accounted for only seven percent of dramas imported into the PRC.[13] Interestingly, Japanese dramas, especially "idol" or "trendy" dramas that portray romance among young urban professionals, were far more popular in Taiwan in the 1990s,

---

[10] Kang 2008, pp. 320–1.

[11] This is the subtitle of a book by Yuezhi Zhao examining the impact of market forces on Chinese media in the 1990s (Zhao 1998).

[12] Zhu, Keane & Bai 2008, p. 3.

[13] Cai 2008, p. 133.

especially among young women. But again by the 2000s, Japanese dramas had been swamped by the "Korean wave" of dramas, especially family dramas and romances. Most commentators attribute the success of the Korean wave, which has swept through popular music as well as TV across Asia, to clever marketing and Korea's cultural proximity to its neighbours.

Historical dramas, set mostly in the Qing dynasty (1644–1912) and Republican China (1912–49) and produced or co-produced in mainland China, Hong Kong and Taiwan, have also been enormously popular. Aside from their lush settings, gorgeous costuming and use of star actors, their popularity can be attributed to three factors. First, because they are set in the pre-Communist past, it has been relatively easy for producers of historical dramas to avoid the heavy hand of state censorship. Many are popular for their satirical humor and criticism of imperial power struggles, corruption and social injustice, which viewers readily identify as reflecting contemporary political realities. Second, the later part of the Qing dynasty and the Republican period were times of particularly great social and cultural upheaval and transition. These periods, therefore, provide useful, dramatic settings for themes of conflict between contending worldviews and moralities, which audiences find highly absorbing but which authorities may find more acceptable when cast in the past than in the present. Third, historical dramas have fed on the imagined glory of a bygone era in China, which in turn has contributed to a growing assertion of nationalist identity and pride in the face of globalization, something we will return to shortly.

A leading example of a historical drama is *Grand Mansion Gate* (*Da Zhaimen*), a CCTV serial first broadcast in 2001. Based on real stories about the tribulations of the family who established the famous Tongrentang Chinese medicine business, it begins in the late Qing dynasty and centers around the disturbances in the family caused by a young man, Bai Jingqi. The drama was not well received by cultural critics and some people complained about its moral messages. However, it was a huge commercial success, receiving the highest ratings of any TV drama in China in 2001.[14]

Grand Mansion Gate is interesting for the hybridized model of masculinity it presents in the figure of Bai. As several scholars have noted, there has been a pluralization and a great deal of flux in popular images of masculinity through the post-Mao period. Nimrod Baranovitch has observed that, since the mid-1990s, "the macho type of manhood has lost much of its past appeal and there has been a return to the more traditional type of soft and delicate manhood, which...many in both

---

[14] Xu 2008, p. 35.

the West and China today see as a 'feminized' type of manhood".[15] All the same, as Song Geng discusses, both *Grand Mansion Gate* and another historical drama popular around the same time, *The Big Dye-house* (*Da Ranfang*, 2003), are noteworthy for their more "macho" male heroes.[16]

Traditionally, there have been two sides to Chinese conceptions of masculinity: *wen*, associated with the refined culture, order and morality of the Confucian scholar-official, and *wu*, associated with martial skills, courage and instinctiveness, and brotherhood, personified by the outlaw heroes of the novel *The Water Margin*. The ideal of masculinity included elements of both *wen* and *wu*, but highest social status was accorded to the scholar-official, the embodiment of *wen*. The character of Bai in *Grand Mansion Gate* challenges this class and gender hierarchy with a *wu*-like homosociality, recklessness and daring, womanizing and violence. He also embodies a relatively new ideal of masculinity as money-making. Merchants were placed at the bottom of the Confucian social hierarchy and the private accumulation of wealth was frowned on during the Maoist period. However, capitalism has brought financial success to the fore in contemporary popular culture.

In the 2000s, new media technologies spurred a significant diversification in TV programming, with efforts to increase the size of youth audiences. The programmers ran more interactive talk shows, reality TV and talent shows, produced online versions of shows, and coupled shows with, for example, SMS voting, actor interviews, audience commentaries and other products and services available online. These efforts were highly successful, with reality TV and talent shows, in particular, garnering huge youth audiences.

The craze for such shows took off in China in 2005, with Hunan Satellite TV's production of *Supergirl*, an all-female singing competition imitating *American Idol*, which attracted tens of thousands of applicants across South China. Two things were particularly striking about *Supergirl* in the Chinese context: the novelty of having ordinary people use text messaging to participate in a direct-voting system; and voters' selection of 21-year-old Li Yuchun as the winner of the competition. Li, who came from a working-class family in Chengdu, had been to music school, but by most accounts her singing and dancing abilities were less than outstanding. She also sang "aggressively", performing loud songs originally written for men, and she matched this repertoire with tomboy clothes and short, roughly cut hair.

Supergirl drew the ire of cultural critics because of these two factors, but it was highly popular among young viewers. Critics voiced the

[15] Baranovitch 2003, p. 132.
[16] Song 2010, pp. 404–34.

Image 9.1   Li Yuchun, winner of the *Supergirl* competition, 2005.
Source: Haibird, Chengdu 2005.

opinion that if *Supergirl*'s model of pop democracy were to be extended
to the political process in the way some international media commentators suggested, the result would be a set of national leaders who lacked
political skills just as Li was deficient in vocal abilities. Li also came under
fire for her supposed lack of femininity, and suffered a great deal of questioning and gossip about her sexuality. CCTV described her as "vulgar
and manipulative".[17] To an even greater extent than the character of Bai
in *Grand Mansion Gate*, then, Li challenged dominant – or at least elite –
norms about culture and class, gender and sexuality. Despite this, or
perhaps because of it, she became an instant celebrity among young people, especially young women. More recently, young women have built a
number of online fan-fiction communities around the stars of *Supergirl*,
especially Li. Some of these have celebrated Li's sexual attractiveness to
men. Others – known as "Girl Love" (GL) fan-fiction communities – have
portrayed her as lesbian and developed stories in which she was paired up
with other *Supergirl* contestants. Ling Yang and Hongwei Bao argue that

[17] Joffe-Walt 2005.

the latter *Supergirl* GL fan-fiction communities have become important spaces of "female homosociality, intimacy and affect in which a new generation of young Chinese women actively enact friendship and female subjectivity in a way that refuses the normalization of gender, sexuality and social relations".[18]

In the early 21st century, television dramas, reality TV and talent shows remained highly popular, but young people in China were spending far less time sitting in front of a television set, preferring to watch shows online – as well as playing games, listening to music, consuming information and interacting with others – on a computer or mobile device. Nationwide, the number of internet users climbed from 620 000 in late 1997 (a couple of years after services first became available to the general public) to 384 million by the end of 2009 and 538 million, or almost 40 percent of the population, by mid-2012.[19]

Most internet users in China have been young and relatively well educated: in mid-2012, 55.6 percent were aged between 10 and 29, and a further 25.5 percent were aged between 30 and 39. Most had junior secondary (37.5 percent) or senior secondary school (31.7 percent) education. Students constituted 28.6 percent of all netizens.[20] The distribution of internet access and usage has been highly uneven, but the rural/urban digital divide has narrowed considerably over time. So too has the gender discrepancy among users. At the end of 2000, only about 0.8 percent of internet users were from rural areas and 70 percent were male. By mid-2012, 27.1 percent were from rural areas and 55 percent were male. In the same year, users' average online time amounted to just under 20 hours per week, most of it spent on a home computer or a mobile device. With the growing availability of home computers and internet services and mobile devices, fewer people now go to internet cafés, particularly in the context of governmental restrictions on such businesses. But still, in mid-2012, 25.8 percent of users accessed the internet in an internet café.[21]

In ethnographic research conducted in a northern city in 2007 and 2008, Fengshu Liu found that most young people used the internet for

---

[18] Yang & Bao 2012, p. 842. Yang and Bao provide a brief account of the emergence of Chinese fan fiction, including "Boy Love" (BL) as well as GL fiction. In recent years, these genres, which are heavily influenced by Japanese anime and other popular culture and by the Chinese tradition of writing sequels to well-known classical novels, have become extremely popular among young women in mainland China, Hong Kong and Taiwan.

[19] Liu, Fengshu 2011, p. 36; CNNIC 2010, p. 2; CNNIC 2012, p. 4.

[20] CNNIC 2012, p. 4.

[21] Liu, Fengshu 2011, pp. 36–7; CNNIC 2012, pp. 15–17.

Image 9.2   10 a.m. in an internet café in Urumqi (Urumchi).
Source: Tom Cliff, Xinjiang 2002.

leisure purposes, and to socialize and escape the boredom, lack of autonomy and pressure of "real" life, dominated, for the majority, by long hours
of school and homework every day, and for others by unemployment and
having "nothing to do". Compared with young people in Britain and
Norway, few Chinese youth used the internet primarily for work and
study purposes, rather than for leisure. Further, while young people in
Norway, for example, tended to see the internet as an extension of their
offline life, Chinese youth were more likely to view it as an alternative
world, and to be attracted to it for this reason.[22]

Chinese parents and the media have held strong concerns about youth
"internet addiction" and, in particular, their playing of online games
in internet cafés. Many people, alarmed by media reports about young
addicts who have dropped out of school, been jailed for crimes including murder, or committed suicide, have tried their utmost to limit the
"corrupting" influence of the internet and internet cafés on their children. However, internet cafés remain particularly popular among young
Chinese as places to socialize with others in person as well as online. For
young people who are financially dependent on their parents, the internet
café is a relatively cheap and accessible form of entertainment as well as a
venue for socializing. As the informants in Liu's study reported, one of the

[22] Liu, Fengshu 2011, pp. 181–2.

attractions of the internet café is that it enables them to escape from their lowly position in the highly competitive, hierarchical social order of their regular life. In the internet café, young people feel that they are among like-minded equals, and they can adopt new, more positive and desirable identities online. They can also achieve successes in exciting, competitive games in which the costs of failure are much lower than in "real" life.

While most young Chinese people use the internet primarily for entertainment and to look for entertainment-related information, it has also been an important site for social and political debate and collective action. Web-based discussion forums, blogs and instant messaging have been particularly important in China. A 2007 study reported, for example, that 70 percent of Chinese internet users reported visiting bulletin boards or online forums, and 77 percent used instant messaging, compared to 39 percent of Americans.[23] A lot of messaging has taken the form of diaries and casual chat about personal feelings, views and experiences. However, such communications have also often been political in the sense that they have challenged dominant social norms. Mu Zimei's blog, discussed in Chapter 2, is one example. Blogs and other online forums have also been popular sites for the expression of nationalist sentiments. This was especially apparent in the lead-up to the Beijing Olympics in 2008, when young Han Chinese, mostly overseas students, came out in huge numbers against Tibetans who were protesting for greater autonomy by intervening in the passage of the Olympic torch around the world. After participating in the demonstrations, the young Han posted their stories online and uploaded photos and video clips. Millions of Chinese internet users read their accounts, sent messages applauding them and joined internet petitions in their support. More than 2 million MSN users attached "I love China" icons to their online profiles.[24]

As Pal Nyíri and Juan Zhang write, this was a striking example of young people competing for a distinctive, individual identity, while simultaneously identifying with, and seeking a sense of belonging in, a (national) community. Praising nationalist heroes and denouncing traitors became an opportunity for contributors to the online discussions to be recognized as "one of us". At the same time, both the demonstrators and those commenting online sought to define themselves as the most passionate, cosmopolitan and sophisticated nationalists, defending the pride of their nation.[25]

---

[23] Cited in Nyíri, Zhang & Varrall 2010, p. 52.

[24] Liu, Fengshu 2011, p. 162.

[25] Nyíri, Zhang & Varrall 2010. In 2012, nationalist protests flared again both in the streets and online, this time in reaction to Japan's claims to the Diaoyu Islands (known as the Senkaku Islands in Japan). At the time of writing, very little sociological or

Summary

Like developments in consumerism, the media boom in contemporary China points to a characteristically modern, global liberation and proliferation of the identities, values and forms of self-expression available to young people. At the same time, it is associated with particular changes in values and identities specific to China. In summing up, we identify five particularly important directions of change in youth identities and values.

First, young people's notions of what constitutes a desirable gender and sexual identity have been multiple and changing. This is apparent in the popularity of shows such as *Grand Mansion Gate*, which challenged and mixed up notions of masculinity, and in *Supergirl* and Mu Zimei's blog, which presented new and alternative images of femininity. For contemporary youth, some of the most popular models of masculinity have been quite different from both Confucian and Maoist models in being highly successful business entrepreneurs. Many, like *Grand Mansion Gate*'s Bai Jingqi, have been rough "macho" types, but more refined "feminized" models of masculinity have also been popular. In recent decades, young people's female models have tended to be far more sexualized than the models that dominated the Maoist era, and also less demure and bolder than the images that dominated the media in the 1980s.

Second, the spread of communications technologies, combined with increases in the population's physical mobility, has made young people across China more worldly-wise and cosmopolitan in their values and tastes than before. Cosmopolitanism has been mostly unidirectional, in that rural residents have gained knowledge and a taste for urban (and foreign) identities and lifestyles, but the reverse has occurred to a much lesser degree. Some argue, though, that in the last few years we have seen the beginnings of an urban, consumer-driven reappraisal of the countryside not unlike the Romantic turn that occurred in European culture following industrialization in the late 18th century. Once considered backward and dirty, villages and "nature" are now seen increasingly as desirable by urbanites. As Michael Griffiths and co-authors write:

For the urban dwellers with the means, the weekend trip out to the *nongjiayuan* [farmers' courtyards] to breathe clean, fresh air and eat natural home-grown food is highly appealing. Where the consumer pioneers are going today, all of China may go tomorrow.[26]

anthropological analysis of these protests was available, although there was plenty of political commentary.

[26] Griffiths, Chapman & Christiansen 2010, p. 353.

Third, a growth in international communications has led to the emergence of globalized youth identities and cultures in China. The impact of modern western values, ideas and tastes has been obvious, but influences from other parts of East Asia have also been extremely significant. We noted the rise of the neo-neo tribe across East Asia and the popularity of Taiwanese and Korean TV dramas among young people in China. In music, "Gang-Tai pop", from Hong Kong and Taiwan, is by far the most popular genre among young people. These shared tastes and fashions suggest that, in fact, a regional East Asian youth identity has been more culturally and socially significant in China in recent decades than any other kind of global identity.

Fourth, a reaction against globalization and a desire to identify with and assert pride in a specifically Chinese cultural identity are also important youth trends. This is apparent both in the enormous popularity of TV dramas set in pre-revolutionary China, and in recent nationalist protests.

Finally, something of a divergence has appeared in post-Mao youth trends between a dominant concern with personal gratification and self-advancement on the one hand, and several incidents of political protest and widespread youth engagement with social and political concerns on the other. Since the early 1980s, commentators have commonly assumed that young people in post-Mao China have become a "me generation", far more pragmatic, materialistic, selfish and apolitical than previous generations of youth. They have then been repeatedly surprised by examples of young people's engagement with political concerns, first in 1989 with the Tian'anmen democracy movement among students and workers, and more recently with migrant-worker protests and growing nationalism. A further puzzle was a surge during the 2000s of youth involvement in volunteer work. This was particularly noteworthy following the Sichuan earthquake of May 2008, when thousands of young people, mostly from urban areas, donated large sums of money and sacrificed many days and weeks of their time to work in the rescue and reconstruction effort in Sichuan.

It is possible, however, to see these trends as different facets of the same process of individualization. Both consumer capitalism and the state's promotion of *suzhi* enjoin Chinese youth to think of themselves as individuals, responsible for their own self-formation and self-development. Further, both encourage them to think that social success and a good life can be achieved through individual effort and by consuming material goods. At the same time, globalization has resulted in a growing consciousness of individual rights. In different ways, many political protests among young people, including the Tian'anmen democracy movement and migrant-worker protests, can be attributed to the frustration of the desire for individual consumption and improvements in social and economic status, combined with a frustration of individual rights, including political, economic and social rights.

With regard to nationalist protests and volunteerism, we noted above that young people's individualized efforts to achieve identity and status for themselves commonly involve attempts to "fit in" with a group, as well as moves to distinguish themselves from others. In this sense, individualization does not necessarily, or only, lead to individualist identities. A dual striving for community as well as individual identity is readily apparent, both in the consumption of fashions and material goods and in nationalist protests. Some scholars suggest that young people's involvement in volunteer work can be seen in a similar light.[27]

In addition, young people's volunteer work, nationalist political protests and cultural nationalism may signal a new cultural and moral development in China. In the 1950s, there was a strong sense of solidarity and optimism in Chinese society and a willingness of people to work for the common good. By the 1980s, that feeling had dissipated and most people heard state calls to work for the collective good as an unwelcome imposition. Today, however, the tide may be turning once more, toward a greater popular, as well as state, interest in collective harmony and well-being, and national pride.

Discussion questions

1. To what extent (if at all) and in what ways can western theories of modernity and identity contribute to an understanding of the formation of youth identities in China?
2. How have ideals of masculinity and femininity among youth in China changed over the last few decades?
3. How do you account for the rise of global cultural identifications and nationalism among young people in China today?
4. To what extent are young people in China today a selfish "me generation"? Explain your answer, comparing contemporary Chinese youth with previous generations and with young people in the society in which you live.

Recommended reading

Baranovitch, Nimrod 2003, *China's New Voices: Popular Music, Ethnicity, Gender and Politics, 1978–1997*. Berkeley: University of California Press.

[27] Rolandsen 2010, pp. 132–63.

Cockain, Alex 2012, *Young Chinese in Urban China*. London: Routledge.

Farrer, James 2002, *Opening Up: Youth Sex Culture and Market Reform in Shanghai*. Chicago: University of Chicago Press.

Hansen, Mette Halskov & Svarverud, Rune (eds) 2010, *iChina: The Rise of the Individual in Modern Chinese Society*. Copenhagen: NIAS Press.

Liu, Fengshu 2011, *Urban Youth in China: Modernity, the Internet and the Self*. London: Routledge.

Liu, Shao-hua 2011, *Passage to Manhood: Youth Migration, Heroin, and AIDS in Southwest China*. Stanford, CA: Stanford University Press.

Wang, Jing 2008, *Brand New China: Advertising, Media and Commercial Culture*. Cambridge, MA: Harvard University Press.

Part 3

Inequalities, Injustices and
Social Responses

10   Social Class and Stratification

In the 1970s, China was considered a comparatively egalitarian society, in which class designation and the rural–urban divide constituted the main sources of social and material inequality. In 2010, there were more than a million millionaires in the country, and *Forbes* magazine listed 64 Chinese citizens among the world's richest billionaires.[1] At the other end of the spectrum, the Chinese government, the United Nations Development Program (UNDP) and the World Bank estimated that between 120 and 150 million Chinese were living on less than US$1.25 (purchasing power parity) per day. Rarely do Chinese citizens speak of this wealth gap in the vocabulary of class. Indeed, other than the term "middle class", the word is not commonly used. And, although inequalities are obviously increasing, wealth is no longer confined to urban areas and poverty is not exclusive to the countryside.

Why, and how, have explanations and indicators of material and social polarization changed so dramatically in China? What are the key axes of polarization, and what are the direction and tempo of trends in inequality? How do people view their relative position in this rapidly changing social order?

Conceptualizing stratification and class in China: historical perspectives

The terms "class" and "stratification" are quintessentially ideological.[2] That is, they encapsulate ideas, beliefs and values about the sources and conditions of inequality, and the principles and structures characterizing relations in an ideal society, as well as efforts to normalize certain experiences of inequality and maintain or transform relations of inequality. Another ideological dimension of these concepts is that governments have used them to classify populations in order to make the social order legible

---

[1] "China ranks No. 2 on Forbes billionaires list" 2010.
[2] Giddens 1977, p. 99.

from, and compatible with, their ideological worldviews, and so more easily governed. In addition to these state projects, citizens use these terms to manipulate social categories rhetorically, position themselves relative to their audience, and try to influence approaches to problems that are unique to their times, places and personal experiences.

Some of the earliest records of Chinese thought contain explanations of how people were rendered different and unequal by state, society, birth and cosmological processes. The collection of texts from the 6th to 4th centuries BCE compiled in the *Book of Documents*, for example, distinguished people according to a rudimentary division of labor (scholars, farmers, artisans and merchants) that defined their obligations to the ruler and each other. The later texts, attributed to Confucius and Mencius, endorsed hierarchies based variously on scholarly merit and the cultivation of moral virtue and civility, political authority, gender, generation and age.

The concepts of inequality these early texts express are significant for several reasons. First, while occupations were unequally rewarded, wealth and poverty were neither fully determined by, nor the inevitable result of, a person's status. Second, although slavery was practiced and, at different periods, intermarriage between certain groups was proscribed, among free people pure mobility – that is, both individuals' occupational mobility and families' intergenerational mobility – was accepted. This is illustrated in Mencius's statement that the legendary Emperor Shun, an "eastern barbarian", had been a farmer, potter and fisherman before he became a sage and ruler. And, owing to the dynamism of the late imperial economy and the orthodox practice of partible patrilineal inheritance (see Chapter 1), families' status and fortunes inevitably waxed and waned. As Qian Yong pointed out: "Wealth and high status are like flowers. They wither in less than a day".[3] Third, status hinged on the acquisition and display of expensive forms of cultural capital, that is, culturally valued knowledge, skills and style. Familiarity with classical texts, which was tested in examinations for bureaucratic office, was particularly important. Fourth, insofar as these concepts were relational, the relationships were idealized as being reciprocal and inspiring ordinary folks' respect and emulation for scholars and bureaucrats, rather than conflict. Ideologically, then, in contrast to rigid stratification systems grounded on racial typologies or religion-based castes, elite imperial Chinese concepts of inequality served to legitimize both large inequalities and a relatively weak social stratification system in which mobility was normalized. Even the poor could imagine that through education, hard work and virtuous actions, they might attain prosperity and prestige. Theoretically, the concepts

---

[3] Qian Yong, quoted in Kuhn 1984, p. 25.

bore more similarity to Weberian strands of thinking, emphasizing commonalities of opportunity, consumption and lifestyles, than to Marxist notions of class.[4]

Though in Chinese the term "social class" (*jieji*) originally referred to stepped social ranks in a hierarchy, since the early 20th century, it explicitly has referenced Marx's theory that conflictual social relationships are structured by modes of production. In modern industrial production, Marx argued, unequal ownership of the means of production, and exploitation of labor, sensitize people to their common material conditions and opposing interests as classes; class-consciousness prompts people to engage in struggle. Conflict, not only economic relations, thereby defines class. In China, this theory-driven lexicon was used to mobilize people in armed struggle and justify radical resource redistribution. The point is underscored in the opening passage of a text penned by a youthful Mao:

Who are our enemies? Who are our friends? . . . To ensure that we will achieve success in our revolution and will not lead the masses astray, we must pay attention to uniting with our real friends in order to attack our real enemies. To distinguish real friends from real enemies, we must make a general analysis of the economic status of the various classes in Chinese society and of their respective attitudes towards the revolution.[5]

This passage also highlights how Maoist class analysis deviated in emphasis and application from Marx's economic determinism. People's support for the Communist revolution – their "redness" – modified the Party's allocation of them to economic classes. This served a pragmatic function in building support for the new regime. Families were assigned a class label based on both their economic origins (determined by an assessment of their ownership of assets and reliance on the exploitation of others' labor), and their political background (which reflected the household head's revolutionary activism and any criminal record). Hence, families' political background – but not their class origin – could be changed by demonstrating support for the Party and the revolution.

Drawing class lines on this basis in the countryside separated "enemy" exploiters such as landlords and usurers, from the vast majority who were classified as "friendly", non-exploitative classes, including some rich peasants; all middle, poor and landless peasants; laborers; shopkeepers; teachers; clerks; artisans; and soldiers who had supported the CCP. In cities and towns, where the Party's predominantly peasant leadership

---

[4] For an introduction to the differences between concepts of class drawing on the work of Max Weber and those referencing Karl Marx's writings, see Breen & Rottman 1995.
[5] Mao 1926, p. 13.

could not dispense with the expertise of professionals, managerial and technical staff, class lines were drawn between "counterrevolutionary" compradors (agents for foreign merchants) and capitalists, and "friendly" members of the "national bourgeoisie", intellectuals and the working class. As with the land reform that reallocated land in the countryside, redistribution of the property of class "enemies" in urban areas, and their transformation into social pariahs, destroyed the material basis and power of the old ruling classes.

To prevent the resurgence of the enemy classes, class designations were inherited patrilineally and recorded in households' *hukou* (household registration) booklets and employees' personnel dossiers. As a famous Cultural Revolution slogan put it: "If the father's a revolutionary, the son's a hero; if the father's a reactionary, the son's a bastard!" Whereas the offspring of the "friendly" or "good" classes were rewarded by the CCP's allocation of political, economic and cultural resources, "enemy" or "bad" class elements were denied opportunities for advancement, and victimized in periodic campaigns to eliminate counterrevolutionaries and rightists. Within Party and government organizations, too, repeated rectification campaigns were supposed to guard against the formation of a new bureaucratic "ruling" class.

In combination with restrictions on geographical and job mobility, the reproduction of class designations impeded status mobility and helped consolidate a system of class stratification. People sought alternative paths to attain and transmit status. Rivalry for entry into the CCP and Communist Youth League, the army and large state-owned *danwei* (work units) intensified. Because politically virtuous "reds" were favored over highly educated "experts", people strove to demonstrate their loyalty to Mao and their socialist, proletarian values. In a twist of hypergamous marital custom,[6] families sought poor and middle peasants, model workers and Party activists as marriage partners for their daughters, and shunned potential bridegrooms whose landlord or capitalist designation would be passed on to offspring. Maoist society was thus characterized by little material inequality, but highly politicized status markers, limited mobility and an inelastic system of stratification.

The post-Mao state rejected the centrality of class antagonisms in socialist society. Instead, its leaders made a strategic decision to correct "unjust, false and wrong" charges of counterrevolutionary and revisionist activity, end class labeling, and mobilize the population behind economic modernization.[7] The subsequent propagation of a new vocabulary of

---

[6] That is, the custom of marrying daughters into families higher up the ladder of social status. See Chapter 1.

[7] CCP 1981.

economic reform, stability, harmony and the construction of a "well-off" society was intended to rebuild CCP support in a population weary of divisive campaigns and eager for improved living standards. The challenge that arose, though, was that while engineering the transformation of the planned economy into a market economy, bureaucrats capitalized on their control over pricing, exports and imports, resources and business licenses, and the commoditization of public enterprises and urban housing, to enrich themselves and their families. Material and social inequalities grew, as public property flowed into private hands. In the popular imagination, the image of the "corrupt official" soon replaced the stock Maoist class villain, the "feudal landlord".

Concerned by protests against corruption and the publication of unfavorable comparisons between levels of inequality in China and other former socialist and developing capitalist countries, China's leaders steered social reportage away from class, and toward the less contentious ideological language of "social strata" (*jieceng*) and stratification. In 2002, the CCP adopted the goal of "controlling the growth of the upper stratum of society, expanding the middle and reducing the bottom".[8] The formulation of this goal was motivated by several assumptions. First, the CCP expected that the middle stratum's educational and professional aspirations and ever-changing tastes would help boost consumerism and thus buoy domestic markets afflicted by investment bubbles and declining exports. Second, the CCP anticipated that the middle stratum would function as a politically stabilizing force. Increased numbers of middle-income earners would moderate income inequalities and the attendant risks of social dissatisfaction. To protect its growing affluence, the middle stratum would choose to support the status quo over the riskier option of political transformation. For this reason, this stratum was granted greater representation in People's Congresses, consultative committees and associations. Third, the values and responsible, self-disciplined behavior that were imputed to the middle stratum were to be promoted by governments and schools as exemplars for improving the *suzhi* (quality) of migrants, semi-skilled workers and villagers.[9] Thus, mounting empirical evidence of growing material and social polarization coincided with the CCP's conceptualization of the middle stratum as an economic and political buffer, and as a model, high-*suzhi* citizenry.

The Party's new emphasis on stratification rather than class prompted intense questioning about the changing sources of status, the trajectories of social mobility and the profile of China's stratification system. We address each of these questions in the next section.

---

[8] Guo 2008, p. 39.
[9] Tomba 2009. See Chapter 8.

Classifying contemporary social structures and relationships

In the satirical science fiction novel *The Fat Years*, the narrator, old Chen, confides to the reader that since the global financial crisis and China's Golden Age of Ascendency began, he has mostly had contact with three types of people. Given old Chen's dream of writing a best seller, the reader is not surprised to learn that media reporters and editors in publishing houses represent two of the three types. His contact with the third type, "ordinary folk", is mediated through his cleaning lady:

I only hire laid-off female workers who live in Beijing with their families. That's because I'm away from home a lot and it makes me feel safer. My current cleaning lady's daughter is a graduate who works for a foreign company so her finances aren't a problem, but she likes to keep busy, likes to work. While she's cleaning, she tells me all about her daughter and her boyfriend. Such details as how much her daughter spends at the hairdresser, or that her daughter's boyfriend might be transferred to Shanghai. She also tells me about the Taiwanese news she sees on Fujian's Southeast Satellite Television. I just sit there working at my computer and listening. Sometimes it gets a little irritating, but sometimes I'm grateful to her for keeping me in touch with ordinary folk.[10]

The excerpt tells us much about the changing conditions influencing Chinese people's perceptions of their social order. It also neatly sums up the challenges that confront scholars who attempt to map the clusters and cleavages of that order. Like old Chen, they rely on a multitude of fragments of information to describe subjects whose positions in the social order are multiple, fluid and inconsistent.

Status inconsistencies and mobility

Sociologists concur that wealth guarantees neither status nor prestige in contemporary Chinese society. Xiaowei Zang, for example, notes that millionaires who profit from their connections with high-ranked officials are sneered at as dishonest, immoral and vulgar arrivistes.[11] A great deal of media attention centers on the high income, fame and lifestyle of actors and sportspeople, but questions are also asked about their paths to riches and their suitability as role models. In contrast, surveys consistently show that officials and highly educated professionals, such as

[10] Chan, Koonchung 2011, p. 46.
[11] Zang 2008.

judges and university professors, enjoy high status and prestige, despite the fact that they, too, have benefited from what might best be dubbed "bureaucratic allocation" – that is, the bureaucracy's allocation of jobs in the public sector, and state-subsidized education, housing and welfare. This inconsistency in status – a discrepancy between high rank according to one criterion (such as income) and low rank according to another (for example, occupation) – springs from the revalorization of cultural capital and the idealization of morality and merit-based stratification processes. Yet the status inconsistencies apparent at the upper end of the stratification spectrum are not mirrored at the lower end of the spectrum. Impoverishment not only coincides with low occupational prestige, but also precludes people's acquisition of the political, economic and cultural capital required for upward mobility.

Overall social mobility in China, while still low in comparison to the United States, has increased as a result of market institutions, industrialization and urbanization. Using data on urban employees from the 2003 Chinese General Social Survey, Yanjie Bian found that 24 percent experienced upward occupational mobility, and 21 percent experienced downward mobility.[12] Yet, although markets have opened new channels for occupational mobility, political capital and bureaucratic allocation still account for the greatest number and magnitude of upward movements. Mobility among young urban men, in particular, is causally associated not only with bureaucratic allocation of state-sector jobs, but also with a generational multiplier effect, because urban parents who acquired state-allocated benefits during the era of central planning now subsidize the education, assets and lifestyle of their sons and daughters in the market economy. The children of industrial workers, in contrast, are unlikely to experience upward mobility unless they gain entrance into university.

Two mobility trends work against the solidification of a stratification system based on political capital and bureaucratic allocations. Adult children who have become geographically and occupationally mobile remit income for investment in the housing, education and marriages of members of their village families, which have always been disadvantaged by bureaucratic allocation. And, as markets enable the conversion of wealth into political, cultural and social capital, the grown-up children of the new rich cross boundaries both between strata and within their own social stratum by achieving qualifications from overseas universities, displaying virtue via charitable sponsorship, and extending their networks through membership of political consultative committees and corporate boards.

---

[12] Bian 2009, p. 185.

The contemporary idealization of morality and merit-based stratification on the one hand, and status inconsistencies and opportunistic use of multiple mobility paths on the other, register the concerns of a complex, rapidly changing society. How, then, do Chinese scholars define the classes, strata or other categories, and how do the members of these conceptual groups view themselves in relation to other categories in this fluid social landscape?

China's social structure of pyramids and diamonds

In her 2002 study of China's "listing social structure", the well-known economist He Qinglian merged heavily modified Marxist arguments with Weberian stratification criteria to explain the causes and map the composition of "elites" and classes.[13] Members of He's categories do not all share a consciousness of class interests, status consistency, or a common trajectory of mobility. One category that possesses all three, however, is the one percent of the population comprising the political–economic "elite". He argues that CCP and bureaucratic leaders have transformed their political power and control over public assets into new, privately owned financial capital, assets and cultural resources. Today, the elite possesses great wealth, has a predilection for luxury consumption, and lacks leisure time. Owing to its kin connections, *guanxi* and continued political influence, it also displays a high degree of intergenerational continuity. He subdivides the elite into three groups differentiated by their positioning relative to the state and market:

1. political and bureaucratic leaders
2. managers of major state enterprises, and banking, media and telecommunications industries
3. the owners of large private companies.

Another small "intellectual elite" is distinguished by its advanced educational qualifications, prestige and influence over public opinion, and is more internally differentiated. While some of its members have gained little materially from market reforms, others, such as lawyers and economists, have been extremely successful in converting their cultural capital into assets and income, and wealth into political connections. Members of the "intellectual elite" also vary in their ideology, political preferences, leisure time and activities. The lower end of the "intellectual elite" is coextensive with the higher rungs of what He refers to as

[13] He, Qinglian 2003.

a new "underdeveloped middle class". The upper end of this new class includes government administrative staff, some private businesspeople, managers of medium-sized firms, doctors and teachers, while the lower end includes upwardly mobile former workers, such as technicians. He suggests that this ill-defined, diverse middle class comprises about 16 per cent of the total workforce.

The lowest class cluster, which He describes as living "either at the bottom or on the margins of society", includes two groups that together make up about 80 percent of China's workforce. Blue-collar workers, who make up around one-fifth of the total workforce, are further subdivided on the basis of their employment in either public or private enterprises, and the extent to which the capital–labor relationship is exploitative. Although employees of large western-invested firms enjoy better salaries, conditions and opportunities than workers in some Asian-invested subcontracting factories and rural enterprises, He asserts that "every part of the working class is in turmoil".[14] This assertion seems to be supported by television dramas centering on rising productivity pressures and layoffs from enterprises; regular news reports of fatal industrial accidents; and findings from the 2002 China household income survey that 89 percent of urban workers judged current income distribution "unfair".[15] The largest proportion of the lowest class cluster, though, is made of up rural-registered people. Suffering from limited assets and income, limited formal education, mobility constraints and a lack of political influence and legal protections, villagers face an insecure future as a result of economic restructuring and global commodity trade. He's depiction of this bottom-heavy pyramidal social structure concludes with a rejection of arguments that China is becoming a diamond-shaped "middle-class" society, and a prediction that the continued exercise of political privilege in markets will exacerbate social polarization.

A second influential analysis of China's social structure, by the sociologist Lu Xueyi, has led to a contrasting prediction. Drawing more directly on Weberian social stratification theory and data from nationwide surveys conducted between 1999 and 2002, Lu's research team classified the population into five socioeconomic strata (defined by possession of organizational, economic and cultural capital) and 10 occupational strata. As illustrated in Figure 10.1, according to Lu's classification, someone who, by occupation, is a private entrepreneur might simultaneously belong to three socioeconomic strata because of his or her upper-level organizational authority, upper-middle levels of income and assets, and middling education. The middle socioeconomic stratum in this diamond-shaped

---

[14] He, Qinglian 2003, p. 172.
[15] Wang & Davis 2010, p. 169.

Socioeconomic strata   % of population by occupation

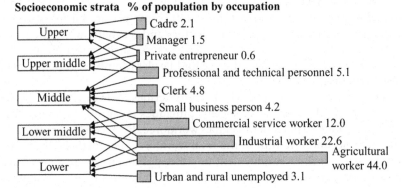

Figure 10.1 Distribution of population into socioeconomic strata and occupational strata.
Source: Adapted from Lu, Xueyi 2002, pp. 9, 44.

structure includes representatives from seven of the 10 occupational strata.

There are limitations in both these frameworks, not least that they have become dated as a result of China's rapid economic restructuring. A more substantive issue is that, like He's account of the "underdeveloped middle class", the socioeconomic strata that Lu's team defined are not classified together as a result of a common causal factor affecting life chances, such as political power, property ownership or transactions in the market economy. Members of the diverse occupational categories that Lu's team assign to the middle stratum would not necessarily share experiences, spheres of social interaction or self-ascribed, positional identities. Take a high-ranking Party official and a company network administrator as examples: although both possess decision-making power in their workplace, postgraduate qualifications and high incomes, they would be unlikely to socialize together after work, much less share a similar perception of their social identity. There is also an unexplained structural anomaly in the profiles Lu's team created: whereas the occupational demographic profile resembles the bottom-heavy pyramidal structure described by He, the clustering of seven of the occupational strata into a bloated middle socioeconomic stratum downplays polarization and suggests that the Party's goal of expanding the middle stratum is within reach. However, one of the key strengths of both these frameworks is that they neatly convey the multi-dimensional, inconsistent identities of the members of various social strata. Next, we will examine two such strata from an insider's perspective, to offer better insight into these complex inconsistencies.

Conflicted identities: the middle stratum

Lu's team had reason to define China's middle socioeconomic stratum as a large, inclusive category. After all, in 2005, Li Chunling calculated that as a percentage of the population, while the middle stratum would comprise only around three percent if occupation, income and consumption were taken into account, it would be almost 47 percent according to self-identification.[16] And in a later survey conducted in Beijing in 2007, Li found that although only 10 percent of mid-ranking respondents described themselves as "middle class", most agreed that they were "middle stratum".[17]

Why, despite clear political, economic and social inequalities, do so many of China's urban citizens identify as middle stratum? An aversion to the conflicts associated with the class labels of the Maoist era might partly account for their choice of terminology. Another explanation reaches beyond terminology, to suggest that state ideology and advertising feed a popular desire to attain, and be treated as, possessing the prestige, property and purchasing power that members of the middle stratum enjoy. But even though, as we suggested in Chapter 9, such desires are central to the construction of modern subjects, it is worth questioning any explanation that treats people merely as the recipients of state and marketing propaganda, rather than as agents capable of critical, selective positioning. Martin King Whyte's research on inequalities suggests a more plausible interpretation, albeit one that also hinges on wishful thinking. Whyte presents evidence showing that most Chinese people would prefer to live

in a society that occupies a middle ground on inequality, one that resembles the welfare state or liberal capitalist ethic promoted in advanced market economies. In such an ideal society, existing inequalities would be equitable in the sense that they would reflect differential skills, contributions, and other merit factors, and the state would provide . . . measures to promote equal opportunities.[18]

There is a considerable gap between that preference and the environment in which they do live. Self-identification as middle stratum might therefore operate as a conversational strategy that signals an ideal and rhetorically attaches the speaker to the moral, behavioral and meritocratic standards they imagine should apply in the ideal society. Simultaneously,

[16] Li, Chunling 2005, pp. 485–99.
[17] Li, Chunling 2010, p. 149.
[18] Whyte 2010a, p. 139.

it distances them from the power structures, bureaucratic allocations and social institutions that contribute to existing inequalities. This explanation seems consistent with studies showing that the middle stratum is strongly optimistic about China's future.

However, on the basis of ethnographic research in the city of Kunming between 2000 and 2007, Li Zhang argues that self-identifying members of the urban middle stratum are torn in a "double movement".[19] On the one hand, they turn inward to perfect the cultural and occupational achievements that are key sources of their status and rising incomes. Convinced that credentials will be essential for upward mobility in the future, the middle stratum spends much of its significant savings and limited leisure time on upgrading its skill-set, personal development and the education of its children. This inward focus also springs from the new middle stratum's preference for discreetly enjoying cultural products and consumer comforts at home. In Chapter 9, we referred to marketing advisors' observation that young people with money tend to spend big on very visible forms of consumption. Li Zhang found, though, that middle-class homeowners in Kunming prefer to invest in the purchase and decoration of private "domestic paradises", shielded from the public gaze by hedges, walls, gates, guards and security systems that protect upscale residential compounds. Within the home, members of middle-stratum families interact rarely with the migrant workers whose household-maintenance services they depend on. Even within their gated residential compounds, they have little to do with their neighbors, in contrast to villages and working-class apartment blocks where old neighbors reciprocate gifts of food, child-minding and invitations to play mah-jongg.

On the other hand, the middle stratum moves into the public sphere to expand its political and social capital, and defend its newly acquired wealth and quality of life. Equipped with high-level communication skills and legal knowledge, its members mobilize to oppose potential threats to their property and personal security by footloose petty criminals, pollution of the environment by industries, and predatory incursions by real-estate developers, commercial property-management companies and local authorities. Modernization theorists typically view these types of middle-class rights activism as precursors to greater political participation and broader demands for stronger civil rights. Zhang cautions, though, that activism by China's middle stratum is directed toward defense of its own right to enjoy a good life. Insofar as it believes that the good life depends on political stability, it will be less likely to participate in broader social struggles aimed at achieving the kind of liberal capitalist ethos and equitable welfare state that Whyte's research suggests it values. Certainly,

[19] Zhang, Li 2010.

as we discuss in Chapter 13, some members of China's middle stratum have become involved in NGO activism in support of the disadvantaged, but there is little evidence of their mobilization into more politically risky collective action to support the claims of the dispossessed. We look at the identities of dispossessed people next.

The dispossessed: laid-off workers and landless villagers

Economic reform has resulted in widespread dispossession among two groups that were ideologically privileged under the Maoist system of class labeling: workers and peasants. The introduction of labor contracts, and the profit-orientation and privatization of state and collective enterprises, combined with the substitution of *danwei*-provided welfare with "user-pays" health and social-insurance schemes, eliminated the cradle-to-grave livelihood guarantees previously enjoyed by the first population, urban workers. Although there is no consensus on how many workers have been retrenched from public sector enterprises since the mid-1980s, estimates put the total somewhere between 30 million and 60 million.[20] Whereas it is the termination of a dependent employment relationship that disadvantages the first group, property expropriation affects the second. Under the impetus of growing market demand for development sites, and fiscal reforms that reduced subnational governments' share of taxes in the mid-1990s, local authorities began to expropriate vast areas of villagers' collectively owned land, to transform it into state-owned land, and to lease it for industrial, residential and commercial uses. By 2004, income from the development of expropriated land generated up to half the revenue of some local authorities. Again, there is no consensus on the size of the population affected, but some scholars calculate that between 60 and 80 million villagers have become landless as a result of expropriation.[21]

So ubiquitous are both these groups today that they are studied as collective categories known by the neologisms *xiagang* (the laid-off) and *shidi nongmin* (landless villagers). When people identify themselves as laid-off or as a landless villager, the terms convey not only a loss of relational status and economic capital, but also an implicit charge that they are casualties of China's modernization process, legislative and policy reforms and corruption. In contrast to the optimism widely expressed by the middle stratum, many laid-off and landless people feel nostalgia for the past, anger about their present situation, and fear for the future.

---

[20] Solinger 2009, p. 43.
[21] Wang, Daoyong 2007, p. 105; Zhang, Dengguo 2007, p. 77.

Stories and songs of material deprivation, blame and alienation are therefore central to the construction of their collective identities, and to the mobilization of these people in protests. As we will discuss in Chapter 13, by the first decade of the 21st century, most large-scale "collective incidents" (*quntixing shijian*) involved precisely these two groups.

LAID-OFF AND LANDLESS PEOPLE'S EXPRESSIONS OF DISCONTENT

Chinese popular culture historically has provided rich vehicles for expressing ridicule, criticism of oppression, and social alienation. As the examples below indicate, laid-off and landless people have been quick to utilize such vehicles to highlight their complaints.

A t-shirt slogan, 1990:

> I don't have the guts to be a smuggler, I don't have the capital to be an entrepreneur, I don't have the cunning to be an official. I mess around; I break my "iron rice bowl"; I am nothing.[22]

The concluding phrase on the T-shirt, "I am nothing", references the song *Nothing to my Name* (*Yi wu suo you*), written and sung by the 1980s rock icon Cui Jian. *Nothing to my Name* was condemned and banned from public performances by the Beijing Party committee, who asked: "How can one of our young people sing about having nothing when he has socialism?" The song became particularly popular among student activists in the Tian'anmen demonstrations of 1989.

Cui continued writing cutting lyrics in the 1990s, as can be seen in this verse from his song *Slackers* (*Hunzi*), 1998:

> No more iron rice bowl, just like my father.
> I don't want everyone fussing over me, like the kids of today.
> We haven't had it rough, haven't had it good;
> So people say we're a generation of uneducated slackers.
> If I had to endure hardship, surely I would cry.
> I could go find a job, but can't lower myself to that level.
> If I talk about anything serious, I always talk around the point,
> But when I do anything serious, I first have to try to save face.[23]

Although landless villagers lacked access to the big audiences available to urban t-shirt printers and Cui, they too found numerous ways to

---

[22] Quoted in Huang, Hao 2001, p. 6.
[23] Cui Jian, *Slackers* from the album "The Power of the Powerless" (*Wu neng de liliang*), quoted in Steen 2000, p. 59.

convey their dissatisfaction publicly, as in this satirical ditty that was being sung in the Zhejiang countryside in 2006:

> In the counties there are development zones,
> In the villages, demolitions and relocated households;
> The subsistence fields of many old folks are enclosed,
> But no prospect of money to support the aged![24]

Yet the collective terms "laid-off" and "landless" mask complex differences among the social and structural identities and attitudes of these people. William Hurst has argued that regional political and economic variations might contribute to these differences. In China's northeastern region, a rust belt where the contraction of state-owned heavy industry has reduced former working-class suburbs to impoverished slums, Hurst found that laid-off workers compared all dimensions of their current lives unfavorably with the past. Many expressed the view that, since economic reforms began, "everything has consistently gotten worse and worse... During the planned economy we were all poor. But we were poor together. We were all proletarians".[25] Others, like the person Mun Young Cho observed berating an official, blamed markets for declining moral and ethical standards: "Are you really serving the people? Truth is, that you do not serve the people. You serve the money!"[26] According to Hurst, such identities and attitudes are less common in the lower Yangzi River Delta, which has a long history of more collective and private banking, manufacturing and commerce and less state-owned industry. Although laid-off workers in the Yangzi River Delta lamented their declining relational status, they felt no hankering for the "egalitarian" ethos of the Maoist era. On the contrary, most believed that living standards and spiritual and social lives had improved. They blamed their situation on their own limited education and lack of competitiveness in labor markets, rather than on the markets or corruption of ethical standards.

Broad regional political–economic variations in people's social and structural identity changes are also evident among the landless. In poorer agricultural areas of central and western China, villagers displaced by large infrastructure projects such as the Three Gorges Dam suffer the greatest deterioration in their political influence, livelihoods and social connections. Where land is taken for residential developments on the outskirts of large cities, there is less evidence of a decline in villagers' relational and economic status. In some of the industrialized, peri-urban villages along the eastern seaboard, landless villagers have even grown

[24] Quoted in Sargeson 2008, p. 657.
[25] Hurst 2009b, p. 123.
[26] Cho 2009, p. 35.

prosperous from sizeable land compensation payments and collective and individual investments in businesses, rental housing and shares. Like members of the middle stratum, these people inhabit expensive homes, spend a great deal on their children's education and have little interaction with the migrants to whom they rent accommodation and whom they employ as cleaners, security guards and factory workers. They also resemble the middle stratum in their capacity to exert considerable political and social influence in local communities.

We should pause to consider what variables might complicate Hurst's argument. The hypothesis that regional political and economic variations explain the social–structural identities and attitudes of the laid-off and landless overlooks individual psychology. The predisposition of individuals toward pessimism or optimism might not correlate with regional or sectoral employment. For example, Guoxin Xing found that laid-off and retirees who had worked in similar state-owned industries and who frequented the same park in their leisure time in Zhengzhou, a city in central China, coalesced into three groups with divergent attitudes.[27] Those in the first group expressed nostalgia for the political, economic and social privileges they (mis)remembered that workers had enjoyed during the Maoist era; those in the second complained about their pensions and medical benefits but were optimistic about market reforms; and those in the third actively blamed Maoist socialism for their present poverty and political and social marginalization.

Self-ascribed identity and attitudes among the laid-off and landless also vary according to age and gender. Irrespective of regional location, because elderly villagers of both sexes and women over the age of 40 have received fewer years of schooling and have less non-agricultural work experience, they are also less successful in creating alternative livelihoods after farmland is expropriated.[28] These people are more likely to experience material deprivation, feelings of disempowerment, and confusion about their social status. Many describe themselves as neither farmers nor urban residents. And, like one 58-year-old Fujian woman whom Sargeson interviewed in 2008, they feel they have no choice but to depend on their family members or the government's payment of the monthly *dibao* (minimum livelihood allowance):

Just speaking of it makes me emotional. We've been farming for generations, endured a lot of hardship. And now the land's gone, I get a benefit of 150 *yuan*[29] each month. People my age can't get any work, even cleaning toilets. You tell me, getting such a pittance, how can we afford food?

[27] Xing 2011, p. 825.
[28] See, for example, Sargeson & Song 2011, pp. 33–5.
[29] At the July 2008 exchange rate, 150 *yuan* was equivalent to US$22.

Conversely, for the majority of young rural people who expect to engage in non-agricultural employment for part or all of their working lives, land-taking represents not the loss of a valued relational status or source of livelihood, but rather an under-compensated transaction that infringes market principles and property law. Having never experienced the privileged class status and welfare guarantees promised to their grandparents' generation, many young people share the middle stratum's expressed preference for a society ordered by a liberal capitalist ethos, secure property rights and a meritocratic system of stratification.

Summary

The shift from class labeling to a focus on social and cultural stratification is symptomatic of China's concurrent transition from an epoch of revolutionary radicalism and Soviet and Maoist economic models to a comparatively stable authoritarian political system and market-based economy. Today, the vast majority of young people in China have little interest in Marx's theory of class relations, and no personal experience of class categorization. Yet, as the foregoing discussion of the self-ascribed identities of middle-class, laid-off and landless people indicates, the concept of social class potentially remains politically potent in the PRC. One of the reasons for its continued potency is that material inequalities between regions and within communities are increasing rapidly. We discuss these increases in the next chapter.

Discussion questions

1. What were the political, economic and social origins of the system of class designation in the Maoist era?
2. What factors are contributing to the intergenerational transmission of social status, and what factors are contributing to intergenerational social status mobility in contemporary Chinese society?
3. Why, and in what ways, have the terms "class" and "stratum" been used ideologically in China since the mid-20th century?

Recommended reading

Gold, Thomas, Hurst, William J, Won, Jaeyoun & Qiang, Li (eds) 2009, *Laid-off Workers in a Workers' State: Unemployment with Chinese Characteristics*. New York: Palgrave Macmillan.
Goodman, David SG (ed.) 2008, *The New Rich in China: Future Rulers, Present Lives*. London: Routledge.

Hanser, Amy 2008, *Service Encounters: Class, Gender and the Market for Social Distinction in Urban China*. Stanford, CA: Stanford University Press.

Li, Cheng (ed.) 2010, *China's Emerging Middle Class: Beyond Economic Transformation*. Washington, DC: Brookings Institution Press.

Mao, Zedong 1979a, "On the correct handling of contradictions among the people", in Mark Selden (ed.) *The People's Republic of China: A Documentary History of Revolutionary Change*. New York: Monthly Review Press, pp. 323–30.

Watson, James L (ed.) 1984, *Class and Social Stratification in Post-Revolution China*. London: Cambridge University Press.

Whyte, Martin King 2010a, *Myth of the Social Volcano: Perceptions of Inequality and Distributive Justice in Contemporary China*. Stanford, CA: Stanford University Press.

Zhang, Li 2010, *In Search of Paradise: Middle-Class Living in a Chinese Metropolis*. Ithaca, NY: Cornell University Press.

11 Regional, Rural–Urban and Within-community Inequalities

It is possible to use many different kinds of indicators to examine changes in regional, rural–urban and within-community inequalities in China. Cultural resources, such as control over knowledge and the ability to influence the values attached to various types of occupation in the public domain, can serve as indicators. In this chapter, though, we focus on material inequalities, including income, wealth and consumption.

Material inequalities are produced by multiple, interacting variables whose significance differs not only over time but also between locations. Much contemporary sociological research focuses on the social and discursive processes through which unequal identities and categories of person are produced, rather than on processes that distribute material resources, goods and services across geographical and economic space. However, the literature on China suggests that the greatest material inequalities are between groups of people defined and differentiated by spatial categorizations. The distribution of material inequalities across space matters for various reasons, not least of which is that people tend to be more tolerant of "inequality at a distance" than of inequality among neighbors. Insofar as growing inequality causes social tension, then, proximate inequality is most likely to produce that tension. Disentangling the spatial components of inequality may therefore better equip us to understand debates about the possible social impacts of changes in inequality.

To this end, in this chapter we present an overview of measures and observations of regional, rural–urban and within-community material inequalities in China. We also review the debate about the sources of these inequalities and about the effectiveness of the welfare system in moderating material inequalities.

Measuring inequality nationwide

Scholars' interpretations of which dimensions of material inequality have changed in China, and where they have changed, are sensitive to a

Regions	Eastern	Northeastern	Central	Western
Provinces	Hebei, Beijing, Tianjin, Shandong, Jiangsu, Shanghai, Zhejiang, Fujian, Guangdong, Hainan	Liaoning, Jilin, Heilongjiang	Shanxi, Anhui, Jiangxi, Henan, Hubei, Hunan	Inner Mongolia, Shaanxi, Gansu, Qinghai, Ningxia, Xinjiang, Tibet, Sichuan, Chongqing, Yunnan, Guizhou, Guangxi
% national population	38.0	8.2	26.8	27.0
% national land area	9.5	8.2	10.7	71.5
% national GDP	53.1	8.6	19.7	18.6
% of the total value of China's exports	87.4	4.0	4.0	4.6

Table 11.1   The composition of China's regions

Source: NBS 2011.

researcher's selection of data and methods of measurement. Changes in the administrative designation of geographical regions in China over time complicate our capacity to compare inequalities. These regional designations are not accurate descriptors of geographical location; rather, they are expressions of how well or how badly different parts of the country are seen to be faring in comparison to an idealized "norm", and thus their eligibility for preferential policies or funding. In the 1950s, China was broadly divided into seven regions: the northeast, north, northwest, central, southwest, south and southeast. Between the 1980s and the 2000s, reporting on regional inequality was based on a division of provinces into three huge regions: east, central and west. There were obvious geographical anomalies in this division. For example, Guangxi, bordering the southeast coast and Vietnam, was classified as part of the western region because of its larger ethnic minority population and lower levels of income compared to other coastal provinces. Since 2007, the National Bureau of Statistics (NBS) has treated the northeastern provinces that were disadvantaged by the contraction of state-owned heavy industries as a fourth region (see Table 11.1).

The ongoing processes of urban expansion and rural-to-urban migration also impede our efforts to track changes in the size of urban and rural inequalities. When government shifts urban boundaries and rezones land use, this radically alters the value of residents' skills and assets, and the roles they play in production, distribution and consumption. As long as cities continue to expand into their hinterlands and absorb the most industrialized, wealthy rural areas, and as long as large cohorts of younger, productive workers continue to flow from poor villages into cities, research will show evidence of material disparities between China's urban and rural areas.

Added to the complications changes in the composition of regions and rural–urban areas produce, researchers who analyze the spatial distribution of material inequalities define income components and populations in different ways. Take urban incomes as an example. Should the value of the state's subsidy of urban residents' food, housing, pensions, health care and education in the 1980s be included as a component of urban income? If so, urban residents' real incomes would be much higher than their nominal incomes. By the same token, although state subsidies to urban residents were rolled back during the 1990s, employer contributions to pensions, health insurance and housing purchases continued to boost the real incomes of urban residents disproportionately, but not so the incomes of rural migrants working in cities. Much of the Chinese data on urban incomes excludes rural migrants' wages, despite the fact that anywhere up to one-third of the people working in a city at any given time might have rural *hukou* (household registration). What happens to estimates of rural–urban income inequality if rural migrants are included in the urban population? On the one hand, migrants generally earn less than urban residents and so their inclusion as urban income earners would reduce estimates of mean urban incomes. On the other hand, excising migrant incomes from the data about rural income also would reduce mean rural incomes, so the ratio of rural to urban incomes might change little. Conversely, the greater the proportion of migrant workers in the population of either rural or urban income earners, the greater will be the within-group income inequality. In addition to these questions of definition, sociologists disagree over whether the unit of analysis should be the household or the individual. If it is the household, gender discrepancies in intra-household incomes will be overlooked; if it is the individual, the extremely rich (who may be too busy to participate in a survey) and the poor (who might be illiterate) are likely to be underrepresented.

To overcome problems in comparing income, some researchers use consumption as an indicator of inequality. Here, too, there are complications, for regional differences in the cost of living significantly affect the purchasing power of a given sum of money. Food prices are high in some

Source	1983	1988	1990	1995	2000	2001	2002	2005	2006	2007	2008	2010
Chen Jiandong et al. 2010	0.25		0.33	0.39	0.40	0.41	0.43		0.44			
Chen Zongsheng, cited in Chen Jiandong et al. 2010				0.36								
Zhao, Shi and Riskin, cited in Chen Jiandong et al. 2010				0.44								
NBS, cited in Fang & Yu 2012					0.41							
World Bank and Development Research Center, State Council, China 2012, pp. 301–2		0.30	0.34			0.44						
Khan & Riskin 2005				0.45			0.45;* 0.44					
Li & Luo 2010, p. 120							0.46;† 0.43					
Yin, Heng 2011, p. 125								West 0.48; Centre 0.41				
Institute of Economics, CASS, cited in Yin, Heng 2011, p. 125			0.38	0.45						0.49		
Zhu & Wang 2012			0.34;† 0.29	0.39;† 0.32	0.41;† 0.34			0.46;† 0.38			0.45;† 0.39	
Mukhopadhaya, Shantakumar & Rao 2011, p. 41											0.50	
Benjamin et al. 2008, p. 729										0.50+		
Chen, Jia 2010												0.47

* adjusted for migrants
† adjusted for prices

Table 11.2 Estimates of China's national Gini coefficient

cities, whereas many rural people consume home-grown produce. Thus, if food costs are factored in, estimates of rural–urban inequalities narrow. Such mundane issues of data selection and methods of measurement can affect not only estimates of the magnitude of regional and rural–urban disparities, but also the identification of trends over time.

The Gini coefficient is one of the most commonly used measures of material inequality. It indicates the extent to which the distribution of income (or consumption) among individuals (or households) within a given population deviates from absolute equality. A Gini coefficient of 0 represents complete equality, whereas a coefficient of 1 implies that one person gets all the measured items and the remainder of the population gets none. Although the Gini coefficient provides a snapshot of the degree to which distribution in a society varies from absolute equality, it does not give any indication of absolute levels of poverty, and so can identify as highly equal a society in which the whole population faces famine. As it usually is based on only one indicator, it also overlooks the variations in inequality caused by the interaction between different income and consumption variables. For this reason, Dwayne Benjamin and colleagues point out, "it is worth reminding ourselves of the limitations associated with summarizing 1 billion people's economic outcomes by any single number".[1]

As Table 11.2 illustrates, because scholars disagree over how to measure income in China, their estimates of China's Gini coefficient also differ. There is, however, no disputing that the trend is in an upward direction. According to most analyses, China's Gini coefficient in the early 1980s was between 0.25 and 0.31, which meant it had one of the lowest levels of overall inequality in the world. By 2008, most analyses indicated that, at somewhere between 0.45 and 0.50, China's Gini coefficient was still lower than in some South American countries such as Brazil (0.55) and Ecuador (0.50), but higher than in its regional neighbors Japan (0.33), Thailand (0.40) and Vietnam (0.35), as well as in other former socialist countries, including Poland (0.34).[2]

Other commonly used measures of material inequality include per-capita Gross Domestic Product (GDP), the distribution of income between population deciles, the percentage of households whose income varies more than 50 percent above or below the national median, and well-being indicators such as the UNDP's Human Development Index (HDI), a composite measure of income, education and health. Like the Gini coefficient, all these measures have shortcomings. Together, though, they confirm that material inequality has indeed grown in China and

---

[1] Benjamin et al. 2008, p. 733.
[2] World Bank 2012; Organization for Economic Cooperation and Development 2012.

provide insights into how the magnitude and trajectories of inequality differ between regions, between urban and rural areas, and within communities.

Inter-regional inequality

All regions in China have experienced rapid economic growth. Yet the disparities between the rich eastern region and the interior remain. In 2010, for example, the total GDP of two of China's wealthiest eastern provinces, Shanghai and Jiangsu, were roughly equivalent to the GDP of Finland and Switzerland, respectively. The GDP comparisons between Shanghai and Jiangsu and China's western provinces, however, can best be described in multiples: Jiangsu's total GDP was 78 times greater than the total GDP of Tibet, while Shanghai's per-capita GDP was around seven times that of the mountainous southwestern province of Guizhou.[3] As critics point out, the fact that a region has a high GDP per capita does not mean that all the people there enjoy a high living standard. Nevertheless, in terms of income, consumption and access to public goods and services, residents of China's eastern region clearly are much better off than those who live in the west. One indicator of this is that, at 0.90–0.94, the HDI of Shanghai is 30 percent higher than that of Tibet (0.60–0.64).[4]

To get a sense of how these inter-regional disparities translate into unequal living standards and life chances for individuals, compare two hypothetical male children who, according to aggregate statistical data, are "typical" of the regions in which they live: Wang, who comes from southern Jiangsu, and Hu, who comes from southern Guizhou. Irrespective of whether he lives in a rural or urban community in his region, we can predict that little Wang will be born in a well-equipped hospital, to a family with substantial bank savings and a comfortable house not only with piped water and electricity, but also a home computer and an internet connection. Members of his extended family and social network will have travelled overseas. Wang will study at senior secondary school or a vocational college and might attend university, before finding a job or starting a business in which he will earn around double the average national per capita income. Like his parents, during his lifetime Wang will accumulate savings, and a pension fund and medical insurance that are sufficient to protect him from poverty. Indeed, according to

---

[3] "Comparing Chinese provinces with countries. All the parities in China. Which countries match the GDP, population and exports of Chinese provinces?" 2010. The gaps remained similar in 2011. See Gu 2012.

[4] UNDP 2010, p. 12.

the absolute measure that sets China's national poverty line, no household in Wang's neighborhood is ever likely to be classified as poor. If,
against the odds, they were to fall into poverty, they would receive a
monthly *dibao* (minimum livelihood allowance) payment from the local
government that would be at least 25 percent higher than that received
by a Guizhou household that also was classified as poor.

Now let's look at Hu, from Guizhou. In this area, only if Hu's family
were to live in a city could we confidently predict that they would have
piped water in their home, and that someone in their neighborhood would
own a home computer with internet access. Once little Hu completes
his nine years of compulsory schooling, he is likely to join many of his
classmates in migrating to find work in an eastern city. Yet even with a
university education, if Hu stays to work in Guizhou there is little chance
that he will earn as high an income as Wang will in his region. So, as Hu
ages, he will find it harder to provide for his elderly, pensionless parents
and any children of his own, much less save enough for a comfortable
retirement. Around five percent of the households in his vicinity will fare
even worse and fall into absolute poverty at some point in Hu's lifetime.
On the basis of where he lives, we also can predict that unfortunately
Hu will die at least five years earlier than Wang. Clearly, inter-regional
disparities matter a great deal to people's lives. Intra-regional inequalities,
however, matter even more.[5]

Rural–urban inequalities

Despite dramatic growth in rural incomes and a fall in the incidence
of absolute poverty in China since the 1970s, there appears to have
been an even more dramatic growth in inequalities between rural and
urban areas. Figure 11.1 presents crude data from the NBS, showing
that China's urban to rural income ratio increased steadily from 1.8:1 in
1985 to 3.22:1 in 2010. The data is not adjusted for non-wage income or
regional price differentials, and does not include migrants. Economists
who have attempted to incorporate these items into their analyses have
drawn divergent and subtle conclusions about changes in the rural–urban
income ratio. For example, after including migrants in their urban income
data set, Azizur Khan and Carl Riskin argue that although, by international standards, the rural–urban gap in China between 1995 and
2002 was exceptionally large, it stabilized during this period.[6] However,
in research on the same period that took into account not only migrant

[5] Yin 2011, p. 131.
[6] Khan & Riskin 2005.

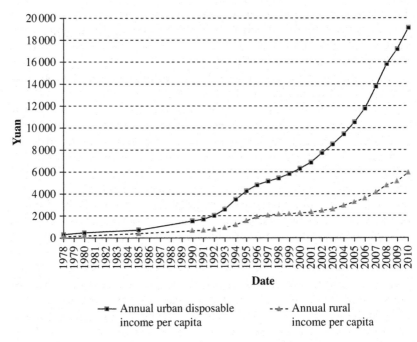

Figure 11.1 Urban and rural annual incomes per capita (unadjusted), 1978–2010.
Source: NBS 2011.

incomes but also the imputed rental value of owner-occupied housing, Björn Gustaffson and colleagues concluded that the contribution of the rural–urban gap to overall inequality grew from 41 percent in 1995 to 46 percent in 2002, while the relative contribution made by inter-regional inequalities, particularly between urban populations, decreased.[7]After adjusting for cost of living differentials as well as migrant and housing-related incomes, Terry Sicular and her colleagues lent support to Khan and Riskin's conclusions: although the rural–urban gap in China was larger than in other developing countries, it contributed only slightly to the growth in overall national inequality between 1995 and 2002.[8]

Although scholars dispute the magnitude and direction of temporal trends, none doubt that the rural–urban income gap produces significant differentials in people's standards of living. Compared to households in which all members are registered as rural residents, for example, there is a far lower probability that any household in which someone has an

[7] Gustaffson, Li & Sicular 2008b, p. 23.
[8] Sicular et al. 2010; Sicular et al. 2007.

urban *hukou* will be absolutely poor.[9] Rural people also fall behind on the commonly used indicators of consumption and well-being.

INDICATORS OF A RURAL–URBAN GAP IN CONSUMPTION AND WELL-BEING

The "Engels coefficient"

Between 1980 and 2010, the percentage of average per capita household income spent on food, known as the "Engels coefficient", declined from 56.9 in urban areas and 61.8 in rural areas to 35.7 in urban areas and 41.1 in rural areas.[10] Although both populations enjoyed increases in the proportion of their surplus income, the gap between them grew. This meant that, in comparison to urban households, rural households had a smaller proportion of a lower net income left over to spend on other essentials such as housing, clothing, health and education, much less to invest in staging the life-cycle rituals, gift-giving and banqueting activities that help to consolidate kinship bonds, forge business deals and facilitate upward social mobility.

Expenditure on education, culture and recreational services

In comparison to rural residents, urban people spent four times more on education, culture and recreational services in 2010. This not only perpetuated inequalities in income-earning potential, but also produced new sources of inequality. For example, 71.16 out of 100 households in urban areas and only 10.37 out of 100 households in rural areas owned a computer.[11] Differentials in computer ownership exacerbate rural–urban differences in access to information, and opportunities to network socially and influence public opinion and policy.

The distribution and affordability of health care

In 2010, the number of hospital beds per thousand people was 5.33 in urban areas and 2.44 in rural areas, while urban people spent 2.6 times more than rural people on health care and medical expenses. As rural medical insurance schemes are under-resourced, rural residents pay high out-of-pocket expenses for medical care. As a village woman interviewed by Sally Sargeson in 2008 explained: "Our medical insurance costs only 20 *yuan* each per year, but it doesn't refund much. The

---

[9] Glauben et al. 2012, p. 790.
[10] NBS 2011.
[11] NBS 2011.

last time my mother-in-law went under the knife, we spent more than 30 000 *yuan* and only got 4000 back." Gaps in health expenditure are reflected in disparities in infant mortality rates, which in 2010 stood at 0.58 percent in urban areas and 1.61 percent in rural areas.[12] Disparities also are apparent in medical treatment of the chronically ill. In 2008, the National Household Health Survey found that the early self-discharge rate among chronically ill patients was 11.5 percent in urban areas and 27.5 percent in rural areas.[13] As poor health reduces income-generating capacity, the rural–urban gap in health care reproduces other rural–urban material inequalities.

Rural–urban disparities across the nation are very high, but recent research shows regional variations in the direction of changes in rural–urban inequality. According to research by Sicular and her colleagues, summarized in Table 11.3, between the 1990s and 2000s, rural–urban inequalities rose in central and western China, but declined in the east. In the northeast of one of China's richest coastal provinces, Zhejiang, because rural incomes grew more rapidly than urban incomes for several years in a row, by 2012 there was relatively little difference between the median incomes of urban and rural-registered populations. Instead, the single greatest contributor to inequality in Zhejiang was within-community inequality.

	Unadjusted		Adjusted to price differentials	
	1995	2002	1995	2002
Urban–rural income ratio				
East	2.99	2.88	2.05	1.89
Center	2.68	3.02	1.95	2.23
West	4.25	4.32	3.33	3.49
% contribution to ratio of				
nationwide inequality	41.00	45.00		
East			23.00	22.00
Center			28.00	36.00
West			51.00	53.00

Table 11.3 Regional variations in the urban to rural income ratio and contributions of the urban to rural ratio to overall inequality

Source: Adapted from Sicular et al. 2010, pp. 94–5.

[12] NBS 2011.
[13] Jian et al. 2010.

Within-community inequality

In 2004, Martin King Whyte found that more than 60 percent of the 3267 Chinese people he surveyed agreed with this statement: "In the last few years, the rich people in our society have gotten richer, while the poor people have gotten poorer."[14] Statistical data, however, tells a slightly different story. Certainly, the rich got richer, yet most of the poor also earned more. Why, then, were so many convinced that poor people were getting poorer?

Two analytically distinct factors combine to produce this common misconception. First, according to Dwayne Benjamin and his colleagues, "at least half, and perhaps as much as two-thirds, of estimated inequality is driven by income differences between 'neighbors' as opposed to income differences based on location".[15] Second, within communities, an increasing incidence of relative poverty – that is, the number of people earning less than half the local median income – leads to stronger feelings of deprivation. Certain forms of conservative political discourse trivialize concern with relative increases in wealth as an expression of envy, or in the Chinese vernacular, *hong yan bing* (red-eye disease). Yet in a market economy, beyond the threshold of absolute poverty, changes in relative wealth might matter just as much to people's sense of well-being as changes in absolute wealth. In lived experience, if one gains in absolute wealth but loses in relative wealth, one may be able to buy more goods for which supply is elastic, but be able to afford fewer goods for which supply is fixed. For the latter category, prices will rise as others who are comparatively richer compete for these goods. So, for example, the price of a house with the best views in an area will become less affordable as one's relative wealth declines. Also, people's sensitivity to relative poverty is most acute when they compare themselves to their own wealthy neighbors rather than the wealthy residents of another city, province or country. The rise in both within-community inequalities and the incidence of relative poverty therefore pose significant challenges for Chinese policy makers, as they are likely to generate social dissatisfaction.

The ratio of per-capita incomes of the richest and poorest deciles among China's urban population grew from 2.9:1 in 1985, to 8.6:1 in 2010.[16] In the mid-1980s, poverty affected less than one percent of the urban population, and that one percent primarily was made up of the "three withouts" (*sanwu*): those who were without family and sick, disabled or elderly. Following a wave of enterprise reforms, retrenchment

---

[14] Whyte 2010a, p. 44.
[15] Benjamin et al. 2008, p. 730.
[16] NBS 2011.

	Yishala	Renhe	Zhuangshang
Mean household per-capita cash income 1988 2006	435 2569* (excl. Party secretary)	1107 5031	462 2904
Gini coefficient 1988 2006	0.31 0.41* (excl. Party secretary); 0.79† (incl. Party secretary)	0.41 0.56	0.24 0.52

* Excluding Party secretary
† Including Party secretary

Table 11.4   Intra-village income disparities and Gini coefficients, 1988 and 2006

Source: Adapted from Zhou, Han & Harrell 2008, pp. 522, 525.

and the withdrawal of state subsidies, the incidence of absolute poverty in urban areas climbed in the 1990s to between 5 and 15 percent. Although some studies suggest it subsequently dropped to around 2 percent at the turn of the century,[17] Benjamin and his colleagues found that the living standards of those who were poor deteriorated.[18] The poor also comprised a different mix of groups of people, as laid-off urban workers and unemployed migrants came to outnumber the "three withouts". There was also a sustained growth in the incidence of relative poverty, with a rise from just over three percent in 1988 to more than 10 percent in 2002.[19] There was a growing mismatch between those who experienced the most severe poverty, and those who felt the strongest sense of relative deprivation. Rural migrants, suffering institutional discrimination that limited their access to welfare benefits, experienced the worst poverty. Yet it was the urban unemployed who felt most deprived, compared both to their own former status as employed people and to the lives of their neighbors.[20]

Rural communities have also witnessed widening inequalities. Insights into the scale of these disparities are offered in Zhou Yingying, Hou Han and Stevan Harrell's longitudinal study of three sites in the western province of Sichuan. As Table 11.4 shows, between 1988 and 2006 both mean household income and the Gini coefficient grew in all three villages. These trends were partly driven by the fact that some households diversified into off-farm work and small business, while others remained in the less profitable agricultural sector. Thus, egalitarian distribution of

[17] He et al. 2008.
[18] Benjamin et al. 2008, p. 750.
[19] Appleton, Song & Xia 2010.
[20] He et al. 2008, p. 125.

collectively-owned land among rural households no longer functioned to moderate intra-village income inequality. But differences in political power and the opportunity to accumulate assets accounted for most of the increase in inequality. In Yishala, for example, the village Party secretary had taken advantage of his positional power to approve contracts and business licenses and sell collective assets to members of his own family. Zhou, Han and Harrell write that these activities "gave the Yishala secretary's family a reported income of over 2 million *Yuan* in 2006, more than 20 times the total income of the second richest family surveyed, and 100 times the village mean of total household income".[21] They note, though, that the *real* income of the secretary's family might have been closer to 4 million *yuan*, or 200 times the village mean. While the average income of ordinary Yishala households had increased, compared to the Party secretary's family they had been left far behind.

Explaining spatial inequalities

There has been a great deal of research on the drivers of rising spatial dimensions of inequality in China. This literature most commonly explains these drivers through analysis of the roles played by geography, state policy and the market economy, and household and individual characteristics. Yet, as we will illustrate now, the interactions between these broad determinants are complex and highly contentious.

The argument that geography is a key contributor to regional inequality in China has recently been revived in academic debates, perhaps because policies premised on alternative explanations have had limited impact on entrenched poverty. Which geographical factors are found to be associated with greater inequality? Characteristically, poorer provinces and counties are located at relatively high altitudes, and have low rainfall and poor soils. Even in the rich coastal provinces, poorer counties are clustered in mountainous areas. Data from China's NBS shows that although mountainous areas accommodated 23 percent of the rural population in 2003, they accounted for 36 percent of the lowest income decile.[22] Conversely, affluent areas, including those in western China, are mostly located in river valleys where they have higher rainfall, more fertile soils and better access to transport, communications and markets.

Of course, physical geography's disequalizing effects have been consolidated by human settlement, because political power, economic infrastructure and commerce have been concentrated in the central and eastern lowlands. We also can disentangle the effects of altitude and climate from

---

[21] Zhou, Han & Harrell 2008, p. 524.
[22] Sanders, Chen & Cao 2007, p. 21.

the effects of some other variables. For example, a high percentage of the people living in China's mountainous west are members of minority ethnic groups. And, as we mentioned in Chapter 7, after accounting for location, human capital and occupation, there still is a residual income gap between the members of some non-Han groups and Han populations, which can be attributed to ethnic discrimination. This suggests, on the one hand, that the ethnic diversity of the population in the west might be exacerbating the dis-equalizing effects of high elevation and low rainfall and, on the other, as China's leaders fear, future temperatures rise and precipitation declines, the geographical features of the western region could reinforce ethnic disadvantage, fanning conflict.

The state's economic policies also have had repercussions on regional and rural–urban disparities, and these repercussions sometimes have been intensified by the growth of markets. Under Mao, state investment was primarily directed toward state-owned heavy industries in northeastern, central and western cities. The coastal region, which China's cold war analysts considered vulnerable to attack, was forced to rely more heavily on local funding to build smaller light enterprises. In the post-Mao era, the contraction of state enterprises therefore disproportionately affected China's northeast and interior. The growth of the non-state sector was slower in the west, and this limited job opportunities for urban school-leavers and rural workers. In the eastern region, in contrast, governments established Special Economic Zones (SEZs) and created preferential policies and tax concessions to attract foreign capital and technology. Much of the story of the coastal manufacturing boom originates in the fact that villagers pooled collective income and created township and village enterprises (TVEs) when agricultural markets were freed up and prices rose in the 1980s. All along the seaboard, clusters of locally capitalized TVEs competed with businesses in the SEZs for export markets, migrant workers and investments from abroad. By the early 2000s, the eastern region had received more than 80 percent of total foreign direct investment, and produced more than 70 percent of exports. Rural incomes there also skyrocketed, as wages, business profits and share dividends comprised an increasing share of household earnings. Thus, the transformation of China's eastern region into "the world's factory" contributed not just to growing regional inequalities and income disparities among migrant and non-migrating rural households in the west, but also to declining rural–urban disparities in the east.

State institutions, most obviously restrictions on rural labor mobility imposed by the *hukou* system, have reproduced other inequalities between urban and rural populations. Two other institutions influenced this. First, China's fiscal system consistently has increased the rural–urban gap. Compared to higher-waged urban households, rural households have not only paid proportionately more tax but also received less expenditure. Although the urban fiscal bias declined somewhat in the 2000s after the elimination of the agricultural tax and increased government spending on rural infrastructure, the tax system still exacerbates rural–urban inequalities. Since the tax system was decentralized in 1994, it also has been influencing regional disparities. Because rich eastern provinces garner high revenues, they can fund far more generous public goods and services than the poorer provinces of the west.

Second, national legislation differentiates between the types of property rights held by urban and rural people. These differentials matter, because disparities in wealth contribute more to the intergenerational reproduction of inequality than do disparities in income. In a market economy, land and housing can earn rental income, appreciate in value over time, and be used as collateral to secure loans for further investment. Wealth can produce future wealth. The creation of markets in urban land leases, and the privatization of urban public housing stock in China in the late 1980s thus delivered a windfall into the hands of urban enterprises and state-sector employees. In the countryside, however, national laws and local practices prohibit villagers in most provinces from leasing collectively owned rural land for commercial development; using land and housing as mortgage collateral; or selling rural housing. Compared to urban people, therefore, most rural people have less capacity to capitalize on their assets. Only after rural land is expropriated by governments can it be transferred to markets. As we noted in Chapter 10, this has led to widespread land expropriation and the displacement of entire villages by revenue-hungry governments. The most notable exception to this situation is Guangdong, where provincial regulations allow village collectives to participate directly in land lease markets. Pointing to the fact that Guangdong's Pearl River Delta is now home to some of China's most prosperous rural communities, some Chinese economists have recommended that villagers be allowed to lease rural land for development. In the opposite camp are those who view rural collective land institutions and access to farmland as an essential safety net for vast numbers of uninsured villagers and migrant workers.

Finally, in China as in other countries, there is an age dimension to spatial distributions of inequality. Higher household-dependency ratios typically correlate with lower per-capita incomes and less asset acquisition and investment. As rural households have higher birth rates, this contributes to rural–urban inequality. It is in the situation of the elderly, though, that the most serious age-related disparities appear. Among both urban and rural populations, per-capita income tends to increase between the ages of 20 and 60 and then declines. But in the countryside, especially in poor counties that cannot afford to fund generous pensions, the income of the elderly deteriorates precipitously. These outcomes raise important questions about the role of social welfare in exacerbating or ameliorating the spatial distribution of material inequalities in China.

Social welfare: progressive or regressive?

In the 20th and 21st centuries, states have attempted to ameliorate inequalities and promote inclusive citizenship through the provision of social welfare. Has welfare in China served similarly progressive ends? Like other late-industrializing East Asian societies, in the second half of the 20th century China established a more comprehensive welfare regime than anything found in the United States or northern Europe at a comparable stage of their economic development. However, under Mao – and in contrast to Japan, Korea and Taiwan, where governments focused on maximizing employment, and welfare was left to families, commercial insurers and charitable organizations – Chinese workers were the owners and masters of the means of production and so, were entitled to benefits from their *danwei*. Another distinctive feature of the Maoist welfare system was that it was bifurcated: the urban workforce enjoyed a very high level of state-subsidized goods, benefits and services, while rural people relied almost entirely on their family and village (see chapters 3 and 4).

That system began to crumble in the context of market reforms. Against a backdrop of declining state-sector employment, growing geographical mobility and an aging population, the state moved to reconstruct China's social welfare system. The aim was to create a welfare mix that would promote economic growth, provide a "safety net" for those who were excluded, left behind or directly harmed by market reforms, and promote social harmony and political order. Government-subsidized schemes, which comprise the main component of this mix, now fall into three main types: insurance against various forms of "social risk", social assistance programs that supplement the incomes of the poor, and poverty-alleviation programs intended to improve the income-earning capacity of poor communities.

Since the mid-1980s, basic unemployment, health insurance and old-age-pension schemes have been launched in both urban and rural areas. Co-contributions from governments, employers and individual participants are pooled at city and county levels. Although the urban and rural basic medical insurance and pension schemes are now comparatively comprehensive, China's other social insurance schemes have very limited coverage and impact. Less than half the urban-registered (non-agricultural) workforce, and very few rural workers, have unemployment insurance, and in rural areas old-age-pension schemes provide pensions that are barely adequate for subsistence.

The social-assistance programs rely primarily on government funding. Because of China's decentralized fiscal system, the scope and level of social assistance available in each government jurisdiction roughly correlate with the overall prosperity of the population. Hence, in rich communities on the coast the basic needs of the poor are met, but in poor jurisdictions even destitute people might miss out. The *dibao* is the widest reaching social assistance program. Introduced in cities in the 1990s and rolled out into the countryside in the 2000s, by 2008, *dibao* was paid to 60 million people nationwide. *Dibao* provides discretionary cash payments to households whose income and assets fall below locally determined thresholds. Nevertheless, coverage among the poor is extremely low, and the average per-capita monthly payment nationwide is less than 20 percent of the average local income. Rural recipients receive only half the amount paid to their urban counterparts. Most recipients would have difficulty surviving without *dibao* payments. However, critics of the program have highlighted its "perverse outcomes". Like social assistance or "dole" programs in other countries, it is susceptible to fraud and embezzlement. Applicants are subjected to invasive investigations and the humiliation of having their circumstances publicized on local notice boards. As recipients who find casual work or invest in equipment or training risk exclusion, the program might discourage them from trying to improve their situation, leading to the reproduction of an unemployed underclass. And, finally, receipt of payments from government might also induce political and social passivity.[23]

Since the 1990s, the state – recognizing that the alleviation of poverty in remote, poor communities requires much more than supportive economic policies – has directly funded subsidized loans for enterprises and households, and public infrastructure and work-for-food projects in designated "poor" counties and communities. In 2009, this designation was accorded to 148 000 villages in China.[24] The programs have been criticized because designations have been politically manipulated and funds embezzled and, as with the other welfare programs, coverage is inadequate. For example, almost half the rural poor lived outside "poor" villages. Nevertheless, without the poverty-alleviation programs, economic growth in the designated areas might have been even lower.

Have these three welfare programs increased or decreased the spatial distribution of material inequalities? In a recent study using nationwide data, Qin Gao concluded that between 1988 and 2002 the distribution of welfare was progressive (inequality reducing) in urban areas, but

---

[23] Solinger 2008.
[24] Li & Liu 2010, p. 316.

regressive (inequality enhancing) in rural areas.[25] Not only did few rural residents have access to any assistance but, because of nepotism and corruption, welfare largely accrued to the rich. Paradoxically, during that period social welfare actually increased rural–urban and within-village inequalities. Since 2002, although the expansion of rural coverage and improved targeting has reduced the socially regressive impact of welfare, social welfare still has a disequalizing effect overall. Undoubtedly, future efforts to make welfare less regressive will be resisted by those who, to this point, have benefited from the biases in the program. But the outcomes of those types of reform also will have important implications for the spatial distribution of material inequalities and for people's changing views on distributive justice as China modernizes.

Summary

Interpretations of the magnitude of material inequality in China, and of its trends, are highly sensitive to variations in data selection and methods of measurement. Dramatic growth in China's economy has improved the standard of living in most urban and many rural households. Yet, at the same time, material inequalities have grown to the point where China now has a less equal society than many comparable postsocialist and developing countries. In different locations around China, these inequalities are diverging, and their different trajectories challenge us to look in greater detail at the way geography, economic and social welfare policies, institutions, expanding markets, and household and individual characteristics interact to influence inequality across space. They also raise important questions about how variations in the magnitude of, and trends in, inequality might influence different Chinese social groups' perceptions of, and possible responses to, distributive justice.

Discussion questions

1. What major factors contribute to the spatial distribution of material inequalities across China? How have interactions between these factors changed since the 1980s?

2. Are increases in the incidence of relative poverty and in people's feelings of relative deprivation both inevitable consequences of economic growth in China?

[25] Gao 2010.

3. Why is it that the poorest people in China's cities do not consistently feel most deprived? Which social group do you think is likely to most strongly feel relatively deprived in the community in which you live?
4. How would you go about measuring temporal trends in material inequalities in different areas of China? What challenges might you encounter in your research?

Recommended reading

Brandt, Loren & Rawski, Thomas (eds) 2008, *China's Great Economic Transformation*. New York: Cambridge University Press.

Davis, Deborah S & Wang Feng (eds) 2009, *Creating Wealth and Poverty in Postsocialist China*. Stanford, CA: Stanford University Press.

Gustaffson, Björn, Li, Shi & Sicular, Terry (eds) 2008a, *Inequality and Public Policy in China*. New York: Cambridge University Press.

Khan, Azizur Rahman & Carl Riskin 2005, "China's household income and its distribution, 1995 and 2002", *The China Quarterly*, no. 182, pp. 356–84.

Shue, Vivienne & Christine Wong (eds) 2007, *Paying for Progress in China: Public Finance, Human Welfare and Changing Patterns of Inequality*. London: Routledge.

Sun, Wanning & Guo, Yingjie (eds) 2013, *Unequal China: The Political Economy and Cultural Politics of Inequality*. London: Routledge.

Whyte, Martin King (ed.) 2010b, *One Country, Two Societies: Rural–Urban Inequality in Contemporary China*. Cambridge, MA: Harvard University Press.

12 The "Woman Question" and Gender Inequalities

In the late 19th and early 20th centuries, debates over what was often referred to as the "woman question" preoccupied the educated social elite in China, just as it did in Europe, Britain and the United States. Leading Chinese intellectuals and political activists viewed patriarchal norms that subordinated women as the epitome of the "backwardness" and degeneration of Confucian social institutions. These (mainly male) reformers and revolutionaries saw women – uneducated, hobbled by foot-binding and subordinated by the "three obediences" (to their father, husband and sons) – both as a metaphor for the weakness of China and the Chinese state, and as literally holding the country back from becoming modern and strong on the world stage. Women were supposedly unproductive, unable to participate in public affairs and poorly equipped to raise their children into modern citizens. Like modernizing elites elsewhere across the world, the reformers viewed the liberation of women and the achievement of gender equality as necessary for national strength and self-determination, modernity and social progress.

In the first half of this chapter, we discuss the lasting impact that the woman question has had in the 20th and 21st centuries on Chinese state policies regarding gender inequalities, and we assess the social consequences of those policies. We also look at the ways in which scholars have approached the topic of gender inequality in China. In the second half, we examine some of the main institutions through which gender inequalities continue to be reproduced today, despite decades of state policies and legislation aimed at overcoming them.

The woman question and state approaches to gender inequality

The woman question put gender equality on the agenda of all revolutionary parties and of both the Nationalist and Communist governments of the 20th century. The CCP, in particular, enshrined gender equality as a core element of its rhetoric, policies and legislation. It also established a "mass organization",[1] the All China Women's Federation (referred to in this chapter as "the Women's Federation"), with an impressive network of representatives at all levels of government, charged with "woman-work", which involved the promotion of women's interests and the mobilization of women for the revolution and national development. However, the CCP's approach to woman-work was limited, precisely because it conceived of gender as a question about women – and for women – rather than as a social issue. One outcome was the marginalization of gender as a low-status set of concerns, isolated from the Party's main work; a marginalization that has persisted to this day, despite efforts since the mid-1990s to address gender as a "mainstream" concern in all government policies and plans.

In addition, while numerous state officials, especially within the Women's Federation, have been passionately dedicated to achieving women's liberation, their efforts have commonly been co-opted for, or subsumed by, the state's other goals. Indeed, state leaders have at times sought to defer or quash active efforts to liberate women, seeing such efforts as potentially diverting attention from more urgent tasks of nation-building, as undermining male support for the revolution, or as threatening the unity of the working class and the cause of class struggle. It was for the last reason, for example, that the Women's Federation was disbanded in the late 1960s, and not fully re-established until 1978.

In the early post-Mao period, the Women's Federation struggled to gain recognition both from state leaders, who generally prioritized market-oriented growth over issues of equity, and from women, who saw the Women's Federation as ineffectual, and as irrelevant to their lives. However, members of the Women's Federation were successful in lobbying for a Women's Rights Protection Law, promulgated in 1992 (and revised in 2005), and Beijing's hosting of the Fourth United Nations World Conference on Women in 1995 greatly boosted the women's movement as well. In the lead-up to that conference, several NGOs for women's rights were set up. These groups and the Women's Federation received funding from overseas development agencies for a number of small-scale development projects that focused on women. The state's introduction of a first Development Plan for Women for the period 2001–10, and a second for 2011–20, gave their activities a further boost. It is noteworthy, though, that into the 2010s, the state and Women's Federation took a highly utilitarian approach to the woman question, especially

---

[1] Mass organizations, including the All China Federation of Trade Unions (ACFTU) and the Youth League, as well as the Women's Federation, are closely linked to the state. In fact, as we note in Chapter 5 with respect to the ACFTU, some scholars consider them part of the state. Certainly, their leadership, national policies and funding come from the state. Officially, however, they are separate from the CCP and the government.

in rural areas, where they focused primarily on improving women's *suzhi* ("quality"), for example through training classes, so that they could better contribute to economic development. As Tamara Jacka and Sally Sargeson have written, the Women's Federation "moved away from remaking the structures, institutions and norms that produce gender inequalities in rural economic participation, towards remaking rural women".[2]

The woman question and scholarship on gender inequality

As Gail Hershatter notes, the framing of the woman question in early modern China shaped not only the way in which its political leaders addressed gender issues but also the questions that scholars have raised, and the answers they have formulated, about gender relations in modern and contemporary China.[3] This was particularly noticeable in the first western feminist studies of contemporary China, written in the late 1970s and early 1980s. For one thing, these studies focused on women and, by and large, they accorded with Chinese modernizers' temporal framing of the woman question. In other words, they reproduced a narrative in which Chinese women progressed from a state of subjugation in the pre-modern period toward liberation in modern times. These studies understood the state to be the driver of that progression, and their dominant questions were about the extent to which state-led socialist revolution and policies had liberated women from traditional patriarchal constraints.

Many of the western feminist scholars of the time looked to Maoist China as an example of a state that could achieve a form of modernity superior to that of the capitalist west. On the whole, though, they were disappointed, especially with progress in the liberation of rural women. They offered two main explanations for this lack of progress. First, they said, state leaders' efforts at implementing marriage reform had stalled in the 1950s and, consequently, some aspects of gender equality – especially equal rights between women and men to control over property – were never fully realized in rural areas. Second, they argued, the state's adoption of Friedrich Engels' emphasis on increasing women's involvement in paid, public production as the key to their liberation failed to overcome gender inequalities in work, let alone other aspects of everyday life.

Between the 1940s and 1970s, state leaders' emphasis on increasing women's participation in the paid workforce waxed and waned, as

---

[2] Jacka & Sargeson 2011b, p. 9.
[3] The following section draws on Hershatter 2007.

their perception of political and economic needs and pressures changed. All the same, official mobilization campaigns, combined with economic imperatives, led to marked increases in women's involvement in paid work so that, by the end of the 1970s, most women of working age were in employment. However, in the paid workforce, and despite state propaganda promoting the notion that "what men can do, women can do too", women were concentrated in trades, occupations and jobs considered either less skilled or less physically demanding than the work that men did, and paid at lower rates. At the same time, with the exception of the establishment of childcare services, and short-lived efforts during the Great Leap Forward to set up communal dining halls, little effort was made by the state to change the assumption that domestic work and the care of children were the responsibility of individual women (not men) in the home. Nor, however, was there much recognition given to the contribution that women made to society through their domestic work and childcare.

While feminist scholars of the 1970s were disappointed with the lack of progress toward gender equality during the Maoist period, those writing in the 1980s were generally no more optimistic about the effects of regime change and the introduction of market-oriented economic reforms that had taken place in the late 1970s and early 1980s. They were concerned that the new leadership rejected the Maoist notion that "what men can do, women can do too", reinforcing instead notions of sexual difference and of conservative models of women as "good wives and mothers" as well as sexual objects. The scholars also worried that the state, having given only secondary priority to overcoming patriarchal family constraints on women, appeared now to be withdrawing from the issues altogether. At the same time, they saw signs that privatization and marketization of the economy and the new drive for economic efficiency and profit were increasing inequalities in employment opportunities and incomes, in much the same way as in the capitalist west. In 1983, their concerns were echoed by Kang Keqing, who at the time was the leader of the newly resurrected Women's Federation. Kang claimed:

The feudal idea of regarding men as superior to women has reappeared, along with other prejudices... What is most intolerable is that some ugly things which had been eliminated since the founding of new China have recurred. Crimes such as female infanticide, abuse of women, maltreatment of mothers who give birth to girl babies and abduction and persecution of women and children have been reported from time to time.[4]

[4] Kang 1983, quoted in Wolf, Margery 1985, p. 262.

Some sociologists and economists countered pessimism about market reforms, hypothesizing that, in a freer market economy, enterprise managers driven by the profit motive would be more "rational" in their employment of labor, and less likely to discriminate on gender grounds. Some survey-based studies lent support to this hypothesis, showing that through the 1980s there was no increase in gender inequality in the urban workforce and, indeed, there were some signs of a decrease. But in later years, the prevailing picture grew increasingly gloomy, with several studies indicating serious increases in gender wage differentials in the urban workforce in the last decade of the 20th century and the first decade of the 21st (we will come back to two of these studies later in this chapter). Other reports bore out Kang Keqing's claim about serious forms of discrimination and the abuse of women, including abduction and trafficking (again, we will return to these issues shortly).

Despite this, very few studies have portrayed Maoist policies as having been more effective overall in achieving gender equality than the policies of the post-Mao period. For one thing, the lack of reliable data about gender inequalities before the 1980s has made any such broad comparison extremely difficult. However, most scholars believe that the gains in gender equality made during the Maoist period were considerably less impressive than Maoist propaganda suggested. Aside from this, in the late 1990s, a shift occurred in the questions that scholars asked about gender inequalities and the framing of their findings on the topic. Previously, the main questions being asked were: "To what extent did the socialist revolutionary state liberate women?" and "What is happening to women's liberation and gender equality with the retreat of the state and a move toward capitalism in China?" Often, these questions were shadowed (implicitly and occasionally explicitly) by more general questions: "Does market transition lead to a reduction or an increase in social inequalities?" and "Which is more conducive to gender equality – capitalism or socialism?" Since the late 1990s, however, most scholars have come to the conclusion that trends in inequalities of all kinds are far too complex and multifaceted to be understood solely in terms of market transition, let alone "socialism" or "capitalism" in themselves.

One of the factors undermining the utility of the "impact of market transition on gender inequalities" framework is that different countries have taken varying approaches to "market transition", with Eastern European countries, Vietnam and China adopting quite different sets of political and economic policies. At the same time, in China, some very different trends have emerged in different kinds of gender inequalities (illustrated in the text box below).

CONTRASTING TRENDS IN GENDER INEQUALITY

Education

Improvements in basic education for girls were one of the success stories of the Maoist era and, since then, China has made further progress in overcoming gender inequalities in this area. In 2000, the average number of years of schooling among women aged 18–64 was 6.1 years, 1.5 years fewer than men. By 2010, this had increased to 8.8 years, just 0.3 years fewer than men.[5]

Sex ratios

China's sex ratio at birth increased at an alarming rate between the 1980s and the 2010s. Normally, between 105 and 107 boys are born for every 100 girls. According to census figures, however, the Chinese sex ratio at birth was 116.86 in 2000, and reached 118.06 by 2010.[6] As we discussed in Chapter 1, the main reason for such skewed sex ratios is that, in rural areas, son-preference and the pressures of the birth-control policy have led some couples to practice sex-selective abortion and others to hide baby girls and not register their births. For an unknown, but probably large, number of rural girls, non-registration seriously undermines even the most basic citizenship entitlements, making it difficult for them to receive schooling, employment and medical care.

Inequalities in employment and wages

Major increases in gender inequalities in urban unemployment rates and in the gender wage gap in the urban workforce have also been recorded. According to data from the Chinese Household Income Project, in 1995 the female unemployment rate was 3.62 percent, just 0.69 percentage points higher than the rate for males. By 2007, it had increased to 9.42 percent, 4.19 percentage points higher than the rate for males. In the same period, among urban waged workers, the ratio of female to male wages declined from 84 percent to 74 percent.[7]

In addition to these contrasting trends, broad comparisons between "women" and "men" as single groups have become less useful and it has become harder to generalize about trends relating even to a single

[5] All China Women's Federation and National Bureau of Statistics 2011.
[6] Hudson 2012.
[7] Li, Song & Liu 2011, pp. 166–7.

Image 12.1   Two women in Ningxia.
Source: Gao Yanqiu 2010.

type of gender inequality, due to increases in a host of other inequalities, including those relating to place, ethnicity and class (we discussed issues of class, regional, rural–urban, and within-community inequalities in chapters 10 and 11). Some of these are illustrated in Image 12.1, which depicts a well-educated and relatively prosperous young urban woman who works for a government bureau, conducting a questionnaire-based interview with an illiterate, elderly subsistence farmer in a poor village in Ningxia. (The basket is normally carried on the back, and the older woman uses it to transport grass she has cut from the mountainside to feed her livestock.) Other forms of inequality intersect and interact with gender inequalities in a number of complex ways.

Partly because of the complexities outlined here, studies of gender in contemporary China have taken an increasingly narrow focus. Sociological studies of gender inequalities most commonly focus on one type of inequality – for example, in education or income – and either confine their research to discrete groups in the population or are careful to identify the numerous variables that shape patterns of inequalities between differently positioned women and men. Methodologically, these studies have become increasingly varied and sophisticated; a trend that has often yielded richer analysis, but at the expense of comparability.

Recent scholarship also tends to be less "state-centric" than earlier studies, underpinned by greater recognition that trends in gender and other inequalities – and indeed, other aspects of social change – are best understood not solely in terms of the impact either of "the state" or "the economy", but as resulting from complex interactions between various institutions with different histories. Much of this recent scholarship has posed challenges to the temporal framing used in earlier studies. For example, early feminist studies largely accepted the state's framing of the woman question and its history as involving a shift away from the "traditional" pre-communist subjugation of women and progress – however slow or halting – toward liberation and increasing levels of equality under communism. However, some recent feminist studies complicate this picture, first by highlighting advances in gender equality achieved by non-CCP women's rights activists before 1949, and second by showing that "traditionally", women may not have been as thoroughly subjugated, or at least subjugated in quite the same ways as we had previously thought.[8] Other recent studies have challenged the Maoist versus post-Mao comparative framework characterizing studies of the 1980s by undertaking an examination of trends in gender inequalities and women's subordination over a longer time frame and across the divide between Maoist and post-Mao periods.[9]

Finally, there has been a trend toward a greater focus on the agency and experiences of ordinary women and men. Today, scholars seek to understand both the reproduction of and change in gender inequalities less in terms of the effect of state policies, and more in terms of complex relationships between women's (and men's) agency and social interactions, and the ways in which these are enabled and constrained by a shifting web of institutions, which have both contributed to, and been shaped by, changes in the political economy. In the rest of this chapter, we present studies that illustrate these complex relationships. The discussion relates to two institutions that have been particularly consequential for gender relations and gender inequalities: those associated with virilocal marriage, and those relating to gender divisions of labor.

Virilocal marriage and gender inequalities in rural China

As we discussed in Chapter 1, most marriages in rural China are virilocal. Scholars have long understood this to be one of the main causes of gender inequality. Parents commonly consider girls to be "temporary"

[8] For examples, see Edwards 2008; Ko 1994.
[9] See, for example, Bossen 2002.

family members, less valuable than boys, because it is likely that they will marry outside of the family's village, and when they do they will belong to someone else. So, parents cannot rely on their daughters to maintain the parents' livelihoods and care when they grow old and infirm. Consequently, in the poorest households in particular, parents have commonly given priority to their sons, and have been less willing to invest resources in girls' education and training. In the 1980s, steep increases in the costs of education for individual households following decollectivization made this a particularly serious problem. More recently, as we noted already, impressive progress has been made in overcoming gender inequalities in basic education. Crucial to this success were increases in state investment in rural education and, from 2006, the abolition of tuition fees for rural children's nine years of compulsory education.

Virilocal marriage is also seen to have a negative impact on women and gender equality after marriage because it separates women from their family members and friends in the village in which they grew up, and moves them to another village in which they have far fewer social connections than their husbands. Despite women's efforts to maintain contact with their natal families, especially their mother, and despite older women's efforts to marry their daughters into villages in which they already have a female relative – an aunt or cousin, for example – most women are more socially isolated than men for at least the first few years of their married life. This has two serious consequences. First, a lack of social connections in their marital village makes it harder for women to start up a business or to become involved in local politics. Second, away from the protection and support of their natal family and friends, married women have less power in their husband's family, and are vulnerable to abuse and violence from their husbands and members of his family.

Institutions relating to property usage rights and inheritance further underpin married women's lack of power and vulnerability in the family. Legally, men and women have equal rights to land and other property. In practice, however, when land usage rights were apportioned to households following decollectivization in the early 1970s and 1980s, they were nearly always contracted to the male head of the household and, in most places, subsequent practices relating to land redistribution and inheritance have been shaped in the interests of the patrilineal family, to the detriment of women. Aging fathers, for example, have usually passed down their land to their sons, but not to their daughters. After decollectivization, land was usually distributed to households according to the number of people they included, male and female. In later years, village adjustments to the size of land holdings over the years were meant to allow for both the entry of wives into the household and the birth of children, and for the reduction in household size through women's marriages and the death of family members. However, such processes of adjustment often discriminated against women by not apportioning land to women on their marriage into a husband's village, and sometimes by giving less land, or none at all, to newborn daughters. In 1998, the state passed a new law, the Land Management Law, which sought to improve farmers' land security by granting them 30-year leases on parcels of land. Consequently, far fewer adjustments to land holdings are made nowadays, and it is the norm for women not to be given land when they marry into a new village.

The consequences of these inheritance and land adjustment practices have been particularly serious for divorced women. Practices vary from one place to another but, very commonly, divorced women lose any entitlement to land they might have had in their husband's village, and are not granted land usage rights anywhere else, including their natal village. In rural areas where people depend on farming for their livelihoods, this means that only the most desperate of women, or those who already have a second marriage partner lined up, contemplate divorce. It also seriously weakens women's bargaining power in the family, since any assertion of a woman's interests in opposition to those of her husband or his relatives can be countered with the threat of divorce and destitution.

These gender inequalities and forms of women's subordination may have been compounded further by the re-emergence of high bride-price payments. Media reports suggest that such payments have contributed to domestic violence against women. A husband and his family who have paid a high bride price, they suggest, are more likely to pressure a woman to undertake a very heavy workload in the family, so that they can get their "money's worth", and are also more likely to be abusive and violent should the woman not meet their expectations. Some reports also note that women find it extremely difficult to escape domestic violence by divorcing, because men commonly demand that the bride-price payment be returned as a condition of divorce, and few women can meet this condition.[10]

High bride-price payments may exacerbate another very serious problem: the kidnapping and sale of women in marriage. No reliable statistics are available on the number of women trafficked each year across China, but localized reports suggest that, in the 1990s, the figure was in the tens

---

[10] For references to such reports, see Jacka 1997, pp. 62–3. We advise, though, that very little research has been conducted on bride-price payments in China. We have no concrete evidence of the causal links made in the media between high bride-price payments and domestic violence and difficulties for women in obtaining divorce. Anti-domestic violence activism is discussed in Chapter 13.

of thousands.[11] Some of these women were sent into prostitution, but many were sold as wives, mostly to poor men in isolated villages in the poorest, interior provinces. It is possible that since the 1990s this problem has been aggravated by a shortage of marriageable women, which has been one of the consequences of skewed ratios resulting from the combination of son-preference and the birth-control policy, as we discussed in Chapter 1. This may have created a market for kidnapped, low-cost wives among men whose poverty makes them unable to attract and pay for a wife at the local rate of bride-price payment.[12] Women who are trafficked tend to be looked down upon by other villagers, and without external support they are particularly vulnerable to abuse in the family. Further, the fact that kin-related men who support each other dominate many villages makes it very difficult for such women to seek help or attempt to escape.

So far, we have focused primarily on the ways in which institutional shifts in the post-Mao period have compounded gender inequalities and difficulties for rural women associated with virilocal marriage. Some studies, however, suggest that in the late 20th and early 21st centuries, state policy changes and economic developments simultaneously weakened the significance of virilocal marriage in shaping social relations, and led to a reduction in some types of gender inequality in rural areas. Next, we will summarize a paper by the anthropologist Hong Zhang as an example. This paper reports on ethnographic research conducted in Zhongshan village in Hubei province in the period 1993–1994 and in 2004.[13]

Zhang finds that, whereas in previous years couples had several children, among women born in Zhongshan between 1978 and 1987, that is, the first cohort of women to have grown up under the "one-child" birth-control policy, 95.5 percent had no more than one sibling. Moreover, 54 of the women (40.9 percent) had no male siblings. Fewer siblings meant less competition in the family for scarce resources and, despite the high costs of education, this made parents more likely to allow and

---

[11] For several such reports, see Biddulph & Cook 1999.

[12] We stress again, though, that there are no reliable statistics on the trafficking of women in China. Counter to the claim made here, official Chinese statistics point to a *decline* in trafficking between the 1990s and the early 2000s. However, as Lu Hong and colleagues suggest, these statistics may reflect changes in the number of people arrested for trafficking, rather than in the number of people trafficked (Lu, Liu & Crowther 2006, p. 861). On the other hand, with Martin Whyte, we warn against assuming that trafficking has in fact increased significantly, either within the post-Mao period, or as compared to the Maoist period. It may be that it was also a serious problem in earlier years, but much less widely reported (Whyte 2000, pp. 162–3). The same is likely to be true of domestic violence, which was not widely recognized as a social problem before the 21st century.

[13] Zhang, Hong 2007.

indeed push their daughters to complete as much schooling as they could. Consequently, by 2004, some 29.1 percent of women in this cohort had continued their schooling beyond the compulsory nine years. This figure was still much lower than the proportion of males in the same cohort who had received education beyond the compulsory level (47.86 percent). However, compared with the few (if any) years of education that most of these women's mothers had received, it represented a major achievement.

Zhang argues that the changes in parental attitudes and practices relating to their children's schooling resulted, first, from the observation that, with education, women could now gain employment as migrant workers and earn as much if not more than sons. In 1993–4, most young women worked at home on the farm. By 2004, however, almost 74 percent of women aged between 16 and 24 worked in urban jobs, in comparison to 59 percent of men in the same age bracket. Growth in the service sector and in export-oriented light industries, in which female workers were preferred, meant that there were more employment opportunities for young women than men. Further, among those with junior secondary school education, young women workers could earn much the same as men. With a senior secondary school education, according to Zhang, women could get office jobs that paid better salaries than most men with similar education could find.[14] For people who had a higher education, however, men's wages were substantially higher than women's.

For Zhongshan parents in the 2000s, improving daughters' employment prospects by giving them an education was particularly important because having fewer or no sons increased the likelihood that parents would have to rely on a daughter to support them financially and in other ways as they grew older and more infirm. In any case, improvements in transport and communication meant that virilocal marriage posed less of an obstacle to daughters' care of elderly parents than before, and that there was less difference between daughters and sons in this regard. This was particularly so because most men and increasing numbers of women were working as migrants and living away from home for many years at a time. This made it harder for both women and men to offer physical care to aging parents, but easier for both to provide financial support. And in this area, many parents told Zhang, daughters were often more reliable and generous than sons.

Further to this, Zhang noted a rise in non-virilocal forms of marriage. Partly this was due to the birth-control policy, which led to an increase

[14] We note, though, that Zhang's findings here are at odds with the national data on the gender wage gap given in the text box above (page 242). They also are at odds with survey findings about the impact of education on the gender wage gap, which we discuss below.

in the number of young women who had no brothers and who sought an uxorilocal marriage rather than marry out and leave their parents with no family support. More novel, though, was the emergence of neolocal marriages, in which newlyweds resided neither with the groom's nor bride's family but established a new household away from the villages of both families. This shift in marriage patterns was clearly associated with the rise of migrant employment among both men and women. In 2004, six young Zhongshan women married neolocally. All had been migrant workers before marriage and all met their partners, who were also rural migrants, in the city. All six women stayed with their husbands in the city after they married, and continued working there.

Zhang's study lends weight to the notion that modernization – more specifically urbanization and industrialization – leads to the disappearance of gender inequalities. However, there is also plenty of evidence to suggest that in an urbanized and industrialized society some gender inequalities and forms of women's subordination are reduced but nevertheless remain, some are little affected, and some increase. Next, we will illustrate this by examining gender divisions of labor, and gender segmentation and income inequalities in the workforce.

Gender divisions of labor, and gender segmentation and income inequalities in the workforce

Household divisions of labor between women and men in China have long been shaped by the notion that "men rule outside, women rule inside" (*nan zhu wai, nü zhu nei*) and by the assumption that "women's work" is lighter and less skilled than "men's work". In addition, as elsewhere, "women's work" is commonly seen as less worthy of recognition and reward than "men's work".

Elsewhere, Tamara Jacka has shown that, in rural China in the post-Mao period, there was a shift in understanding about what constituted "inside work" suitable for women and what was men's "outside work".[15] In the late 1970s, the former included cooking, cleaning and other domestic work, caring for a few domestic livestock, and tending the family's small, private plot of land. Agricultural work for the collective was considered "outside work" and, despite the mobilization of women for such work, it continued to be seen primarily as men's domain. However, after the introduction of decollectivization and, in particular, with industrialization taking place, men were the first to move out of agriculture and take up better paid employment opportunities off the farm.

[15] Jacka 1997.

Increasingly, outside work involved work outside the village, not just the family. Meanwhile, except for harvesting and ploughing, most agricultural work came to be viewed as women's inside work, to be undertaken in conjunction with domestic work and childcare.

Between the 1980s and the 2000s, most studies point to a feminization of agriculture across China. In other words, the proportion of agricultural work undertaken by women increased. Simultaneously, across the nation, the proportion of rural women employed in non-agricultural work was smaller, and grew at a slower rate than that of men. In 2000, only 10.2 percent of the rural female workforce was employed primarily in non-agricultural work, compared to 18.9 percent of the rural male workforce. By 2010, the proportion of the rural female workforce engaged primarily in non-agricultural work had increased to 24.9 percent, but the proportion of their male counterparts in such work had increased even faster, to 36.8 percent.[16]

In many places, this trend, combined with the low and declining profitability of agriculture relative to non-agricultural employment, created a large gap between the cash incomes of rural men and women. This was very apparent in the poor area of Ningxia, where Jacka conducted research between 2010 and 2012. There, most of the products of women's agricultural labor were not sold but rather kept for personal consumption. Married women generally had very little, if any, cash income of their own and relied heavily on the wages their migrant-worker sons and husbands earned. This compounded their relative lack of power in the family because, as villagers put it, "he earns the money, so he decides [how it's spent]".[17]

In the non-agricultural workforce, also, there have been marked divisions and inequalities between women and men. These are apparent in both the rural- (including rural migrant) and urban-registered workforces. Here, we confine ourselves to a discussion of gender inequalities in income in the urban-registered, non-agricultural workforce, as this has been the focus of most analysis of gender inequalities in work.

As in all modern economies, gender segmentation characterizes the contemporary Chinese urban labor market. This means that women are consistently overrepresented in lower paid jobs. In part, this is related to differences in human capital, such as technical qualifications and years of schooling attained. In particular, gender inequalities in education translate into differences in the occupations and trades in which women and men are concentrated. Norms and practices relating to the gendered divisions between inside/outside, light/heavy and skilled/unskilled also feed

[16] All China Women's Federation and National Bureau of Statistics 2011.
[17] Jacka 2012, p. 16.

into this. For example, both employers and employees often assume that work in the service sector, which can be associated with wives' and mothers' nurturing roles "inside", are better suited to women, while women should not (or are not equipped to) undertake "heavy" work in heavy industry, mining and construction. Women are also often seen as poor leadership material, in part because official and business negotiations are seen to belong traditionally to the male, "outside" domain.

Despite these attitudes, until recently gender segmentation and gender wage differentials were less severe than in other industrializing and industrialized economies. Scholars attribute this to the lasting effects of Maoist interventions, because although the state under Mao did not prevent or remove gender divisions and inequalities from the fledgling urban, industrial economy of the first half of the 20th century, it did ameliorate them. However, recent surveys point to increases in the gender wage gap since the 1990s. To begin to understand how and why these increases may have occurred, we turn now to two studies that draw on national survey data on urban incomes and employment.

In 1999, sociologists Philip Cohen and Wang Feng found that, although gender segmentation by occupation was low by international standards, it had a significant impact on wage differentials.[18] Gender segmentation by ownership sector also had an impact, albeit smaller, but there was no overall correlation between industry and earnings. The relationship between gender composition and average monthly wage earnings by sector, occupation, and industry is shown in Figure 12.1 overleaf. The occupation with the highest average monthly income (1351 *yuan*) but lowest proportion of women in the workforce (7.4 percent) was that of high-level official. Among ownership sectors, the collective sector had the lowest average income (567 *yuan*) but the highest proportion of women in the workforce (55.6 percent). Among industries, it was health and social welfare that employed the largest proportion of women (61.8 percent), with an average income of 861 *yuan*.[19]

Examining wages, gender wage differentials and the gender composition of the workforce in different sectors of the economy suggested a yet more complex story. In the state sector, average wages were not as high as in some other sectors, but wage inequalities, including by gender, were low. In contrast, in "other organizations" (comprising mainly joint ventures and private businesses) and among individual private business owners, average incomes were the highest of all sectors, but so too were gender wage and other wage inequalities. Compared with the state sector, the gender wage gap between male and female employees was about

---

[18] The following discussion summarizes findings from Cohen & Wang 2009.

[19] For further explanation of this figure, see Table 3.1 in Cohen & Wang 2009, p. 42.

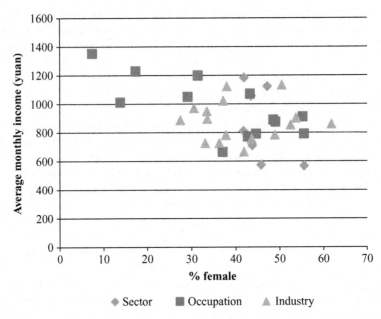

Figure 12.1   Gender composition and average income by sector, occupation and industry, urban China, 1999.
Source: Cohen & Wang 2009, p. 43. © The Board of Trustees of the Leland Stanford Jr University 2009. All rights reserved. Used with the permission of Stanford University Press, www.sup.org.

5 percent higher in "other organizations" and 17 percent higher among individual business owners. Among employees in individual businesses, also, the gender wage gap was 15 percent higher than in the state sector. In other words, the state sector was far less discriminatory than the private and joint-venture sectors.

Factors such as the ongoing decline of the state sector and growth of the private and joint-venture sectors go a long way toward explaining increasing levels of gender inequality in the urban Chinese workforce, and lend weight to the notion that, as marketization increases, so too do gender wage inequalities. However, this hypothesis does not take into account trends in education. Cohen and Wang found that education had a significant impact on wages, with employees whose education ended with junior secondary school suffering at least a 50 percent pay penalty compared with those who had university education. It is possible that the high returns that come from completing tertiary education might lead to a reduction in gender wage inequalities in coming years, since the number of women going to university is rising both in absolute terms and as a proportion of the total. In 1995, women comprised 35.4 percent of all students enrolled in university. By 2004, the figure had increased 10.3 percentage points, to 45.7 percent.[20] However, even these increases may not offset gender segmentation in the workforce or the impact of such segmentation on wage distribution. Cohen and Wang hint at this:

[I]n the urban labor market, a growing service economy – in the non-state sector – could pull women into nurturing roles, where they earn lower incomes and have fewer opportunities for advancement.[21]

In this regard, it is worth noting that neither the state, nor women's activists nor educators have made any significant effort to change norms with respect to gender divisions of labor. In both secondary and tertiary education sectors, men and women are concentrated in areas of learning seen as naturally more appropriate to their gender. This is partially due to students' and parents' gender norms, and partially due to gender discrimination among educators. For example, as we noted in Chapter 8, in recruiting students for majors deemed to relate to "men's work", some universities require higher University Entrance Examination (UEE) scores for women than for men. Such practices both reflect and further intensify gender segmentation in the workforce.

A second, more recent study led by the economist Li Shi confirms a less optimistic perspective on the potential for education to overcome gender inequalities in the workforce. Li and colleagues found that in the 2000s, the gender wage gap increased significantly. Cohen and Wang claimed that in 1999, female employees earned about 22 percent less than men. In comparison, Li and colleagues found a gender wage gap of 10.5 percent and 17.4 percent in 1995 and 2002 respectively, but that increased sharply to 29.7 percent by 2007. Similar to Cohen and Wang, they claimed that there was a continuous increase in the rate of return to education and experience in the labor market between 2002 and 2007. However, the return to education for men increased more than it did for women. This meant a particularly sharp rise in the gender wage gap among the highest income earners.[22]

Meanwhile, discrimination against women, based purely on their gender, increased across the board, but was most severe among those earning the lowest wages, that is, in industries, occupations and ownership

---

[20] Yu & Huang 2010, p. 94.
[21] Cohen & Wang 2009, p. 52.
[22] Li, Song & Liu 2011.

sectors that had a high concentration of women. Li and colleagues conclude that, in the early 21st century:

market discrimination against female employees kept increasing year by year. Young women with low educational levels and poor jobs were subject to severe and increasing discrimination. As most of the female workforce is employed in low-end jobs and competitive industries and in the private sector, some of the factors leading to labor market segregation also exert a marked influence on the expansion of the gender wage gap.[23]

Summary

Over the last few decades, there have been several changes in women's status and patterns of gender inequality in China. However, not all of the changes have been in one direction: some types of gender inequality have become less common, while others appear to have changed relatively little. Yet other types of gender inequality and some problems for women appear to have been exacerbated or created in the post-Mao period. Among the changes of most benefit to women has been a reduction in gender inequalities in education. In the early 21st century, building on earlier gains made in this area, enrollment rates in compulsory education reached close to 100 percent among girls as well as boys across most of China. However, shifts in gender income disparities in urban industrial employment present a contrasting picture. By the 2000s, there was growing evidence that increases in the gaps between men's and women's earnings resulted from discrimination against women, as well as gender segmentation of the workforce and, to a lesser and declining extent, from differences in their human capital. In addition, some problems for women, especially rural women, appear to have re-emerged or been exacerbated in the post-Mao period, relative to the Maoist period. Trafficking in girls and women is one example. To complicate matters even further, already significant differences and inequalities between women of differing socioeconomic backgrounds multiplied in the post-Mao period as a result of market-oriented economic reforms.

In part because of the growing multiplicity and complexity of patterns of gender inequality, the types of questions posed by scholars interested in gender relations in contemporary China have changed. In the 1980s, scholars asked "Has the Communist Party liberated women?", "Have post-Mao reforms benefited or set back the cause of gender equality?" and "Which does more to further gender equality: socialism or capitalism?" Today, however, it is generally recognized that, in response to

---

[23] Ibid., p. 177.

such broad questions, one can only say "it depends". Studies of gender inequality and other aspects of gender relations in contemporary China have taken a narrower focus. They have also moved away from an exclusive concern with state policies. In addition, in the late 20th and early 21st centuries, there has been some interest among scholars, both within and outside China, in the circumstances of Chinese men. On the whole, however, most studies of gender relations in China continue to be framed by the "woman question".

Discussion questions

1. How has the "woman question" shaped the Chinese state's approaches to gender inequality in the 20th and 21st centuries?
2. What can we learn from studies of China about the relationship between market transition and trends in gender inequalities?
3. How do you explain recent evidence in China of decreasing gender inequality in education on the one hand, and increasing gender income inequalities among urban workers on the other?

Recommended reading

Entwisle, Barbara & Henderson, Gail E (eds) 2000, *Re-drawing Boundaries: Work, Households, and Gender in China*. Berkeley: University of California Press.

Hershatter, Gail 2007, *Women in China's Long Twentieth Century*. Berkeley: University of California Press.

Jacka, Tamara 1997, *Women's Work in Rural China: Change and Continuity in an Era of Reform*. Cambridge, UK: Cambridge University Press.

Jacka, Tamara & Sargeson, Sally (eds) 2011a, *Women, Gender and Rural Development in China*. Cheltenham, UK: Edward Elgar.

Judd, Ellen R 1994, *Gender and Power in Rural North China*. Stanford, CA: Stanford University Press.

Stacey, Judith 1983, *Patriarchy and Socialist Revolution in China*. Berkeley: University of California Press.

Zang, Xiaowei 2011c, *Islam, Family Life, and Gender Inequality in Urban China*. London: Routledge.

13 Collective Action and Social Change

In previous chapters, we have discussed several kinds of social change that have taken place in China during the 20th and 21st centuries, including changes in the organization of society, cultures, values and identities and patterns of inequality. We have attributed these changes mostly to changing Chinese state policies and to the processes of modernization. But what about the role of ordinary Chinese citizens in creating social change?

As we noted in the introduction, scholars characterize China today as governed by an authoritarian, single-party state. However, Chinese government is highly decentralized. Far from being united under one homogeneous authority, uniformly enforcing a single set of policies on a mass populace, the policy behavior of state actors and their relationships with non-state actors varies according to their location in different parts of the country, at different levels of government, and in different bureau-cracies, coalitions and alliances. In addition, as suggested in previous chapters, high levels of differentiation and inequality also have character-ized Chinese society over the past few decades, and there is a great deal of variation between different citizens' outlooks and interests. Also, both leaders and ordinary citizens are increasingly exposed to an array of new and changing non-state as well as state behaviors, norms, expectations and desires. Together, these trends have created both opportunities and pressures for people to initiate, organize and act for social change.

In the western media, individual intellectual dissidents, their calls for political change, and the human rights abuses they have suffered at the hands of the Chinese state have received a lot of attention. In this chapter, however, we focus on *collective* action among different population groups in society, including intellectuals but also others. In recent years, scholars have considered a vast array of different forms of collective action. Here, we confine our discussion to those that are aimed primarily at challenging and changing some aspect of the sociopolitical order on the grounds that it is unjust. In this relatively narrow definition of collective action, we include environmental activism and women's NGOs campaigning against domestic violence, student demonstrations calling for democracy and freedom of expression, workers' strikes, and collective petitions and protests by villagers against land expropriation. However, we exclude the activities of business associations, religious groups and criminal gangs.[1]

We focus on three types of collective action: collective petitions, protest actions – what the state refers to as "collective public security incidents" (CoPSI) – and the activities of NGOs.

COLLECTIVE PETITIONS, PROTESTS AND ORGANIZING

Collective petitions

Petitions and complaints to "letters and visits" (*xinfang*) offices are one of the main ways in which Chinese citizens voice their grievances. According to official figures, in 2000 a total of 10.2 million petitions (collective and individual) were submitted to provincial, county and municipal offices; 115 percent more than in 1995. Between 1995 and 2000, the number of *collective* petitions (defined as involving five or more people) and collective petitioners also increased, by 280 percent and 260 percent, respectively. In 2000, over 76 percent of all petitioners were involved in collective petitions.[2]

Collective public security incidents

Official reports indicate that the number of "collective public security incidents" (CoPSI) – defined as incidents in which a group of more than five people "illegally gather to disrupt public order and destroy public property" – have risen, from 8700 in 1994 to 87 000 in 2005. Unofficial reports suggest that there have been further increases since then, with a figure of 180 000 reported for 2010.[3]

The average number of participants in CoPSI has also risen. During the first quarter of 1998, a total of 202 000 people participated

---

[1] Not all China scholars would agree with these exclusions. Patricia Thornton, for example, discusses the activities of internet-based religious sects, or "cybersects", as a form of collective political action (Thornton 2008). Jae Ho Chung and colleagues group the activities of religious groups and criminal organizations together with protest actions, but discuss these as sources of political and social instability, rather than as forms of collective action (Chung, Lai & Xia 2006). We do not know of any studies that discuss the activities of business associations as collective action. However, such associations are seen as contributing to civil society by Gordon White, Jude Howell and Shang Xiaoyuan (1996, pp. 184–207).

[2] Lee 2007b, pp. 230–1.

[3] Chung, Lai & Xia 2006, pp. 5–7; "Wen pledges to curb graft, income inequality as police head off protests" 2011.

in CoPSI. By 2003, CoPSI participants numbered 3.1 million, or an average of 767 500 per quarter.[4] In the seven-year period between 2003 and 2009, the researchers Yanqi Tong and Shaohua Lei recorded 248 large-scale CoPSI, that is, CoPSI involving more than 500 participants. Of these, the majority involved workers or the laid-off and concerned labor disputes in either the state sector (26 percent) or non-state sector (18 percent), or involved villagers protesting against land expropriation or villager relocation (10.5 percent). In addition, 12 of the incidents concerned pollution, seven involved students, and six were ethnic disturbances.[5]

NGO organizing

The number of people involved in non-governmental activism has increased rapidly since the mid-1990s. By 2005, official figures put the number of NGOs registered as "social organizations", "non-profit" entities or "foundations" at about 320 000, and researchers estimate that there were another 1.4 million informal grassroots groups. By 2012, the total number of NGOs registered in these three categories was estimated at about 500 000, and that figure was expected to double within a few years, as a result of reforms aimed at making registration easier.[6]

Some differences can be seen in the involvement of different groups in different types of collective action. NGOs tend to be dominated by middle-class urbanites, whose professed aims are mostly to help and empower those they believe are less fortunate than themselves, such as poor rural women and migrant workers, and to address broad social problems, such as environmental degradation, domestic violence and discrimination against HIV/AIDS sufferers. NGO efforts to achieve the first aim commonly include training and consciousness-raising activities, and services, such as legal aid, counselling hotlines and microcredit programs. They address broader social problems through media campaigns, school education programs and lobbying to change policy or legislation. In contrast, collective petitioning and mass protest actions occur more often among disgruntled villagers or industrial workers seeking to defend or further their own interests and those of their families and

---

[4] Chung, Lai & Xia 2006, p. 7.
[5] Tong & Lei 2010, pp. 489–91.
[6] Watson 2008, p. 37; "China set to give NGOs equal status" 2012. Bear in mind that these figures include all sorts of groups with a variety of aims, including many that do not accord with our focus on forms of collective action aimed primarily at challenging and changing the social order.

communities. These distinctions, however, have never been clear-cut, and over time have become less and less so. Thus, in the early 21st century, middle-class urbanites participated in increasingly numerous, strident and large-scale protests against threats to their personal interests, such as industrial pollution from chemical companies set up in their neighborhood, safety and health hazards resulting from tainted and counterfeit products, the demolition of housing and the broken promises of real-estate developers in gated residential communities. To give another example, while in the 1990s NGOs seeking to improve the rights of rural migrant workers were staffed mostly by middle-class urbanites, more recently rural migrant workers themselves have taken the reins at several NGOs. In addition, several long-running campaigns have emerged that combine repeated protest actions among local residents with lobbying and other efforts on the part of both local leaders and non-local NGOs. Campaigns against dam construction are a good example of this type of collective action.[7]

In the 1990s, many studies of collective action in China were framed by the concept of "civil society" – roughly speaking, an autonomous sphere of citizen debate and activity around public affairs, separate from the state, the market and the family. Perceiving that civil society groups had played a major role in the collapse of state socialism in Russia and Eastern Europe, several scholars went "in search of civil society"[8] in China, looking for signs among NGOs, in particular, of the development of a sphere of associations that were independent of the state and that would contribute to democratization and the end of one-party rule. By the end of the 20th century, however, interest in the search for civil society was fading, for there were few signs that NGOs were independent of the state, or that they were working to overthrow the CCP. However, there *were* signs that the actions of NGOs and other forms of collective action were contributing to other kinds of social and political change.

Since the 1990s, studies of collective action in China have more commonly focused on a different set of questions, namely: "How do collective action and social movements arise?", "Why do they take the forms they do?" and "What makes some succeed and others fail to achieve social or political change?" Inspired by social movement theorists, such as Sidney Tarrow, Doug McAdam and Charles Tilly, they have addressed these questions primarily in terms of "political opportunities", "mobilizing structures", "repertoires of contention" and "collective action frames". In the rest of this chapter, we draw on several of their studies to discuss NGOs, collective petitions and protest actions that challenge and seek

---

[7] Mertha 2008.
[8] White, Howell & Xiaoyuan 1996.

to change the sociopolitical order on the grounds that it is unjust, and the contribution that these kinds of collective action have made to social change in contemporary China.

Political opportunities

How does collective action get started, what keeps it going, and what leads some types of activism to develop into broader movements, while others fail or fizzle out? In seeking to answer these questions, recent studies begin from the observation that dissatisfaction is a poor indicator of when, and among whom, collective action will start. Some people who are disgruntled or concerned band together with others to protest, while others who are equally dissatisfied keep quiet. Rather than focusing on people's grievances, therefore, studies of social movements focus, first of all, on changes in political opportunities and resources as being important factors enabling and motivating the initiation, escalation and scaling-back of collective action.

It is often observed that in contemporary China economic liberalization has proceeded much more rapidly than political liberalization. All the same, since the 1980s there have been significant shifts in political opportunities for collective action. One such shift has resulted from the state's efforts to put in place a rule of law. Laws enacted in recent years, such as the Women's Rights Protection Law, the Labor Law and the Property Law, and legal mechanisms such as litigation, have not been very effective in protecting citizens' legal rights. However, they have cultivated a new understanding that citizens *have* legal rights and they have also provided both legitimacy to and avenues for certain types of collective action.

A range of different groups has mobilized these legal resources. For example, migrant workers have taken employers to court for violations of the Labor Law. In addition, and perhaps even more crucially, widespread outrage at the violation of legal rights, combined with the repeated frustration of workers' efforts to achieve justice through the courts, have served as resources for the mobilization of migrant workers into illegal protest actions, such as strikes. In the countryside, a growing awareness of legal rights and knowledge of specific laws and regulations have enabled the mobilization of thousands of people into what Kevin O'Brien and Lianjiang Li refer to as "rightful resistance", a form of resistance that "entails the innovative use of laws, policies and other officially promoted values to defy disloyal political and economic elites".[9] As an example, villagers frequently draw on the Organic Law of Village Committees to lodge complaints and petitions with township and county officials about

[9] O'Brien & Li 2006, p. 2.

Image 13.1   Protest in Wukan, Guangdong province.
   Villagers are protesting against land expropriation and corruption among local officials. Several of their banners appeal to the national leadership of the CCP.
Source: AFP/Getty Images 2011.

rigged village elections and to push for the removal of corrupt or unresponsive village leaders. Others accuse village leaders of failing to carry out policies or breaking contracts. In the 21st century, the main target of rural rightful resistance has been the expropriation of land for industrial and urban development without adequate compensation to farmers.

   Other shifts in governance have provided further opportunities for collective action. Since the late 1980s, state leaders influenced by the concept of "small government, big society" have become increasingly tolerant of NGOs, and have even encouraged them as a means of addressing needs for welfare and services and of contributing to social harmony and sustainable development. This has opened up opportunities for some NGO activism, especially in relation to women's rights, community development and environmental protection. Activism in these areas has also been able to draw on opportunities afforded by global development agendas. Beijing's hosting of the 1995 Fourth United Nations World Conference on Women and specifically its accompanying NGO Forum, was particularly important in this regard, for it raised the profile of women's issues and alerted the state to the potential for NGOs to serve as a marker of China's status as an advanced, modern nation and a conduit for funding from the United Nations and other overseas development agencies. Consequently, many NGOs – including groups campaigning for environmental protection as well as women's rights – were established in the years leading up to and immediately following this conference. All the same, there has remained a great deal of wariness among China's leaders about the potential threat to state power that NGOs pose. Today, foreign entities and those with close connections to overseas groups are particularly likely to suffer restrictions and crackdowns, as are those working in the politically sensitive areas of labor rights and HIV/AIDS.

The commercialization and privatization of the media and developments in communication technologies have provided other resources and opportunities for collective action. Thus, editors and journalists on the lookout for eye-catching stories that will increase newspaper sales or television ratings have been an important resource for activists seeking to mobilize others around issues such as village leaders' corruption and industrial pollution. The significance of new communications technologies in mobilizing collective action first became apparent in China in the 1989 Tian'anmen demonstrations, when student leaders used faxes and, to a lesser extent, the internet to spread the word quickly and drum up support for the demonstrations, both in China and abroad. Since that time, greater internet access and mobile telephones have served the same purpose to even greater effect.

So far, and in line with theorizations of the emergence of collective action and social movements in Europe and North America, we have focused on opportunities and resources for activism that have emerged in spaces outside the state as a result of a loosening of the state's grip on society. As Xi Chen and others note, though, in high-capacity authoritarian regimes such as China, the state still controls most resources for mobilization, so "what matters most is not whether 'free spaces' or a civil society free from state domination exist but whether ordinary people can locate resources and support from state actors".[10] The question is, then, what sort of resources and opportunities *within* the state can be mobilized for collective action? Here, we focus on two aspects of the Chinese state that provide such opportunities.

First, as we have already observed, the Chinese state is not a homogeneous monolith: there are many differences and divisions between the interests of actors and institutions in different parts of the state, which can be and are exploited by canny activists and protestors. We noted above, for example, that a key strategy among rightful resisters in rural China is

[10] Chen, Xi 2008, p. 54.

to seek the support of higher level officials in curbing the malpractices of local village leaders. Another example is provided by China's first legal environmental NGO, Friends of Nature, and its founder, Liang Congjie, who once said:

> It is hard to generalize what the government thinks about us. The government is not a monolithic bloc in this regard. SEPA [the State Environmental Protection Administration] supports us and has called us their "natural ally". The MOWR [Ministry of Water Resources] probably likes us much less and the provincial government in Yunnan undoubtedly hates us.[11]

The ability of Friends of Nature to forge connections with members of SEPA, to create and maintain the sense that they are "natural allies", and to use those connections to get around other, hostile state entities, is undoubtedly an important factor contributing to the survival of this NGO and their achievements, including in protecting endangered species such as the Tibetan antelope and the snub-nosed monkey.[12]

The personal background and connections of Liang Congjie are not incidental to these successes. His grandfather was the famous reformer of the late Qing period, Liang Qichao, a pedigree that afforded Liang Congjie considerable respect and influence among powerful actors in SEPA, and protection against enemies. Few other activists today can lay claim to quite such a pedigree, but many of the most successful have had either elite family connections, a revolutionary past or positions within a state institution or media outlet. These have given them distinct advantages in mobilizing support and other resources from within the state.

A second aspect of many state institutions that has provided opportunities for collective action has been "amphibiousness". Scholars use this term to refer to the fact that some institutions serve multiple purposes for the state, and can also be "converted" or "appropriated" for purposes other than those for which they are intended. In China, several organizations are officially intended both to support state power and policies and to serve as avenues for the articulation of the interests and opinions of "the masses". These include, most importantly, the mass organizations, including the Women's Federation (see Chapter 12), state media outlets and the "letters and visits" (*xinfang*) system. Xi Chen and other scholars suggest that all of these can and have been subject to "appropriation" and "conversion" by those seeking to mobilize collective action.[13] Next, we discuss the *xinfang* system as an example.

---

[11] Quoted in Mertha 2008, p. 27.
[12] See Friends of Nature no date.
[13] Chen, Xi 2008.

Xinfang is a system of offices, set up at most levels of government and in most CCP and government departments, as an outlet for citizens' grievances and a mechanism for the state to obtain information about the behavior of local officials and the mood of the populace. As their name suggests, the *xinfang* offices receive petitions both in writing and in person. They may pass on the complaints to other government departments, as well as monitor and pass back information on the progress of the dispute. They can also make suggestions themselves about how complaints should be addressed, but they do not have the power to resolve disputes formally.[14]

As noted above, in the late 1990s, there were huge increases in the number of petitions, especially *collective* petitions to the *xinfang* system. Xi Chen discusses these increases in terms of citizens' "conversion" of the *xinfang* system into a vehicle for noisy, sometimes violent collective protests against official wrongdoing. In the post-Mao period, the *xinfang* system has encouraged such protests. This stems in part from a decline (or at least a perceived decline) in the potential risks to troublemaking petitioners. This has occurred because of the weakening hold of state officials over people's lives, due to decollectivization and the erosion of the *danwei* (work unit) system and because higher level authorities, increasingly concerned about social stability and harmony, have tried to discourage coercion on the part of local officials. In this context, petitioners have learned that "the squeaky wheel gets the oil" and that collective petitions are more likely to be effective than those presented by an individual. It also pays to take one's complaints to higher levels of government. At lower levels, complaints are more likely to be ignored and official misdeeds covered up, owing to close ties among local officials. Higher authorities' interests are not necessarily the same as those of local officials, over whom they have power. As Xi Chen explains:

Whereas ordinary petitioners seldom get a chance to talk to top city leaders if they petition the municipality directly, they often can if they "skip levels" (*yueji*). When a group of petitioners march on a provincial capital, for example, a city leader is likely to rush in to try to stop them. So there is a saying: "If you want to meet the county head, go to the municipal government; if you want to see the mayor, go to the provincial capital".[15]

In the first decade of the 21st century, faced with escalating collective petitions resulting from this situation, state leaders introduced measures aimed at increasing the authority and responsibilities of *xinfang* offices and at making the system more responsive. At the same time, though,

[14] Liebman 2011, p. 274.
[15] Chen, Xi 2008, p. 63.

they sought to reduce the incidence of petitions by introducing rules out-lawing certain types of petitioning, including *yueji* and the presentation of petitions by any more than five representatives at a time. They also intro-duced (lack of) petitioning and the maintenance of social order as criteria for the evaluation of grassroots officials' performance by higher levels of government. These measures may have backfired. Most of the rules lim-iting petitioning have been routinely violated, with at least some local officials reluctant to reject or punish "illegal" petitions, partly because there are so many of them. Xi Chen argues that the inclusion of social order as a criterion in their performance evaluation puts local officials under greater pressure than before to address complaints before they get out of hand. This, he suggests, increases the bargaining power of peti-tioners and enhances the power of collective petitioning, in particular, as a strategy for having claims addressed.[16] This may, however, suggest an overly rosy picture of the bargaining power of petitioners: petitioners are often very fearful and with justification, for they face serious threats to their physical safety and freedom from local officials. More recent analyses suggest that local officials may respond in a variety of ways to increased pressure to reduce the number of complaints and petitions on their watch, with some not registering petitions and others responding by threatening or even "disappearing" petitioners.[17]

Mobilizing structures, repertoires of contention and collective action frames

We have given several examples of NGO leaders and protestors seizing opportunities they saw opening up, and converting them into resources for the mobilization of collective action. But while opportunity or, at any rate, the *perception* of opportunity, is a necessary precondition for the initiation of social activism, it alone cannot explain how people are mobilized and pulled together into collective action, often in the face of considerable risk, how they attract further participants and support for their cause, and how they push for change. For this, students of social movement theory turn to what Sidney Tarrow has called "repertoires of contention", "collective action frames" and "mobilizing structures" (including social networks). As Tarrow writes:

Contention crystallizes into a social movement when it taps embedded social networks and connective structures and produces collective action frames and supportive identities able to sustain contention with powerful

[16] Ibid., pp. 68–70.
[17] Godement 2012.

opponents. By mounting familiar forms of contention, movements become focal points that transform external opportunities into resources. Repertoires of contention, social networks, and cultural frames lower the costs of bringing people into collective action, induce confidence that they are not alone, and give broader meaning to their claims. Together, these factors trigger the dynamic processes that have made social movements historically central to political and social change.[18]

Some elements of "repertoires of contention" – the toolkits of tactics that social activists draw upon in their efforts to achieve change – have spread across the modern world. The strike, for example, is as familiar a tactic to industrial workers in contemporary China as it is to their counterparts in Europe and the United States, having been learned from generations of workers' protests.[19] Other mobilizing tools and strategies are more specific to particular cultures. Petitioning is a very old tool in the Chinese repertoire of contention. The CCP established the *xinfang* system we described above, but this system in fact builds on a long, pre-communist tradition in which citizens sought justice by taking their petitions to higher and higher levels of officialdom, including travelling to the capital, if necessary, to present their complaints to the imperial court. Collective petitioning, with this long history, is thus embedded in Chinese culture, and this helps to explain its effectiveness as a strategy for mobilizing large numbers of protestors.

A similar mix of old and new, local and international, can be seen in "collective action frames", that is, the shared understandings, values and identities that frame the actions of social activists, and the language and imagery they use to mobilize support and disarm opponents. For example, labor protestors and rightful resistors in the countryside sometimes invoke Mao and use the Maoist language of egalitarianism to justify their claims and garner support, while simultaneously drawing on the language of legality and citizens' legal rights (*gongmin de hefa quanyi*). In 2002, among tens of thousands of workers who marched in the northeastern city of Liaoyang to protest against government corruption and state enterprise leaders' failure to pay back wages, pensions and unemployment allowances, some carried huge portraits of Mao, and one elderly woman cried out "Chairman Mao should not have died so soon!"[20] In addition, protestors put up posters and open letters that insisted on their legal rights and melded the new legal language with an older, Maoist style of mobilizational rhetoric. One open letter read:

[18] Tarrow 2011, p. 23.
[19] For a discussion of Chinese workers' strikes and other forms of protest before and after 1949, see Perry 1993.
[20] Lee 2007c, p. 3.

We the working masses decide that we cannot tolerate such corrupt elements who imposed an illegal bankruptcy on our factory... Our respected compatriots, brothers and fathers, we are not anti-Party, antisocialism hooligans who harm people's lives and disrupt social order. Our demands are all legal under the Constitution and the laws... Let's join forces in this action for legal rights and against corruption. Long live the spirit of Liaoyang![21]

The Tian'anmen demonstrations of 1989 involved a particularly interesting mix of local and international mobilizing strategies and frames.[22] Student leaders of the demonstrations framed their demands primarily in terms of "democracy" and "free speech". This language may have held little meaning for most villagers in China, but it resonated strongly with westerners and the educated, urban Chinese middle class. For the latter, the demonstrations were particularly powerful because they were seen as belonging to a tradition of protest going back to the May 4th Movement of 1919, a student-led movement for cultural revolution, enshrined in both official and unofficial culture as the beginnings of modernity and national pride in China. The Tian'anmen demonstrators marched, just as their May 4th predecessors had done, holding high banners proclaiming their university affiliation and calling for others to join their fight to "save the nation". And throughout the month of May, they staged huge gatherings in Tian'anmen Square, the heart of the capital, displacing the official anniversary celebrations for May 4th.

Besides this, the demonstrators made use of a host of strategies and frames in both Chinese and foreign (specifically western) repertoires of contention. Three students knelt on the steps of the Great Hall of the People to present a petition – a core element in the Chinese cultural repertoire of contention; others went on hunger strike – a more international form of activism. Toward the end of May, students revived flagging interest in the demonstrations by constructing a 10-meter-tall Goddess of Democracy and placing it in Tian'anmen Square, between a giant portrait of Mao and the Monument to the People's Heroes. The statue attracted enormous attention, partly because it looked so much like the American Statue of Liberty. As Joseph Esherick and Jeffrey Wasserstrom note, though, it also bore resemblance to Buddhist images of the Bodhisattva, as well as to the socialist–realist sculptures of revolutionary heroes already present in Tian'anmen Square, and it brought to mind the giant statues of Mao that were carried through the square during National Day parades in the 1960s.

It can be seen that leaders of collective action in China make use of various mobilizational structures, including registered and unregistered

---

[21] Ibid., p. 4.
[22] The following discussion draws on Esherick & Wasserstrom 1990.

NGOs, internet forums, strikes and demonstrations. In all cases, though, networking has been crucial to success in recruiting participants, countering opposition and achieving goals for social change. We have already discussed this in the case of Friends of Nature, and another example comes from the women's movement and its efforts to combat domestic violence. In 1998, three women's activists from Beijing attended a symposium on domestic violence in India. Inspired, they returned to China and called together members of up to 30 women's groups, to ask them about their understanding of domestic violence and what they might do to combat it. Later, in 2000, several of these activists launched a project entitled "Combating domestic violence against women: research, countermeasures and intervention". The project ran until 2003, after which time it was transformed into the Anti-Domestic Violence Network (ADVN). In 2012, the ADVN comprised 118 individual members and 75 group members, including branches of the Women's Federation, research institutes and NGOs.[23] As in other areas of the women's movement, the inclusion of members of the Women's Federation is extremely important, not only because these women are often able to influence central state officials more effectively than non-state actors, but because such inclusion gives activists access to the Women's Federation's national network of organizations and representatives. This enables them to share their message far more broadly than would otherwise be possible.

Together, ADVN members maintain a domestic violence resource center and website, run gender awareness and anti-domestic violence training programs, organize media campaigns, provide legal aid to domestic violence victims and lobby for legislative change. These activities were a major contributing factor in the emergence of domestic violence as an issue of public concern in the early 21st century. In addition, lobbying by ADVN members contributed to the inclusion of clauses on domestic violence in the revised Marriage Law of 2001 and the revised Women's Rights Protection Law of 2005. Most importantly, ADVN members helped draft a new Anti-Domestic Violence Law, which, after several years of lobbying, was finally included in the 2012 legislative plans of the NPC.

Of course, some activists are better at organizing and networking than others, and some mobilizing strategies and frames are more effective in garnering support and countering opposition than others. Failures in these areas can have a decisive impact on the outcomes of collective action, as Andrew Mertha demonstrates in his account of protests against Pubugou Dam in Hanyuan county, Sichuan. In late 2004, some 100 000 people demonstrated for several weeks against the imminent completion

---

[23] Keech-Marx 2008, p. 179; Wang, Zheng 2010, pp. 111–13; Qin 2012.

of the dam and the local government's acquiescence in the resettlement of almost half of Hanyuan's population. These protests followed years of complaints and resistance on the part of Hanyuan locals. They were said to be the biggest demonstrations since Tian'anmen in 1989 and the largest rural protests since the founding of the PRC, but they came to nothing: although shortly after the protests, local officials were dismissed and arrested for corruption, several villagers were also imprisoned and one was executed. Construction of the dam went ahead and after a protracted period of resistance, most villagers were forced to agree to unsatisfactory relocation compensation packages and, by late 2006, the majority had been moved out of their homes.

Mertha attributes this failure primarily to the fact that most of the villagers' resistance, including before and after the 2004 protests, was spontaneous and lacked leadership and coordination. There was no NGO involvement and protestors did not find influential government allies, who might have been able to leverage support for the protestors. In addition, by 2004, the Sichuan provincial authorities had already succeeded in publicly framing resistance to the dam in terms of political crisis and social instability. So, after that point, media outlets were unable to report favorably on the dam protests and it was too politically risky for any NGO or local official, however sympathetic to the protestors, to come out in their support.[24]

Social change

The question "To what extent does collective action result in social change?" is problematic because it is often very hard to measure the full impact of collective action, which includes its unintended as well as intended consequences and its long-term as well as short-term contributions to social change. When looking at the relationship between a particular type of activism, such as environmental campaigns, and a form of social change, such as a shift in public attitudes toward the environment, it can also be challenging to correctly identify what is a cause and what is an effect, and to say whether a third factor is influencing events (for example, pressure from overseas).

Nevertheless, we can point to some broad shifts in society and sociopolitical relations, to which collective action has clearly contributed. One

---

[24] Mertha 2008, pp. 65–93. Elsewhere in his book, Mertha contrasts the failure at Pubugou with the success of protestors campaigning against dam construction at Dujiangyan, also in Sichuan, and the partial success of those campaigning against the Nu River Dam project in Yunnan.

of these is a shift in values, understandings and expectations. The role that environmental NGOs such as Friends of Nature have played in fostering public concern about environmental degradation is one example of this. The role of the ADVN network and other women's NGOs in raising public awareness of domestic violence as a social concern is another. More generally, NGO activism, labor protests, rural rightful resistance and other forms of collective action have heightened public awareness, concern and outrage about a range of injustices.

Such increased awareness and outrage, often expressed in the form of increased collective action, have put a great deal of pressure on state authorities, who have responded sometimes with repression and sometimes with policy measures aimed at more positively addressing social concerns. Most notably in rural China, increasingly frequent and large-scale expressions of discontent led the state leadership to introduce direct elections at the village level in the 1990s, and a raft of measures aimed at reducing peasant burdens and "constructing a new socialist countryside" in the 2000s. This highlights a broad change in governance, to which collective action has contributed: an increase in the number and range of people shaping public decision-making processes and policy outcomes, whether through direct participation or indirect pressure.

We can also note the types of change that collective action has so far *not* brought about. To date, it has not resulted in revolution, the overthrow of the CCP, or the introduction of a system of multi-party democracy. The question of whether such systemic changes will take place in China, in a similar fashion to events in other countries in the late 20th and early 21st centuries, has been the subject of some debate in recent years. Some commentators talk of China as a "social volcano" that could erupt at any time as a result of mounting discontent over inequalities and injustices. As we have already suggested, though, rising discontent does not always or inevitably result in increased collective action, let alone revolution. Also, as Martin King Whyte notes, most Chinese citizens are quite tolerant of high levels of inequality, and the most disadvantaged are not always angrier about inequality and distributive injustice than those in more advantaged groups in society.[25] In general, rural residents, especially farmers, express less anger about such matters than urbanites. This does not mean that reports of rising anger in rural areas are incorrect, or that inequalities are not associated with social tension (see Chapter 11). However, according to Whyte, widening inequalities are not the immediate trigger of most rural protest incidents. Rather, the majority of such incidents in recent years have focused on procedural injustices, such as

---

[25] This discussion summarizes points made in Whyte 2010a. Whyte's claims are based on the findings of a survey conducted in 2004. Chapter 11 also refers to this survey.

the expropriation of land without proper consultation or compensation, rather than distributive injustices.

Most rural protest has been localized, and has not challenged central state policies or leaders. Rather, it has focused on the injustices of local procedures (or the lack of procedure), the corruption of local leaders and their failure to properly implement state policies and laws. The same is essentially true of almost all other protests. To date, with only a few exceptions, they have been confined to single communities, or, in the case of workers' protests, single factories,[26] and they complain about particular local authorities, rather than the regime. We conclude with the words of the leading historian Elizabeth Perry:

The genius of the Chinese political order – whether in imperial times, in Mao's day, or today – has been its capacity to sustain (and on occasion even to stimulate) massive popular protest without jeopardizing the fundamental underpinnings of the system. So long as Chinese popular protests target "men" rather than "principles", a revolutionary challenge to the legitimacy of the regime remains unlikely. Yet it seems appropriate to close this brief historical overview on a note of caution: . . . [H]istorically grounded forecasts, in China as elsewhere, have a way of being overtaken by history itself.[27]

Summary

Since the 1990s, there has been an upsurge in collective action in China, including in the formation of NGOs and in NGO-led campaigning, and rises in the frequency and number of people involved in collective petitions, and strikes, riots and other forms of protest. Changes in political opportunities have enabled and spurred on these forms of collective action. For example, the state's increased tolerance of NGOs and its efforts to promote the rule of law have created openings for certain types of collective action. Perhaps even more significantly, efforts to promote the rule of law have created a stronger consciousness of citizens' legal rights and have lent popular and official legitimacy to types of collective action that seek to protect these rights or to protest against the behavior of local officials, employers and others who violate them. The commercialization of the media and advances in communication technology have opened further opportunities for mobilizing people for collective action, and so too have aspects of state structures themselves. Divisions between

---

[26] For a discussion of the Liaoyang protests as "the exception that proves the rule", see Lee 2007b.

[27] Perry 2008, p. 215.

different bureaucracies and levels of government and the "amphibious-ness" of some state bodies (meaning that they can be converted for purposes other than those intended by the state) provide resources for collective action.

Political opportunities and resources have been taken up in collective actions that have had a range of goals and have been framed in a variety of ways. Some of the most influential and effective NGOs have worked in the areas of women's rights, especially anti-domestic violence activism, and environmental protection. The largest and commonest forms of collective petitioning and protest action have focused on violations of workers' rights and the illegal and corrupt behavior of village leaders, especially around land expropriation. These different types of collective action most often have been framed in terms of legal rights, while some-times also drawing on a Maoist discourse of equality and justice for "the masses".

Collective actions have made an important contribution to social and political change but, to date, they have not resulted in the kind of regime change that occurred in the Soviet Union in 1989. However, both NGOs and protest actions have achieved some concrete changes with respect to specific goals; have contributed to shifts in public awareness and attitudes to a range of issues; and have brought about significantly greater popular participation in decision-making processes.

Discussion questions

1. What are the main forms of collective action in contemporary China? Why has collective action taken these forms?
2. To what extent, and in what ways, has collective action con-tributed to social change in contemporary China? Illustrate your answer with reference to one or two types or areas of collective action.
3. What arguments can you propose for and against the notion of China as a "social volcano" that will erupt in large-scale, regime-changing collective action in the near future as a result of mounting discontent over inequalities and injustices? What are the difficulties of making such a diagnosis or prediction?

Recommended reading

Cai, Yongshun 2010, *Collective Resistance in China: Why Popular Protests Succeed or Fail*. Stanford, CA: Stanford University Press.

Ho, Peter & Edmonds, Richard Louis (eds) 2008, *China's Embedded Activism: Opportunities and Constraints of a Social Movement*. London: Routledge.

Hsing, You-tien & Lee, Ching Kwan (eds) 2010, *Reclaiming Chinese Society: The New Social Activism*. London: Routledge.

Hsiung, Ping-Chun, Jaschok, Maria, Milwertz, Cecilia & Chan, Red (eds) 2001, *Chinese Women Organizing: Cadres, Feminists, Muslims, Queers*. Oxford, UK: Berg.

Lee, Ching Kwan 2007c, *Against the Law: Labor Protests in China's Rustbelt and Sunbelt*. Berkeley: University of California Press.

Mertha, Andrew C 2008, *China's Water Warriors: Citizen Action and Policy Change*. Ithaca, NY: Cornell University.

O'Brien, Kevin J (ed.) 2008, *Popular Protest in China*. Cambridge, MA: Harvard University Press.

O'Brien, Kevin J & Li, Lianjiang (eds) 2006, *Rightful Resistance in Rural China*. Cambridge, UK: Cambridge University Press.

Unger, Jonathan (ed.) 2008, *Associations and the Chinese State: Contested Spaces*. Armonk, NY: ME Sharpe.

Glossary of Chinese Terms

Pinyin	Characters	English translation
baojia	保甲	pre-communist form of social control through inter-household mutual responsibility
caizi jiaren	才子佳人	the scholar and the beauty
chaxu geju	差序格局	differential mode of association
chengzhongcun	城中村	villages-in-cities
cun	村	village
dagong	打工	temporary or seasonal employment
danwei	单位	work unit
dibao	低保	minimum livelihood allowance
fenliezhuyifenzi	分裂主义分子	a traitor who wishes to split up the country (lit. "splittist")
ganqing	感情	true feelings
gongmin de hefa quanyi	公民的合法权益	citizens' legal rights
gongzuo	工作	work, a "proper job"
guanxi	关系	connections, relationships with people outside of the family
hukou	户口	household registration
jia	家	family
jieceng	阶层	(social) stratum
jiedao	街道	street or ward (the lowest level of state administration in urban areas)
jieji	阶级	(social) class
laoban jidutu	老板基督徒	boss Christians
laodong	劳动	labor, work, toil
li	礼	rituals and rules of social behavior
minzu	民族	a nationality, ethnic group
nan zhu wai, nü zhu nei	男主外, 女主内	saying: "Men rule outside, women rule inside."
pinwei	品位	good taste
putonghua	普通话	Mandarin Chinese (lit. "the common language")
qigong	气功	physical exercise involving the manipulation of *qi* (the vital energy of life)

Pinyin	Characters	English translation
sanwu	三无	the "three withouts": those without family, who are sick, disabled or elderly
sheng	省	province
shequ	社区	residential community
shequ jumin weiyuanhui	社区居民委员会	community residents' committee
shidi nongmin	失地农民	landless villager
suzhi	素质	(human) quality
suzhi jiaoyu	素质教育	education for quality
tongzhi	同志	comrade, homosexual
tuchan	土产	special local product (lit. "product from the earth")
wang zi cheng long de xinli	望子成龙的心里	the psychology of hoping one's child becomes a dragon
wenming	文明	civilization
xiagang	下岗	laid-off, retrenched
xian	县	county
xiang	乡	town
xinfang	信访	petitions (lit. "letters and visits")
yizu	蚁族	ant tribe, an expression referring to university graduates working in large numbers in low-paid jobs and living in poor-quality rental accommodation in cities
yueji	跃级	skip levels (of government), for example, when petitioning authorities
zhen	镇	township
zhigong	职工	employees (lit. "staff and workers")
zhongdian renkou	重点人口	targeted persons

References

Ahern, Emily Martin 1981, *Chinese Ritual and Politics*. Cambridge, UK: Cambridge University Press.

All China Women's Federation and National Bureau of Statistics 2011, "*Di san qi Zhongguo funü shehui diwei diaocha: zhuyao shuji baogao*" [The third survey of Chinese women's status: A report on key figures], retrieved 27 February 2012 at <http://www.china.com.cn/zhibo/zhanti/ch-xinwen/2011-10/21/content_23687810.htm>

Appleton, Simon, Song, Lina & Xia, Qingjie 2010, "Growing out of poverty: trends and patterns of urban poverty in China, 1988–2002", *World Development*, vol. 38, no. 5, pp. 665–78.

Asad, Talal 1993, *Genealogies of Religion: Discipline and Reasons of Power in Christianity and Islam*. Baltimore: Johns Hopkins University Press.

Bakken, Børge 2000, *The Exemplary Society: Human Improvement, Social Control, and the Dangers of Modernity in China*. New York: Oxford University Press.

Baranovitch, Nimrod 2003, *China's New Voices: Popular Music, Ethnicity, Gender and Politics, 1978–1997*. Berkeley: University of California Press.

Barmé, Geremie (ed.) 1996, *Shades of Mao: The Posthumous Cult of the Great Leader*. Armonk, NY: ME Sharpe.

Benjamin, Dwayne, Brandt, Loren, Giles, Wang, & Wang, Sangui 2008, "Income inequality during China's great economic transformation", in Loren Brandt & Thomas Rawski (eds) *China's Great Economic Transformation*. New York: Cambridge University Press, pp. 729–75.

Berman, Marshall 1982, *All That is Solid Melts into Air: The Experience of Modernity*. New York: Simon & Schuster.

Bian, Yanjie 1994, "*Guanxi* and the allocation of urban jobs in China", *The China Quarterly*, no. 140, pp. 971–99.

Bian, Yanjie 2009, "Urban occupational mobility and employment institutions: hierarchy, market and networks in a mixed system", in Deborah S Davis & Wang Feng (eds) *Creating Wealth and Poverty in Postsocialist China*. Stanford, CA: Stanford University Press, pp. 172–90.

Bianco, Lucien 1971, *Origins of the Chinese Revolution, 1915–1949*. Stanford, CA: Stanford University Press.

Biddulph, Sarah & Cook, Sandy 1999, "Kidnapping and selling women and children: the state's construction and response", *Violence against Women*, vol. 5, no. 12, pp. 1437–68.

Billioud, Sebastien & Thoraval, Joel 2007, "*Jiaohua*: The Confucian revival in China as an educative project", *China Perspectives*, no. 4, pp. 4–20.

Bossen, Laurel 2002, *Chinese Women and Rural Development: Sixty Years of Change in Lu Village, Yunnan.* Lanham, MD: Rowman and Littlefield.

Bramall, Chris 2008, *Chinese Economic Development.* London: Routledge.

Brandt, Loren & Rawski, Thomas (eds) 2008, *China's Great Economic Transformation.* New York: Cambridge University Press.

Brandtstadter, Susanne & dos Santos, Goncalo (eds) 2009, *Chinese Kinship: Contemporary Anthropological Perspectives.* New York: Routledge.

Bray, David 2005, *Social Space and Governance in Urban China: The* Danwei *from Origins to Reform.* Stanford, CA: Stanford University Press.

Breen, Richard & Rottman, David B 1995, *Class Stratification: A Comparative Perspective.* New York: Harvester Wheatsheaf.

Brooks, David 2000, *Bobos in Paradise: The New Upper Class and How they Got There.* New York: Simon & Schuster.

Buckingham, Will & Chan, Kam Wing 2008, "Is China abolishing the *hukou* system?" *The China Quarterly*, vol. 195 (September), pp. 582–606.

Bulag, Uradyn E 2003, "Mongolian ethnicity and linguistic anxiety in China", *American Anthropologist*, vol. 105, no. 4, pp. 753–63.

Cai, Hua 2001, *A Society without Fathers or Husbands: The* Na *of China* (trans. Asti Hustverdt). Cambridge, MA: Zone Books.

Cai, Rong 2008, "Carnivalesque pleasure: The audio-visual market and the consumption of television drama", in Ying Zhu, Michael Keane and Ruoyun Bai (eds) *TV Drama in China.* Hong Kong: Hong Kong University Press, pp. 129–44.

Cai, Yongshun 2010, *Collective Resistance in China: Why Popular Protests Succeed or Fail.* Stanford, CA: Stanford University Press.

Cao, Nanlai 2011, *Constructing China's Jerusalem.* Stanford, CA: Stanford University Press.

Chan, Anita 2001, *China's Workers Under Assault: The Exploitation of Labor in a Globalizing Economy.* Armonk, NY: ME Sharpe.

Chan, Anita (ed.) 2011a, *Walmart in China.* Ithaca, NY: ILR Press.

Chan, Anita 2011b, "Introduction", in Anita Chan (ed.) *Walmart in China.* Ithaca, NY: Cornell University Press, pp. 1–12.

Chan, Anita 2012, "Strikes in China's export industries in comparative perspective", *The China Journal*, no. 65, pp. 27–51.

Chan, Anita, Madsen, Richard & Unger, Jonathan 2009, *Chen Village: From Revolution to Globalization.* Berkeley: University of California Press.

Chan, Anita & Siu, Kaxton 2010, "Analyzing exploitation", *Critical Asian Studies*, vol. 42, no. 2, pp. 167–90.

Chan, Koonchung 2011, *The Fat Years.* London: Doubleday.

Chase, Thomas 2012, "Problems of publicity: online activism and discussion of same-sex sexuality in South Korea and China", *Asian Studies Review*, vol. 36, no. 2, pp. 151–70.

Chau, Adam Yuet 2006, *Miraculous Response: Doing Popular Religion in Contemporary China.* Stanford, CA: Stanford University Press.

Chen, Calvin 2008, *Some Assembly Required: Work, Community and Politics in China's Rural Enterprises.* Cambridge, MA: Harvard University Press.

Chen, Feng 2003, "Between the state and labour: the conflict of Chinese trade unions' double identity in market reform", *The China Quarterly*, no. 176, pp. 1006–28.

Chen, Jia 2010, "Country's wealth divide past warning level", *China Daily*, retrieved 28 November 2012 at <http://www.chinadaily.com.cn/china/2010-05/12/content_9837073.htm>

Chen, Jiandong, Dai, Dai, Pu, Ming, Hou, Wenxuan & Feng, Qiaobin 2010, "The trend of the Gini coefficient in China". University of Manchester, Brooks World Poverty Institute Working Paper 109.

Chen, Xi 2008, "Collective petitioning and institutional conversion", in Kevin J O'Brien (ed.) *Popular Protest in China*. Cambridge, MA: Harvard University Press, pp. 54–70.

Cheng, Joseph Yu-shek, Ngok, King-lun & Huang, Yan 2012, "Multinational corporations, global civil society and Chinese labour: workers' solidarity in China in the era of globalization", *Economic and Industrial Democracy*, vol. 33, no. 3, pp. 379–401.

China Labor Watch 2012, "Samsung supplier factory exploiting child labor – investigative report on HEG Electronics (Huizhou) Co., Ltd, Samsung supplier", China Labor Watch, 7 August, retrieved 29 November 2012 at <http://www.chinalaborwatch.org/pro/proshow-175.html>

China Labour Bulletin 2007, *Small Hands: A Survey Report on Child Labour in China*. *China Labour Bulletin*, Research Report No. 3, September, retrieved 20 November 2012 at <http://www.clb.org.hk>

"China: migrants" 2012, *Migration News*, retrieved 16 November 2012 at <http://migration.ucdavis.edu/mn/comments.php?id=3794_0_3_0>

China Net Network Information Center [CNNIC] 2010, "*Zhongguo hulian wang luo fazhan zhuangkuang tongji baogao*" [Statistical report on internet development in China], retrieved 21 May 2012 at <http://www.cnnic.net.cn/en/index/>

China Net Network Information Center [CNNIC] 2012, "*Zhongguo hulian wang luo fazhan zhuangkuang tongji baogao*" [Statistical report on internet development in China], retrieved 21 May 2012 at <http://www.cnnic.cn/hlwfzyj/hlwxzbg/hlwtjbg/201207/P020120723477451202474.pdf>

"China ranks No. 2 on Forbes billionaires list" 2010, *China Daily*, 11 March, retrieved 29 October 2012 at <http://www.chinadaily.com.cn/business/2010-03/11/content_9575101.htm>

"China set to give NGOs equal status" 2012, 8 May, retrieved 14 May 2012 at <http://www.china.org.cn/china/2012-05/08/content_25325862.htm>

"China's floating population exceeds 221 million" 2011, *Xinhua*, 1 March, retrieved 28 May 2012 at <http://www.china.org.cn/china/2011-03/01/content_22025827.htm>

Chinese Communist Party [CCP] 1981, "Resolution on certain questions in the history of our party since the founding of the People's Republic of China", retrieved 29 November 2012 at <http://www.marxists.org/subject/china/documents/cpc/history/01.htm>

Chinese Women's Research Network 2011, "Shanghai sustains late marriage trend", retrieved 17 December 2012 at <http://en.wsic.ac.cn/academicnews/2095.htm>

Cho, Mun Young 2009, "On the edge between "the people" and "the population:" ethnographic research on the minimum livelihood guarantee", *China Quarterly*, no. 201, pp. 20–37.

Chung, Jae Ho, Lai, Hongyi & Xia, Ming 2006, "Mounting challenges to governance in China: Surveying collective protestors, religious sects and criminal organizations", *The China Journal*, no. 56 (July), pp. 1–31.

Cliff, Tom 2012, "The partnership of stability in Xinjiang: State–society interactions following the July 2009 unrest", *The China Journal*, no. 68 (July), pp. 79–105.

Coale, Ansley J 1989, "Marriage and childbearing in China since 1940", *Social Forces*, vol. 67, no. 4, pp. 833–50.

Cockain, Alex 2012, *Young Chinese in Urban China*. London: Routledge.

Cohen, Philip N & Wang, Feng 2009, "Market and gender pay equity: Have Chinese reforms narrowed the gap?" in Deborah S Davis & Wang Feng (eds) *Creating Wealth and Poverty in Postsocialist China*. Stanford, CA: Stanford University Press, pp. 37–53.

"Comparing Chinese provinces with countries. All the parities in China. Which countries match the GDP, population and exports of Chinese provinces?" 2010, *The Economist*, retrieved 28 October 2012 at <http://www.economist.com/content/chinese_equivalents>

"Constitution of the People's Republic of China" 1982 (amended 2004), retrieved 7 June 2012 at <http://www.npc.gov.cn/englishnpc/Law/2007-12/05/content_1381903.htm>

Cook, Sarah & Dong, Xiaoyuan 2011, "Harsh choices: Chinese women's paid work and unpaid care responsibilities under economic reform", *Development and Change*, vol. 42, no. 4, pp. 947–65.

Davis, Deborah S & Wang Feng (eds) 2009, *Creating Wealth and Poverty in Postsocialist China*. Stanford, CA: Stanford University Press.

Diana, Antonella 2009, "Re-configuring belonging in post-socialist Xishuangbanna, China", in Andrew Walker (ed.) *Tai Lands and Thailand. Community and State in Southeast Asia*. National University of Singapore Press, pp. 192–213.

Dryburgh, Marjorie 2011, "Foundations of Chinese identity: place, past and culture", in Xiaowei Zang (ed.) *Understanding Chinese Society*. London: Routledge.

Duhigg, Charles & Barboza, David 2012, "In China, the human costs that are built into an iPad", *The New York Times*, 26 January, retrieved 29 November 2012 at <http://www.nytimes.com/2012/01/26/business/ieconomy-apples-ipad-and-the-human-costs-for-workers-in-china.html?pagewanted=all>

Dutton, Michael 1992, *Policing and Punishment in China: From Patriarchy to "the People"*. Cambridge, UK: Cambridge University Press.

Dutton, Michael 1998, *Streetlife China*. Cambridge, UK: Cambridge University Press.

Economist Intelligence Unit 2012, "Supersized cities: China's 13 megalopolises", retrieved 29 November 2012 at <http://www.eiu.com/megalopolis>

Edwards, Louise 2008, *Gender, Politics and Democracy: Women's Suffrage in China*. Stanford, CA: Stanford University Press.

Elvin, Mark 1973, *The Pattern of the Chinese Past: A Social and Economic Interpretation*. Stanford, CA: Stanford University Press.

Entwisle, Barbara & Henderson, Gail E (eds) 2000, *Re-drawing Boundaries: Work, Households, and Gender in China*. Berkeley: University of California Press.

Esherick, Joseph W & Wasserstrom, Jeffrey N 1990, "Acting out democracy: political theater in modern China", *The Journal of Asian Studies*, vol. 49, no. 4, pp. 835–65.

Evans, Harriet 1997, *Women and Sexuality in China: Dominant Discourses of Female Sexuality and Gender since 1949*. Cambridge, UK: Polity Press.

Eyferth, Jacob 2006, *How China Works: Perspectives on the Twentieth-Century Industrial Workplace*. Milton Park, UK: Routledge.

Fan, Cindy 2008, *China on the Move: Migration, the State, and the Household*. London: Routledge.

Fang, Xuyan & Yu, Lea 2012, "China refuses to release Gini coefficient", *Caixin*, 19 January, retrieved 23 January 2012 at <http://marketwatch.com/story/china-refuses-to-release-gini-coefficient-2012-01-18>

Farrer, James 2002, *Opening Up: Youth Sex Culture and Market Reform in Shanghai*. Chicago: University of Chicago Press.

Farrer, James 2007, "China's women sex bloggers and dialogic sexual politics on the Chinese internet", *China Actuell*, vol. 36, no. 4, pp. 1–36.

Fauna 2011, "New Chinese Marriage Law protects men's assets, angers women", chinaSMACK, 17 August, retrieved 18 May 2012 at <http://www.chinasmack.com/2011/stories/new-chinese-marriage-law-prot-ects-mens-assets>

Fei, Hsiao Tung [Fei, Xiaotong] 1983 [first published 1936], *Chinese Village Close-Up*. Beijing: New World Press.

Fei, Hsiao Tung [Fei, Xiaotong] 1992, *From the Soil: The Foundations of Chinese Society, A Translation of Fei Xiaotong's Xiangtu Zhongguo* (trans.Gary Hamilton & Wang Zheng). Berkeley: University of California Press.

Feuchtwang, Stephan 2001, *Popular Religion in China: The Imperial Metaphor*. Richmond, UK: Curzon.

Fitzgerald, John 1996, *Awakening China: Politics, Culture, and Class in the Nationalist Revolution*. Stanford, CA: Stanford University Press.

Fong, Vanessa L 2002, "China's one-child policy and the empowerment of urban daughters", *American Anthropologist*, vol. 104, no. 4, pp. 1098–1109.

Fong, Vanessa L 2011, *Paradise Redefined: Transnational Chinese Students and the Quest for Flexible Citizenship in the Developed World*. Stanford, CA: Stanford University Press.

Friedman, Eli & Lee, Ching Kwan 2010, "Remaking the world of Chinese labor: a 30-year retrospective", *British Journal of Industrial Relations*, vol. 48, no. 3, pp. 507–33.

Friedman, Sara L 2006, *Intimate Politics: Marriage, the Market, and State Power in Southeastern China*. Cambridge, MA: Harvard University Press.

Friends of Nature no date, retrieved 16 May 2012 at <http://www.fon.org.cn/channal.php?cid=616>

Gaetano, Arianne & Jacka, Tamara (eds) 2004, *On the Move: Women and Rural-to-Urban Migration in Contemporary China*. New York: Columbia University Press.

Gao, Qin 2010, "Redistributive nature of the social benefit system: progressive or regressive?" *The China Quarterly*, no. 201, pp. 1–19.

Giddens, Anthony 1977, *Studies in Social and Political Theory*. London: Hutchinson.

Giddens, Anthony 1991, *Modernity and Self-Identity: Self and Society in the Late Modern Age*. Cambridge, UK: Polity Press.

Gillette, Maris B 2000, *Between Mecca and Beijing: Modernization and Consumption among Urban Chinese Muslims*. Stanford, CA: Stanford University Press.

Gladney, Dru 1990, "The ethnogenesis of the Uighur", *Central Asian Survey*, vol. 9, no. 1, pp. 1–28.

Gladney, Dru (ed.) 1998, *Making Majorities: Constituting the Nation in Japan, Korea, China, Malaysia, Fiji, Turkey and the United States*. Stanford, CA: Stanford University Press.

Gladney, Dru 2004a, "Representing nationality in China: Refiguring majority/minority identities", *Journal of Asian Studies*, vol. 53, no. 1, pp. 92–123.

Gladney, Dru 2004b, *Dislocating China: Reflections on Muslims, Minorities, and Other Subaltern Subjects*. Chicago: University of Chicago Press.

Glauben, Thomas, Herzfeld, Scott, Rozelle, Scott, & Wang, Xiaobing 2012, "Persistent poverty in rural China: Where, why and how to escape?" *World Development*, vol. 40, no. 4, pp. 784–95.

Godement, Francois 2012, "Control at the grassroots: China's new toolbox", retrieved 28 June 2012 at <http://ecfr.eu/page/-/China_Analysis_Control_at_the_Grassroots_June_2012.pdf>, pp. 6–7.

Goffman, Erving 1961, *Asylums: Essays on the Social Situation of Mental Patients and Other Inmates*. New York: Doubleday.

Gold, Thomas, Guthrie, Doug & Wank, David L (eds) 2002, *Social Connections in China: Institutions, Culture and the Changing Nature of Guanxi*. New York: Cambridge University Press.

Gold, Thomas, Hurst, William J, Won, Jaeyoun & Li, Qiang (eds) 2009, *Laid-off Workers in a Workers' State: Unemployment with Chinese Characteristics*. New York: Palgrave Macmillan.

Goldstein, Melvyn C, Childs, Geoff & Wangdui, Puchung 2011, "Beijing's 'people first' development initiative for the Tibet Autonomous Region's rural sector: A case study from the Shigatse area", *The China Journal*, no. 63 (January), pp. 57–75.

Goldstein, Melvyn C, Jiao, Ben & Lhundrup, Tanzen 2009, *On the Cultural Revolution in Tibet: The Nyemo Incident of 1969*. Berkeley: University of California Press.

Golley, Jane & Meng, Xin 2011, "Has China run out of surplus labour?" *China Economic Review*, vol. 22, pp. 555–72.

Goodman, David SG (ed.) 2008, *The New Rich in China: Future Rulers, Present Lives*. London: Routledge.

Goossaert, Vincent & Palmer, David A 2011, *The Religious Question in Modern China*. Chicago: University of Chicago Press.

Greenhalgh, Susan 2003, "Planned births, unplanned persons: 'Population' in the making of Chinese modernity", *American Ethnologist*, vol. 30, no. 2: 196–215.

Greenhalgh, Susan 2008, *Just One Child: Science and Policy in Deng's China*. University of California Press.

Greenhalgh, Susan & Winckler, Edwin A 2005, *Governing China's Population: From Leninist to Neoliberal Politics*. Stanford, CA: Stanford University Press.

Griffiths, Michael B, Chapman, Malcolm & Christiansen, Flemming 2010, "Chinese consumers: The romantic reappraisal", *Ethnography*, vol. 11, no. 3, pp. 331–57.

Grose, Timothy 2010, "The Tibet and Xinjiang *neidi* classes: the aims, strategies, and difficulties of educating a new generation of ethnic minority students", *Chinese Education and Society*, vol. 43, no. 3, pp. 3–9.

Gu, Julia 2012, "China's provincial GDP figures in 2011", *China Briefing*, 27 January, retrieved 28 October 2012 at <http://www.china-briefing.com/news/2012/01/27/chinas-provincial-gdp-figures-in-2011.html>

Guo, Yingjie 2008, "Class, stratum and group: the politics of description and prescription", in David SG Goodman (ed.) *The New Rich in China: Future Rulers, Present Lives*. London: Routledge, pp. 38–52.

Gustaffson, Björn, Li, Shi & Sicular, Terry (eds) 2008a, *Inequality and Public Policy in China*. New York: Cambridge University Press.

Gustaffson, Björn, Li, Shi & Sicular, Terry 2008b, "Inequality and public policy in China: Issues and trends", in Björn Gustaffson, Li Shi & Terry Sicular (eds) *Inequality and Public Policy in China*. NY: Cambridge University Press, pp. 1–34.

Han, Min 2001, *Social Change and Continuity in a Village in Northern Anhui, China: A Response to Revolution and Reform*. Osaka, Japan: National Museum of Ethnology.

Hansen, Mette Halskov 1999, *Lessons in Being Chinese: Minority Education and Ethnic Identity in Southwest China*. Seattle: University of Washington Press.

Hansen, Mette Halskov & Svarverud, Rune (eds) 2010, *iChina: The Rise of the Individual in Modern Chinese Society*. Copenhagen: NIAS Press.

Hanser, Amy 2008, *Service Encounters: Class, Gender and the Market for Social Distinction in Urban China*. Stanford, CA: Stanford University Press.

Harrell, Stevan (ed.) 1995, *Cultural Encounters on China's Ethnic Frontiers*. Seattle: University of Washington Press.

He, Qinglian 2003, "A listing social structure" in Wang Chaohua (ed.) *One China, Many Paths*. London: Verso, pp. 163–88.

He, Shenjing, Liu, Yuting, Wu, Fulong & Webster, Chris 2008, "Poverty incidence and concentration in different social groups in urban China: a case study of Nanjing", *Cities*, vol. 25, pp. 121–32.

He, Xuefeng 2010, "Nongcun tudi de zhengzhixue [The politics of rural land]", *Xuexi yu Tansuo* [Study and exploration], vol. 2, no. 187, pp. 70–5.

Hershatter, Gail 2007, *Women in China's Long Twentieth Century*. Berkeley: University of California Press.

Hershatter, Gail 2011, *The Gender of Memory: Rural Women and China's Collective Past*. Berkeley: University of California Press.

Hess, Steve 2010, "Dividing and conquering the shop floor: Uyghur labor export and labour segmentation in China's industrial east", *Central Asian Survey*, vol. 28, no. 4, pp. 403–16.

Hinton, William 1966, *Fanshen: A Documentary of Revolution in a Chinese Village*. Harmondsworth, UK: Penguin.

Ho, Loretta Wing Wah 2010, *Gay and Lesbian Subculture in Urban China*. London: Routledge.

Ho, Peter & Edmonds, Richard Louis (eds) 2008, *China's Embedded Activism: Opportunities and Constraints of a Social Movement*. London: Routledge.

Hsing, You-tien & Lee, Ching Kwan (eds) 2010, *Reclaiming Chinese Society: The New Social Activism*. London: Routledge.

Hsiung, Ping-Chun, Jaschok, Maria, Milwertz, Cecilia & Chan, Red (eds) 2001, *Chinese Women Organizing: Cadres, Feminists, Muslims, Queers*. Oxford, UK: Berg.

Hsu, Francis LK 1971 [1948], *Under the Ancestors' Shadow: Kinship, Personality, and Social Mobility in China*. Stanford, CA: Stanford University Press.

Huang, Chien-Yu Julia & Weller, Robert P 1998, "Merit and mothering: Women and social welfare in Taiwanese Buddhism", *The Journal of Asian Studies*, vol. 57, no. 2, pp. 379–96.

Huang, Hao 2001, "*Yaogun yinyue*: rethinking mainland Chinese rock 'n' roll", *Popular Music*, vol. 20, no. 1, pp. 1–11.

Huang, Jikun, Zhi, Huayong, Huang, Zhurong, Rozelle, Scott & Giles, John. 2011, "The impact of the global financial crisis on off-farm employment and earnings in rural China", *World Development*, vol. 39, no. 5, pp. 797–807.

Huang, Philip, Yuan, Gao & Peng, Yusheng 2012, "Capitalization without proletarianization in China's agricultural development", *Modern China*, vol. 38, no. 2, pp. 139–73.

Huang, Xianbi 2008, "*Guanxi* networks and job searches in China's emerging labour market: a qualitative investigation", *Work, employment, society*, vol. 22, no. 3, pp. 467–84.

Huang, Yuqing 2011, "Labour, leisure, gender and generation: the organization of '*wan*' and the notion of 'gender equality' in contemporary rural China", in Tamara Jacka & Sally Sargeson (eds) *Women, Gender and Rural Development in China*. Cheltenham, UK: Edward Elgar, pp. 49–70.

Hudson, Valerie M 2012, "China's census: The one-child policy's gender-ratio failure", *World Politics Review*, 26 February, retrieved 27 February 2012 at <http://www.worldpoliticsreview.com/articles/8731/chinas-census-the-one-child-policys-gender-ratio-failure>

Human Rights Watch 2009, "'An alleyway in hell': China's abusive 'black jails'" retrieved 29 November 2012 at <http://www.hrw.org/reports/2009/11/12/alleyway-hell>

Hung, Ho-fung 2008, "Rise of China and the global accumulation crisis", *Review of International Political Economy*, vol. 15, no. 2, pp. 149–79.

Hurst, William 2009a, *The Chinese Worker After Socialism*. New York: Cambridge University Press.

Hurst, William J 2009b, "The power of the past: nostalgia and popular discontent in contemporary China", in Thomas Gold, William Hurst, Jaeyoun Won, & Li Qiang (eds) *Laid-off Workers in a Workers' State: Unemployment with Chinese Characteristics*. New York: Palgrave Macmillan, pp. 115–32.

Ikels, Charlotte (ed.) 2004, *Filial Piety: Practice and Discourse in Contemporary East Asia*. Stanford, CA: Stanford University Press.

International Labor Organization 2010, "Main statistics – economically active population", retrieved 27 November 2012 at <http://laborsta.ilo.org/applv8/data/c l e.html>

Jacka, Tamara 1997, *Women's Work in Rural China: Change and Continuity in an Era of Reform*. Cambridge, UK: Cambridge University Press.

Jacka, Tamara 2006, *Rural Women in Urban China: Gender, Migration, and Social Change*. Armonk, NY: ME Sharpe.

Jacka, Tamara 2007, "Population governance in the PRC: Political, historical and anthropological perspectives", *The China Journal*, no. 58 (July), pp. 111–26.

Jacka, Tamara (ed.) 2009, "Quality and Citizenship in China", *positions: east asia cultures critique*, vol. 17, no. 3 [special issue].

Jacka, Tamara 2012, "Migration, householding, and the well-being of left-behind women in rural Ningxia", *The China Journal*, no. 67, pp. 1–21.

Jacka, Tamara & Sargeson, Sally (eds) 2011a, *Women, Gender and Rural Development in China*. Cheltenham, UK: Edward Elgar.

Jacka, Tamara & Sargeson, Sally 2011b, "Introduction: conceptualizing women, gender and rural development in China", in Tamara Jacka & Sally Sargeson (eds) *Women, Gender and Rural Development in China* (Cheltenham, UK: Edward Elgar, 2011), pp. 1–24.

Jankowiak, William R 1988, "The last hurrah? Political protest in Inner Mongolia", *The Australian Journal of Chinese Affairs*, no. 19/20, pp. 269–88.

Jeffreys, Elaine (ed.) 2006, *Sex and Sexuality in China*. London: Routledge.

Jenkins, Richard 1996, *Social Identity*. London: Routledge.

Jian, Weiyuan, Chan, Kit Lee, Reidpath, Daniel & Xu, Ling. 2010, "China's rural–urban care gap shrank for chronic disease patients, but inequities persist", *Health Affairs*, vol. 29, no. 12, pp. 2192–4.

Jiang, Chenghcheng 2011, "In Beijing, students in limbo after migrant schools closed", *Time*, 14 September, retrieved 18 December 2011 at <http://www.time.com/time/world/article/0,8599,2093175,00.html>

Joffe-Walt, Benjamin 2005, "Mad about the girl: a pop idol for China", *The Guardian*, 7 October, retrieved 29 November 2012 at <http://www.guardian.co.uk/media/2005/oct/07/chinathemedia.broadcasting>

Judd, Ellen R 1989, "*Niangjia*: Chinese women and their natal families", *The Journal of Asian Studies*, vol. 48, no. 3, pp. 525–44.

Judd, Ellen R 1994, *Gender and Power in Rural North China*. Stanford, CA: Stanford University Press.

Kang, Liu 2008, "Media boom and cyber culture: Television and the internet in China", in Kam Louie (ed.) *The Cambridge Companion to Modern Chinese Culture*. Cambridge, UK: Cambridge University Press, pp. 318–38.

Keech-Marx, Samantha 2008, "Airing dirty laundry in public: anti–domestic violence activism in Beijing", in Jonathan Unger (ed.) *Associations and the Chinese State: Contested Spaces*. Armonk, NY: ME Sharpe, pp. 175–99.

Khan, Azizur Rahman & Carl Riskin 2005, "China's household income and its distribution, 1995 and 2002", *The China Quarterly*, no. 182, pp. 356–84.

Kipnis, Andrew 1997, *Producing Guanxi: Sentiment, Self, and Subculture in a North China Village*. Durham, NC: Duke University Press.

Kipnis, Andrew 2001, "The flourishing of religion in post-Mao China and the anthropological category of religion", *The Australian Journal of Anthropology*, vol. 12, no. 1, pp. 32–46.

Kipnis, Andrew 2002, "Zouping Christianity as gendered critique? The place of the political in ethnography", *Anthropology and Humanism*, vol. 27, no. 1, pp. 80–96.

Kipnis, Andrew 2004, "Anthropology and the theorisation of citizenship", *The Asia Pacific Journal of Anthropology*, vol. 53, pp. 257–78.

Kipnis, Andrew 2006, "*Suzhi*: A keyword approach", *The China Quarterly*, vol. 186 (June), pp. 295–313.

Kipnis, Andrew 2011a, "Chinese nation building as, instead of, and before globalization", *ProtoSociology*, vol. 28, pp. 25–48.

Kipnis, Andrew 2011b, *Governing Educational Desire: Culture, Politics, and Schooling in China*. Chicago: University of Chicago Press.

Kipnis, Andrew 2012, "Constructing commonality: Standardization and modernization in Chinese nation-building", *Journal of Asian Studies*, vol. 71, no. 3, pp. 731–55.

Kleinman, Arthur, Yan, Yunxiang, Jing, Jun, Lee, Sing, Zhang, Everett, Pan, Tianshu, Wu, Fei, & Guo, Jinhua 2011, *Deep China: The Moral Life of the Person*. Berkeley: University of California Press.

Knight, John & Yueh, Linda 2008, "The role of social capital in the labour market in China", *Economics of Transition*, vol. 16, no. 3, pp. 389–414.

Ko, Dorothy 1994, *Teachers of the Inner Chambers: Women and Culture in China, 1573–1722*. Stanford, CA: Stanford University Press.

Kuan, Teresa 2011, "'The heart says one thing but the hand does another': a story about emotion-work, ambivalence and popular advice for parents", *The China Journal*, no. 65 (January), pp. 77–100.

Kuhn, Philip 1984, "Chinese views of social classification", in James L Watson (ed.) *Class and Social Stratification in Post-Revolution China*. London: Cambridge University Press, pp. 16–28.

Lee, Ching Kwan (ed.) 2007a, *Working in China: Ethnographies of Labor and Workplace Transformation*. Milton Park, UK: Routledge.

Lee, Ching Kwan 2007b, "Is labor a political force in China?" in Elizabeth J Perry & Merle Goldman (eds) *Grassroots Political Reform in Contemporary China*. Cambridge, MA: Harvard University Press, pp. 228–52.

Lee, Ching Kwan 2007c, *Against the Law: Labor Protests in China's Rustbelt and Sunbelt*. Berkeley: University of California Press.

Lee, Ching Kwan 2010, "Workers and the quest for citizenship" in You-tien Hsing & Ching Kwan Lee (eds) *Reclaiming Chinese Society: The New Social Activism*. London: Routledge, pp. 42–63.

Lee, Ching Kwan & Shen, Yuan 2009, "China: the paradox and possibility of a public sociology of labor", *Work and Occupation*, vol. 36, no. 2, pp. 110–25.

Leibold, James 2010, "The Beijing Olympics and China's conflicted national form", *The China Journal*, no. 63 (January), pp. 1–24.

Li, Cheng (ed.) 2010, *China's Emerging Middle Class: Beyond Economic Transformation*. Washington, DC: Brookings Institution Press.

Li, Chunling 2005, Duanlie yu Suipian – Dangdai Zhongguo Shehui Jieceng Fenhua Shizheng Fenxi [*Cleavages and Fragments: An Empirical Analysis of Social Stratification in Contemporary China*]. Beijing: Shehui Kexue Wenxian Chubanshe.

Li, Chunling 2010, "Characterizing China's middle class: heterogeneous composition and multiple identities", in Cheng Li (ed.) *China's Emerging Middle Class: Beyond Economic Transformation*. Washington, DC: Brookings Institution Press, pp. 135–56.

Li, Huaiyin 2009, *Village China under Socialism and Reform: A Micro-History, 1948–2008*. Stanford, CA: Stanford University Press.

Li, Qiang 2012, "Testimony for Congressional Executive Commission on China", 31 July, retrieved 2 August 2012 at <http://www.cecc.gov/pages/hearings/general/hearing7/CECC%20Hearing%20-%20Working%20Conditions%20and%20Worker%20Rights%20in%20China%20-%20Li%20Qiang%20Witness%20Statement.pdf>

Li, Shi & Luo, Chuliang 2010, "Reestimating the income gap between urban and rural households in China", in Martin King Whyte (ed.) *One Country, Two Societies Perceptions of Inequality and Distributive Justice in Contemporary China*. Stanford, CA: Stanford University Press, pp. 105–24.

Li, Shi, Song, Jin & Liu, Xiaochuan 2011, "Evolution of the gender wage gap among China's urban employees", *Social Sciences in China*, vol. 32, no. 3, pp. 161–80.

Li, Xiaoyun & Liu, Xiaoqian 2010, "Stalemate of participation: participatory village development planning for poverty alleviation in China", in Norman Long, Ye Jingzhong & Wang Yihuan, (eds) *Rural Transformations and Development – China in Context*. Cheltenham, UK: Edward Elgar, pp. 312–26.

Liebman, Benjamin L 2011, "A populist threat to China's courts?" in Margaret YK Woo & Mary E Gallagher (eds) *Chinese Justice: Civil Dispute Resolution in Contemporary China*. Cambridge, UK: Cambridge University Press, pp. 269–313.

Litzinger, Ralph A 2000, *Other Chinas: The Yao and the Politics of National Belonging*. Durham, NC: Duke University Press.

Liu, Fengshu 2011, *Urban Youth in China: Modernity, the Internet and the Self*. London: Routledge.

Liu, Petrus & Rofel, Lisa (eds) 2010, "Beyond the Strai(gh)ts: Transnationalism and Queer Chinese Politics", *Positions: East Asia Cultures Critique*, vol. 18, no. 2 [special issue].

Liu, Shao-hua 2011, *Passage to Manhood: Youth Migration, Heroin, and AIDS in Southwest China*. Stanford, CA: Stanford University Press.

Liu, Xin 2002, *The Otherness of Self: A Genealogy of the Self in Contemporary China*. Ann Arbor: The University of Michigan Press.

Lu, Hong, Liu, Jianhong & Crowther, Alicia 2006, "Female criminal victimization and criminal justice response in China", *British Journal of Criminology*, vol. 46, pp. 859–74.

Lu, Ming & Gao, Hong 2011, "Labour market transition, income inequality and economic growth in China", *International labour review*, vol. 150, nos 1–2, pp. 101–26.

Lü, Xiaobo and Perry, Elizabeth (eds) 1997, Danwei: *The Changing Chinese Workplace in Historical and Comparative Perspectives*. New York: ME Sharpe.

Lu, Xueyi (ed.) 2002, *Dangdai Zhongguo shehui jieceng yanjiu baogao [Research Report on Social Stratification in China]*. Beijing: Shehui Kexue Wenxian Chubanshe.

Mackerras, Colin 1994, *China's Minorities: Integration and Modernization in the 20th Century*. Hong Kong: Oxford University Press.

Makley, Charlene 2009, "Review of 'On the Cultural Revolution in Tibet: The Nyemo Incident of 1969'", *The China Journal*, no. 62 (July), pp. 127–30.

Mao, Zedong 1926, "Analysis of the classes in Chinese society", in *Selected Works of Mao Tse-Tung*, vol. 1. Peking: Foreign Languages Press.

Mao, Zedong 1979a, "On the correct handling of contradictions among the people", in Mark Selden (ed.) *The People's Republic of China: A Documentary History of Revolutionary Change*. New York: Monthly Review Press, pp. 323–30.

Mao, Zedong 1979b. "Report to the Second Plenary Session of the Seventh Central Committee of the Communist Party of China', in Mark Selden (ed.) *The People's Republic of China: A Documentary History of Revolutionary Change*. New York: Monthly Review Press, pp. 180–6.

"Marriage Law of the People's Republic of China" 2007, *China Procedural Law Network*, retrieved 18 May 2012 at <http://www.procedurallaw.cn/english/law/200807/t20080724_40987.html>

Marshall, Thomas Humphrey 1963, *Sociology at the Crossroads and Other Essays*. London: Heinemann.

Meisner, Maurice 1986 [first published 1977], *Mao's China and After: A History of the People's Republic [Mao's China]*, revised and expanded edition. New York: The Free Press.

Meriam, Beth 2012, *China's "Tibetan" Frontiers: Sharing the Contested Ground*. Leiden, Netherlands: Global Oriental.

Mertha, Andrew C 2008, *China's Water Warriors: Citizen Action and Policy Change*. Ithaca, NY: Cornell University.

"Migrant workers in China" 2008, *China Labour Bulletin*, 6 June, retrieved 28 May 2012 at <http://www.clb.org.hk/en/node/100259#part1_1>

Millward, James A 2009, "Introduction: does the 2009 Urumchi violence mark a turning point?", *Central Asian Survey*, vol. 28, no. 4, pp. 347–60.

Mueggler, Erik 2001, *The Age of Wild Ghosts: Memory, Violence, and Place in Southwest China*. Berkeley: University of California Press.

Mukhopadhaya, Pundarik, Shantakumar, G & Rao, Bhanoji 2011, *Economic Growth and Income Inequality in China, India and Singapore*, London: Routledge.

Mullaney, Thomas S 2011, *Coming to Terms with the Nation: Ethnic Classification in Modern China*. Berkeley: University of California Press.

National Bureau of Statistics [NBS], Rural Office 2009, *Nongmingong Jiance Diaocha Baogao [Report on a Survey of Rural Migrant Workers]*, retrieved 28 May 2012 at <http://wenku.baidu.com/view/065bc38a6529647d27285255.html>

National Bureau of Statistics [NBS] 2011. *ZhongguoTongji Niangjian 2011 [China Statistical Yearbook 2011]*. Beijing: Zhongguo Tongji Chubanshe. Retrieved 29 November at <http://www.stats.gov.cn/tjsj/ndsj/2011/indexeh.htm>

Nie, Hongping Nannie 2008, *The Dilemma of the Moral Curriculum in a Chinese Secondary School*. Latham, MD: University Press of America.

Nyíri, Pal, Zhang, Juan & Varrall, Merriden 2010, "China's cosmopolitan nationalists: "heroes" and "traitors" of the 2008 Olympics", *The China Journal*, no. 63 (January), pp. 25–55.

O'Brien, Kevin J (ed.) 2008, *Popular Protest in China*. Cambridge, MA: Harvard University Press.

O'Brien, Kevin J & Li, Lianjiang (eds) 2006, *Rightful Resistance in Rural China*. Cambridge, UK: Cambridge University Press.

Organization for Economic Cooperation and Development 2012, *OECD Factbook 2011–2012: Economic, Environmental and Social Statistics*, retrieved 29 November 2012 at <http://www.oecd-ilibrary.org/sites/factbook-2011-en/03/05/01/index.html?contentType=&itemId=/content/chapter/factbook-2011-31-en&containerItemId=/content/serial/18147364&accessItemIds=&mimeType=text/h>

Osborg, John 2013, *Anxious Wealth: Money and Morality Among China's New Rich*. Stanford, CA: Stanford University Press.

Ownby, David 2002, "Approximations of Chinese bandits: Perverse rebels, romantic heroes, or frustrated bachelors?" in Susan Brownell & Jeffrey N Wasserstrom (eds) *Chinese Femininities/Chinese Masculinities: A Reader.* Berkeley: University of California Press, pp. 226–50.

Palmer, David A 2007, Qigong *Fever: Body, Science, and Utopia in China.* New York: Columbia University Press.

Perry, Elizabeth J 1993, *Shanghai on Strike: The Politics of Chinese Labor.* Stanford, CA: Stanford University Press.

Perry, Elizabeth J 2008, "Permanent rebellion? Continuities and discontinuities in Chinese protest", in Kevin J O'Brien (ed.) *Popular Protest in China.* Cambridge, MA: Harvard University Press, pp. 205–16.

Pieke, Frank N 2012, "Immigrant China", *Modern China,* vol. 38, no. 1, pp. 40–77.

Population Census Office 2012, *Zhongguo 2010 Nian Renkou Pucha Ziliao [Tabulation on the 2010 Population Census of the People's Republic of China].* Vol. 1. Beijing: China Statistics Publishing.

Postiglione, Gerard A (ed.) 2006, *Education in Social Change in China: Inequality in a Market Economy.* Armonk, NY: ME Sharpe.

Potter, Sulamith Heins & Potter, Jack 1990, *China's Peasants: The Anthropology of a Revolution.* Cambridge, UK: Cambridge University Press.

Pun, Ngai 2005, *Made in China: Women Factory Workers in a Global Workplace.* Durham, NC: Duke University Press.

Pun, Ngai & Chan, Jenny 2012, "Global capital, the state and Chinese workers: the Foxconn experience", *Modern China,* vol. 38, no. 4, pp. 384–410.

Pun, Ngai & Lu, Huilin, 2010, "A culture of violence: the labor subcontracting system and collective action by construction workers in post-socialist China", *The China Journal,* no. 64, pp. 143–58.

Qin, Liwen 2012, "Gender equality and combating domestic violence", *IIP Digital,* 10 September, retrieved 29 January 2013 at <http://iipdigital.usembassy.gov/st/english/publication/2012/02/20120227160902ael0.5071309.html#axzz1vfrXSNwy>

Qing, Deqing 2006, "Follow-up research on the Potters' investigation of Chashan, South China", *Chinese Sociology and Anthropology,* vol. 38, no. 2, pp. 77–93.

Ramsey, S Robert 1987, *The Languages of China.* Princeton: Princeton University Press.

Read, Benjamin 2012, *Roots of the State: Neighborhood Organization and Social Networks in Beijing and Taipei.* Stanford, CA: Stanford University Press.

Reynolds, Bruce (ed.) 1987, *Reform in China: Challenges and Choices, A Summary and Analysis of the CESRRI Survey.* Armonk, NY: ME Sharpe.

Rofel, Lisa 2010, "The traffic in money boys", *positions: east asia cultures critique,* vol. 18, no. 2, pp. 425–58.

Rofel, Lisa 2013, "Grassroots activism: non-normative sexual politics in post-socialist China", in Wanning Sun & Yingjie Guo (eds) *Unequal China: The Political Economy and Cultural Politics of Inequality.* London: Routledge, pp. 155–67.

Rolandsen, Unn Målfrid H 2010, "A collective of their own: Young volunteers at the fringes of the Party realm", in Mette Halskov Hansen & Rune Svarverud (eds) *iChina: The Rise of the Individual in Modern Chinese Society*. Copenhagen: NIAS Press, pp. 132–63.

Ross, Andrew 2007, "Outsourcing as a way of life?" in Ching Kwan Lee (ed.) *Working in China: Ethnographies of Labor and Workplace Transformation*. London: Routledge, pp. 188–208.

Rudelson, Justin Jon 1997, *Oasis Identities: Uyghur Nationalism along China's Silk Road*. New York: Columbia University Press.

Sanders, Richard, Chen, Yang & Cao, Yiying 2007, "Marginalisation in the Chinese countryside: the question of rural poverty", in Heather Zhang, Bin Wu & Richard Sanders (eds) *Marginalisation in China: Perspectives on Transition and Globalisation*. Aldershot, UK: Ashgate, pp. 15–34.

Sargeson, Sally 1999, *Reworking China's Proletariat*. Houndmills, UK: Macmillan.

Sargeson, Sally 2002, "Subduing the rural house-building craze: attitudes toward housing construction and land use controls in four Zhejiang villages", *The China Quarterly*, no. 172, pp. 927–55.

Sargeson, Sally 2008, "Women's property, women's agency in China's 'new enclosure movement': evidence from Zhejiang", *Development and Change*, vol. 39, no. 4, pp. 641–65.

Sargeson, Sally & Song, Yu 2010, "Land expropriation and the gender politics of citizenship in the urban frontier", *The China Journal*, no. 64 (July), pp. 19–45.

Sargeson, Sally & Song, Yu 2011, "Gender, citizenship and agency in land developments", in Tamara Jacka & Sally Sargeson (eds) *Women, Gender and Development in Rural China*. London: Edward Elgar, pp. 25–48.

Scharping, Thomas 2003, *Birth Control in China, 1949–2000: Population Policy and Demographic Development*. London: RoutledgeCurzon.

Schein, Louisa 2000, *Minority Rules: The Miao and the Feminine in China's Cultural Politics*. Durham, NC: Duke University Press.

Selden, Mark 1993. *The Political Economy of Chinese Development*. Armonk, NY: ME Sharpe.

Shi, Nai'an 2010 [first published in Chinese in 1592], *The Water Margin: Outlaws of the Marsh* (trans. JH Jackson). Hong Kong: Periplus Editions Ltd.

Shi, Shih-Jiunn 2012, "Toward inclusive social citizenship? Rethinking China's social security in the trend towards urban–rural harmonization", *Journal of Social Policy*, vol. 41, no. 4, pp. 789–810.

Shue, Vivienne 1988, *The Reach of the State: Sketches of the Chinese Body Politic*. Stanford, CA: Stanford University Press.

Shue, Vivienne & Wong, Christine (eds) 2007, *Paying for Progress in China: Public Finance, Human Welfare and Changing Patterns of Inequality*. London: Routledge.

Sicular, Terry, Yue, Ximing, Gustafsson, Björn & Li, Shi. 2007, "The urban–rural income gap and inequality in China", *Review of Income and Wealth*, vol. 53, no. 1, pp. 93–126.

Sicular, Terry, Yue, Ximing, Gustafsson, Björn & Li, Shi 2010, "How large is China's rural–urban income gap?" in Martin King Whyte (ed.) *One Country, Two Societies: Rural–Urban Inequality in Contemporary China*. Cambridge, MA: Harvard University Press, pp. 85–103.

Skinner, G William 1971, "Chinese peasants and the closed community: an open and shut case", *Comparative Studies in Society and History*, vol. 13, no. 3, pp. 270–81.

Solinger, Dorothy J (ed.) 1984, *Three Visions of Chinese Socialism*. Boulder, CO: Westview Press.

Solinger, Dorothy J 1999, *Contesting Citizenship in Urban China: Peasant Migrants, the State, and the Logic of the Market*. Berkeley: University of California Press.

Solinger, Dorothy J 2008, "The *Dibao* recipients: mollified anti-emblem of urban modernization", *China Perspectives*, no. 4, pp. 36–46.

Solinger, Dorothy J 2009, "*Xiagang* and the geometry of urban political patronage in China: celebrated state (once) workers and state chagrin", in Thomas Gold, William Hurst, Jaeyoun Won & Li Qiang (eds) *Laid-off Workers in a Workers' State: Unemployment with Chinese Characteristics*. New York: Palgrave Macmillan, pp. 39–60.

Song, Geng 2010, "Chinese masculinities revisited: Male images in contemporary television drama serials", *Modern China*, vol. 36, no. 4, pp. 404–34.

Song, Geng & Lee, Tracy K 2010, "Consumption, class formation and sexuality: reading men's lifestyle magazines in China", *The China Journal*, no. 64 (July), pp. 159–77.

Stacey, Judith 1983, *Patriarchy and Socialist Revolution in China*. Berkeley: University of California Press.

Stafford, Charles 1995, *The Roads of Chinese Childhood: Learning and Identification in Angang*. Cambridge, UK: Cambridge University Press.

Steen, Andreas 2000, "Sound, protest and business: Modern Sky Co. and the new ideology of Chinese rock", *Berliner China-Hefte*, no. 19, pp. 40–64.

Stockman, Norman 2000, *Understanding Chinese Society*. Cambridge, UK: Polity Press.

Sun, Wanning 2013, "Inequality and culture: a new pathway to understanding social inequality", in Wanning Sun & Yingjie Guo (eds) *Unequal China: The Political Economy and Cultural Politics of Inequality*. London: Routledge, pp. 27–42.

Sun, Wanning & Guo, Yingjie (eds) 2013, *Unequal China: The Political Economy and Cultural Politics of Inequality*. London: Routledge.

"Swimming against the tide: a short history of labour conflict in China and the government's attempts to control it" 2010, *China Labour Bulletin*, 12 October, retrieved 15 November 2012 at <http://www.clb.org.hk/en/node/100896>

Tanghe County People's Procuratorate 2011, "Case of Dong Pingling accepting bribes, embezzlement and misappropriating public funds", Tanghe County People's Procuratorate of Henan Province, 30 November, retrieved 23 November 2012 at <http://app.westlawchina.com/maf/china/app/document?&docguid=i3cf76ad500000133ddc193e2c16f534c&hitguid=i3cf76ad500000133ddc193e2c16f534c&srguid=ia744c0690000013b3f6d1cdbd142505d&spos=1&epos=1&td=1&crumb-action=append&context=16&lang=en>

Tarrow, Sidney 2011, *Power in Movement: Social Movements and Contentious Politics*, revised 3rd edition. Cambridge, UK: Cambridge University Press.

Tatlow, Didi Kirsten 2012, "Women in China face rising university entrance barriers", *The New York Times*, 7 October, retrieved 1 December 2012 at <http://www.nytimes.com/2012/10/08/world/asia/08iht-educlede08.html?pagewanted=all>

Taylor, Bill 2012, "Supply chains and labour standards in China", *Personnel Review*, vol. 41, no. 5, pp. 552–71.

Taylor, Bill & Li, Qi 2007, "Is the ACFTU a union and does it matter?" *Journal of Industrial Relations*, vol. 49, no. 5, pp. 701–15.

Thøgersen, Stig 2002, *A County of Culture: Twentieth-Century China Seen from the Village Schools of Zouping, Shandong*. Ann Arbor: University of Michigan Press.

Thompson, Warren S 1929, "Population", *American Sociological Review*, vol. 34, no. 6, pp. 959–75.

Thornton, Patricia M 2008, "Manufacturing dissent in transnational China", in Kevin J O'Brien (ed.) *Popular Protest in China*. Cambridge, MA: Harvard University Press, pp. 179–204.

Tien, H Yuan 1983, "Age at marriage in the People's Republic of China", *The China Quarterly*. vol. 93 (March), pp. 90–107.

Tomba, Luigi 2009, "Of quality, harmony and community: civilization and the middle class in urban China", *positions: east asia cultures critique*, vol. 17, no. 3, pp. 591–616.

Tong, Sarah Y & Wong, John 2008, "China's economy", in Robert Gamer (ed.) *Understanding Contemporary China*, 3rd edition. Boulder, CO: Lynne Rienner, pp. 117–61.

Tong, Yanqi & Lei, Shaohua 2010, "Large-scale mass incidents and government responses in China", *International Journal of China Studies*, vol. 1, no. 2, pp. 487–508.

Tönnies, Ferdinand 1955, *Community and Association*. London: Routledge & Kegan Paul.

Unger, Jonathan 1982, *Education under Mao: Class and Competition in Canton Schools, 1960–1980*. New York: Columbia University Press.

Unger, Jonathan (ed.) 2008, *Associations and the Chinese State: Contested Spaces*. Armonk, NY: ME Sharpe.

United Nations Development Program [UNDP] 2010, *China Human Development Report 2009/2010*. Beijing: China Translation and Publishing Corporation.

United Nations Educational, Scientific and Cultural Organization [UNESCO] no date, "World Heritage list: Three Parallel Rivers of Yunnan Protected Areas", retrieved 6 October 2012 at <http://whc.unesco.org/en/list/1083>

United Nations Trade and Development Board 2011, "Integration of developing countries in global supply chains, including through adding value to their exports", UN Conference on Trade and Development, Geneva, 21 March, retrieved 29 November 2012 at <http://unctad.org/en/Docs/cid16_en.pdf>

Veeck, Gregory, Pannell, Clifton W, Smith, Christopher J & Huang, Youqin 2011, *China's Geography: Globalization and the Dynamics of Political, Economic, and Social Change*, 2nd edition. Lanham, MD: Rowman and Littlefield.

Walder, Andrew G 1986, *Communist Neo-Traditionalism: Work and Authority in Chinese Industry*. Berkeley: University of California Press.

Wang, Daoyong 2007, "*Shidi nongmin 'wentihua' de zhidu luoji ji duice*" ["Systemic logic and counter-measures of the landless farmers' problematic"], *Shanghai Xingzheng Xueyuan Xuebao*, no. 8, pp. 105–10.

Wang, Fei-Ling 2005, *Organizing through Division and Exclusion: China's* Hukou *System*. Stanford, CA: Stanford University Press.

Wang, Haiyan, Appelbaum, Richard, Degiuli, Francesca and Lichtenstein, Nelson 2009, "China's new labour contract law: Is China moving towards increased power for workers?" *Third World Quarterly*, vol. 30, no. 3, pp. 485–501.

Wang, Jianying & Davis, Deborah 2010, "China's new upper middle classes: the importance of occupational disaggregation", in Li Cheng (ed.) *China's Emerging Middle Class: Beyond Economic Transformation*. Washington, DC: Brookings Institute Press, pp. 157–78.

Wang, Jing 2005, "Bourgeois bohemians in China? Neo-tribes and the urban imaginary", *The China Quarterly*, vol. 183 (September), pp. 532–48.

Wang, Jing 2008, *Brand New China: Advertising, Media and Commercial Culture*. Cambridge, MA: Harvard University Press.

Wang, Zheng 2010, "Feminist networks", in You-tien Hsing & Ching Kwan Lee (eds) *Reclaiming Chinese Society: The New Social Activism*. London: Routledge, pp. 101–18.

Watson, Andrew 2008, "Civil society in a transitional state: the rise of associations in China", in Jonathan Unger (ed.) *Associations and the Chinese State: Contested Spaces*. Armonk, NY: ME Sharpe, pp. 14–47.

Watson, James L (ed.) 1984, *Class and Social Stratification in Post-Revolution China*. London: Cambridge University Press.

Wei Chen & Liu Jinyu 2009, "Future Population Trends in China: 2005–2050", General Paper no. G 191. Center of Policy Studies, Monash University, pp. 19–20.

Weller, Robert P 1987, *Unities and Diversities in Chinese Religion*. Seattle: University of Washington Press.

"Wen pledges to curb graft, income inequality as police head off protests" 2011, *Bloomberg News*, 28 February, retrieved 14 May 2012 at <http://www.bloomberg.com/news/2011-02-27/china-police-blanket-planned-jasmine-protest-sites-in-beijing-shanghai.html>

Wharton School of the University of Pennsylvania 2011, "Marketing to China's youth: fitting in and standing out", retrieved 9 January 2011 at <http://www.knowledgeatwharton.com.cn/index.cfm?fa=article&articleid=2442&languageid=1>

White, Gordon, Howell, Jude & Shang, Xiaoyuan 1996, *In Search of Civil Society: Market Reform and Social Change in Contemporary China*. Oxford, UK: Clarendon Press.

Whittaker, D Hugh, Zhu, Tianbao, Sturgeon, Timothy, Tsia, Mon Han & Okita, Toshie 2010, "Compressed development", *Studies in Comparative International Development*, vol. 45, pp. 439–67.

Whyte, Martin King 2000, "The perils of assessing trends in gender inequality in China", in Barbara Entwisle & Gail E Henderson (eds) *Re-drawing Boundaries: Work, Households, and Gender in China*. Berkeley, CA: University of California Press, pp. 157–70.

Whyte, Martin King 2010a, *Myth of the Social Volcano: Perceptions of Inequality and Distributive Justice in Contemporary China*. Stanford, CA: Stanford University Press.

Whyte, Martin King (ed.) 2010b, *One Country, Two Societies: Rural–Urban Inequality in Contemporary China*. Cambridge, MA: Harvard University Press.

Wolf, Arthur P (ed.) 1974a, *Religion and Ritual in Chinese Society*. Stanford, CA: Stanford University Press.

Wolf, Arthur P 1974b, "Gods, ghosts and ancestors", in Arthur P Wolf (ed.) *Religion and Ritual in Chinese Society*. Stanford, CA: Stanford University Press, pp. 131–82.

Wolf, Margery 1972, *Women and the Family in Rural Taiwan*. Stanford, CA: Stanford University Press.

Wolf, Margery 1985, *Revolution Postponed: Women in Contemporary China*. Stanford, CA: Stanford University Press.

Wong, Edward 2012, "Test that can determine the course of life in China gets a closer examination", *New York Times*, 30 June, retrieved 29 November 2012 at <http://www.nytimes.com/2012/07/01/world/asia/burden-of-chinas-college-entrance-test-sets-off-wide-debate.html?_r=0>

World Bank 2012, "Gini index", retrieved 28 November 2012 at <http://data.worldbank.org/indicator/SI.POV.GINI?order=wbapi_data_value_2010+wbapi_data_value&sort=asc>

World Bank and Development Research Center, State Council, China 2012, *China 2013: Building a Modern, Harmonious and Creative High-Income Society*. Washington, DC: World Bank, pp. 301–2.

Woronov, Terry E 2011, "Learning to serve: urban youth, vocational schools and new class formations in China", *The China Journal*, no. 66, pp. 77–99.

Wu, Fei 2010, *Suicide and Justice: A Chinese Perspective*. London: Routledge.

Xing, Guoxin 2011, "Urban workers' leisure culture and the 'public sphere:' a study of the transformation of the Workers' Cultural Palace in reform-era China", *Critical Sociology*, vol. 37, no. 6, pp. 817–35.

Xu, Janice Hua 2008, "Family saga serial dramas and reinterpretation of cultural traditions" in Ying Zhu, Michael Keane & Ruoyun Bai (eds) *TV Drama in China*. Hong Kong: Hong Kong University Press, pp. 33–46.

Xue, Hong 2008, "Local strategies of labor control: a case study of three electronics factories in China", *International Labor and Working-Class History*, vol. 73, pp. 85–103.

Yan, Yunxiang 2003, *Private Life under Socialism: Love, Intimacy and Family Change in a Chinese Village 1949–1999*. Stanford, CA: Stanford University Press.

Yang, Ling & Bao, Hongwei 2012, "Queerly intimate: friends, fans and affective communication in a *Super Girl* fan fiction community", *Cultural Studies*, vol. 26, no. 6, pp. 842–71.

Yang, Mayfair Mei-hui 1994, *Gifts, Favors, and Banquets: The Art of Social Relationships in China*. Ithaca, NY: Cornell University Press.

Yin, Heng 2011, "Characteristics of inter-regional income disparities in China", *Social Sciences in China*, vol. 32, no. 3, pp. 123–44.

Yoshida, Jun 1990, "On intellect and intelligence in Qing China: languages, education and philology", *Senri Ethnological Studies*, vol. 28, pp. 49–65.

Yu, Dongmei & Huang, Rentao 2010, Zhongguo xingbie pingdeng yu funü fazhan dituji [*Atlas of gender equality and women's development in China*]. Beijing: Zhongguo Ditu Chubanshe.

Yu, Xingzhong 2002, "Citizenship, ideology and the PRC constitution", in Merle Goldman & Elizabeth J Perry (eds) *Changing Meanings of Citizenship in Modern China*. Cambridge, MA: Harvard University Press, pp. 288–307.

Zang, Xiaowei 1993, "Household structure and marriage in urban China: 1900–1982", *Journal of Comparative Family Studies*, vol. 24, no. 1, pp. 35–43.

Zang, Xiaowei 2008, "Market transition, wealth and status claims", in David SG Goodman (ed.) *The New Rich in China: Future Rulers, Present Lives*. London: Routledge, pp. 53–70.

Zang, Xiaowei 2011b, "Uyghur-Han earnings differentials in Urumchi", *The China Journal*, no. 65 (January), pp. 141–55.

Zang, Xiaowei 2011c, *Islam, Family Life, and Gender Inequality in Urban China*. London: Routledge.

Zhang, Dengguo 2007, "*Shehui gongzheng shiye xia de shidi nongmin quanyi baohu yanjiu*" ["Study of safeguards for land-losing villagers' rights and interests from a social justice viewpoint"], *Ningxia Dangxiao Xuebao*, vol. 9, no. 4, pp. 77–80.

Zhang, Everett Yuehong 2007, "The birth of *Nanke* men's medicine in China: the making of the subject of desire", *American Ethnologist*, vol. 34, no. 3, pp. 491–508.

Zhang, Hong 2004, "'Living alone' and the rural elderly: strategy and agency in post-Mao rural China", in Charlotte Ikels (ed.) *Filial Piety: Practice and Discourse in Contemporary East Asia*. Stanford, CA: Stanford University Press, pp. 63–87.

Zhang, Hong 2007, "China's new rural daughters coming of age: downsizing the family and firing up cash-earning power in the new economy", *Signs*, vol. 323, pp. 671–98.

Zhang, Li 2010, *In Search of Paradise: Middle-Class Living in a Chinese Metropolis*. Ithaca, NY: Cornell University Press.

Zhang, Q Forrest & Donaldson, John A 2010, "From peasants to farmers: peasant differentiation, labor regimes and land-rights institutions in China's agrarian transition", *Politics and Society*, vol. 38, no. 4, pp. 458–89.

Zhao, Yuezhi 1998, *Media, Market, and Democracy in China: Between the Party Line and the Bottom Line*. Champaign, IL: University of Illinois Press.

Zheng, Tiantian 2009, *Red Lights: The Lives of Sex Workers in Postsocialist China*. Minneapolis: University of Minnesota Press.

Zhongguo Jiaoyu Tongji Nianjian 2009 [*China Education Statistical Yearbook 2009*]. Beijing: Renmin Jiaoyu Chubanshe.

Zhongguo Renkou Nianjian 2007 [*China Population Yearbook 2007*]. Beijing: Institute of Population and Labor Economics, China Academy of Social Sciences.

Zhou, Yingying, Han, Hou & Harrell, Stevan 2008, "From labour to capital: intra-village inequality in rural China, 1988–2006", *The China Quarterly*, no. 195, pp. 515–34.

Zhu, Cuiping & Wang, Guanghua 2012, "Rising inequality in China and the move to a balanced economy", *China and World Economy*, vol. 20, no. 1, pp. 83–104.

Zhu, Ying, Keane, Michael & Bai, Ruoyun 2008, "Introduction", in Ying Zhu, Michael Keane & Ruoyun Bai (eds), *TV Drama in China*. Hong Kong: Hong Kong University Press, pp. 1–18.

Zhu, Ying, Warner, Malcolm & Feng, Tongqing 2011, "Employment relations 'with Chinese characteristics': the role of trade unions", *International Labour Review*, vol. 150, nos 1–2, pp. 127–43.

Zweig, David 1989, *Agrarian Radicalism in China, 1968–1981*. Cambridge, MA: Harvard University Press.

Index

Lightning Source UK Ltd.
Milton Keynes UK
UKOW06f0425081117
312389UK00007B/109/P